Hugh Johnston, William Morley Punshon

Toward the sunrise

Being sketches of travel in Europe and the East. Fourth Edition

Hugh Johnston, William Morley Punshon

Toward the sunrise

Being sketches of travel in Europe and the East. Fourth Edition

ISBN/EAN: 9783337206123

Printed in Europe, USA, Canada, Australia, Japan

Cover: Foto ©Andreas Hilbeck / pixelio.de

More available books at www.hansebooks.com

TOWARD THE SUNRISE.

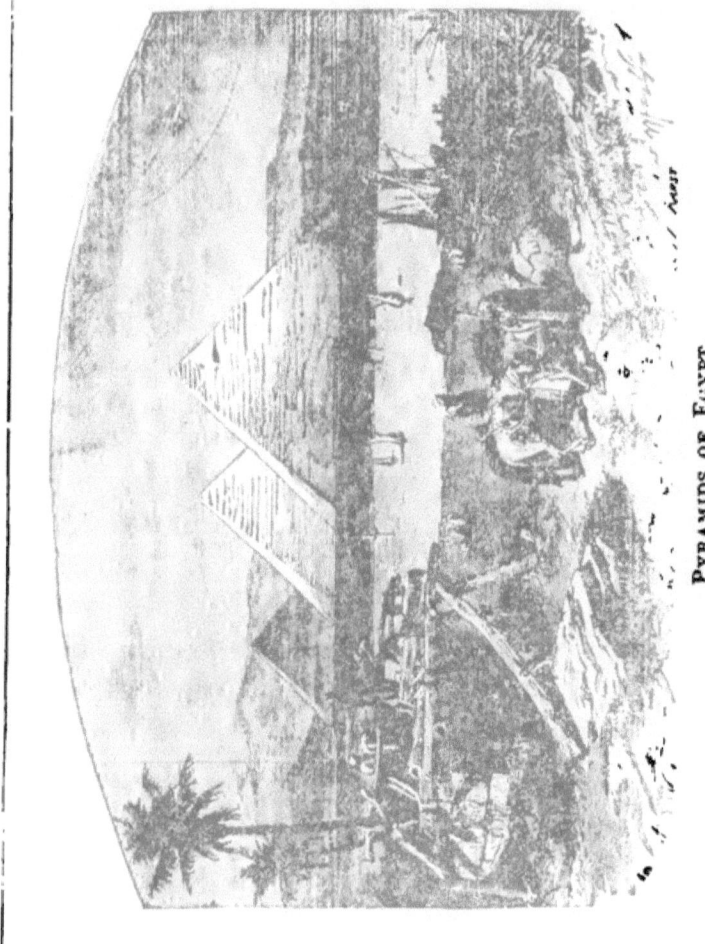

PYRAMIDS OF EGYPT.

TOWARD THE SUNRISE;

BEING

SKETCHES OF TRAVEL IN EUROPE & THE EAST.

TO WHICH IS ADDED

A Memorial Sketch

OF THE

REV. WILLIAM MORLEY PUNSHON, LL.D.

BY

HUGH JOHNSTON, M.A., B.D.

WITH ILLUSTRATIONS.

FOURTH EDITION.

TORONTO:
WILLIAM BRIGGS, 78 & 80 KING STREET EAST.
MONTREAL: C. W. COATES.
HALIFAX: S. F. HUESTIS.

1883.

Dedication.

TO THE

HONORABLE JAMES FERRIER, SENATOR,

OF MONTREAL,

A PATRIOTIC STATESMAN, AN EXTENSIVE TRAVELLER,

AND A TRUE FRIEND,

This Volume

IS RESPECTFULLY DEDICATED

AS A TOKEN

OF

GRATITUDE, ESTEEM, AND AFFECTION

BY

The Author.

PREFACE.

JOHN FOSTER, in his Essay on the Alarming Increase of Books of Travel, is distressed to think of the literary hardships of posterity in having to read the accumulating thousands of volumes of travel. There is one comfort, however, which the great reading public enjoy—a privilege of which they cannot be deprived—and that is the inalienable right to read only such books as they choose to read.

If an apology for another book of travel is necessary, the writer has only to say, that having published during his journey a series of letters in the *Christian Guardian*, which interested some of its readers at the time, he has, at the request of many friends, presumed to revise, enlarge, and supplement the series, with the hope that they may serve a better purpose in this more permanent form. Our warmest thanks are due to the Rev. W. H. WITHROW, Editor of the *Canadian Methodist Magazine*, who has kindly furnished the larger portion of the excellent engravings with which this volume is illustrated. While endeavoring to reflect exact images of the scenes and events witnessed in many lands, the writer is indebted to various authors for helps and suggestions, and in some instances he has "conveyed," as Ancient Pistol puts it, the facts furnished by them to these pages, making them contributory to his design to impart instruction as well as pleasure. If the reader should find entertainment or profit, or should have awakened in his mind new interest in the historic lands of Europe, and the more ancient and sacred lands of the Bible, the purpose of the author will have been fully accomplished.

H. J.

MONTREAL, *December*, 1881.

CONTENTS.

CHAPTER I.

Reasons for the Journey—Starting—The Dominion Steamship Company—The *Mal de Mer*—Fog Banks—Old Ocean in Winter—Grand Sights—Lessons of the Sea—Chief Occupation on Shipboard—Land Ahead—On English soil 1–17

CHAPTER II.

Sights of Liverpool—Hotel Life—Chester—Its Walls and Rows—The Cathedral—Dean Howson—Eaton Hall—Railways—English Scenery—Manchester—Bedford—On to London 18–34

CHAPTER III.

The World's Metropolis—The People—The Streets—The River—Hyde Park—A Diversion—St. Paul's Cathedral—Westminster Abbey—Jerusalem Chamber—Houses of Parliament—Exciting Debates—Cleopatra's Needle—Her Majesty's Tower 35–55

CHAPTER IV.

The Heart of London—The Bank—Exchange—Mansion House—National Gallery—Madame Tussaud—Zoological Gardens—South Kensington—The British Museum—City Road Chapel—Bunhill Field's Cemetery—The Children's Home 56–72

x   *Contents.*

CHAPTER V.

London Preachers—Charles H. Spurgeon—Archibald G. Brown —Dean Stanley—Cathedral Music—Canon Liddon—The Establishment — Cardinal Manning — Dr. Parker—Dr. Donald Fraser—Dr. Pope—Dr. Rigg—Dr. Wm. Morley Punshon 73–102

CHAPTER VI.

Alexandra and Crystal Palaces—Kew Gardens—Windsor Castle —Crossing the Channel—France—Paris—First Impressions—French Language—Avenues—Arch of Triumph— Palace of the Tuileries—The Louvre—The Nude in Art— The Luxembourg—Madeleine—Notre Dame—St. Germain l'Auxerrois—Saint Chapelle—Pantheon—Hotel des Invalides—Tomb of Napoleon—Père La Chaise—Les Gobelins —Versailles—Parisian Life—A Sunday in the City......103–131

CHAPTER VII.

Railway Ride to Turin—Bribing a Guard—Mountain Scenery Mont Cenis Tunnel — Turin — Marengo — Bologna—A Pleasant Incident—The Shores of the Adriatic—Italians— Brindisi—Scapegraces on the Adriatic—Corfu—Charming Scenery—The People—Greek Church—The Ionian Sea— Classic Lands—Byron's Isles of Greece—Crete and Fair Havens—A Storm—The Mediterranean—Arrival in Alexandria 132–160

CHAPTER VIII.

Alexandria Landing—The Donkey Boys—The Streets and Bazaars—Khedive's Palace—Pompey's Pillar—The Ancient City of the Ptolemies—Library—Arab Quarter— Drives—On Shipboard Again—Aboukir Bay and Nelson's Victory—A Lovely Sunset—Port Said—Landing at Joppa —An Ancient City—The Holy Land 161–179

Contents.

CHAPTER IX.

First Day in the Holy Land—House of Simon the Tanner—Miss Arnott's School—Orange Gardens—A Feast—Getting Ready to Start—A Caravan—The Plain of Sharon—The Philistines—Beit Dejân—Ludd—Ramleh, or Arimathea—The Tower—A Noble Act—Encampment—Dinner—First Night under Canvas — A Jackass — Gimzo — Scripture Scenes—Valley of Ajalon—Dr. Tyndall and Joshua's Miracle—Gezer—Amwâs—The Gate of the Valley—The Mountains of Judea—Abu-Gosh—Kirjath Jearim—Valley of Elah—A Magnificent View—Valley of Koloniah—The Mountains round about Jerusalem—Arrival in the City..180-205

CHAPTER X.

The Holy City—First Feeling of Disappointment—Topography of the City—The Walls—The Gates—Mount Zion—Tower of Hippicus—Armenian Convent and Church of St. James—House of Caiaphas—Tomb of David—Cœnaculum—Zion "as a Ploughed Field"—Lepers—Jews' Quarter—Wailing Place—An Affecting Scene—Robinson's Arch—Bridge over the Tyropœan Valley—Mosque of Omar—Haram Area—Interior of the Noble Sanctuary—The Sacred Rock—El Aksa—A Chance of Heaven—Solomon's Stables—View from the Eastern Wall—Mount Moriah and the Jewish Temple—Christ in the Temple—An Angry Sheik—The Tower of Antonia—Pool of Bethesda—St. Stephen's Gate—Outside the City—A Mohammedan Funeral—Climbing the Mount of Olives—View from the Summit—Garden of Gethsemane—The Brook Kedron—Re-entering by the East Gate—Arch of Ecce Homo—*Via Dolorosa*—Lying Frauds—The Church of the Holy Sepulchre—The Court—Appearance of the Interior—Conflicting Opinions as to the True Site—Weight of Testimony in favor of the Traditional *Locale*—Calvary—The Holy Sepulchre itself—Chapels of the Latins, Greeks, Armenians, &c.—Chapel of St. Helena—Mediæval Legends—Impressive Associations—Church of the Holy Sepulchre, the "Holy of Holies" of Jerusalem...206-253

xii   *Contents.*

CHAPTER XI.

PAGE.

Bethlehem—The Dead Sea and the Jordan—An Oriental Salutation—Journey to Bethlehem—"Through Hell"—Plains of Rephaim—Rachel's Tomb—Zelzal—Solomon's Pools—Hebron—Cave of Machpelah—Etham—Bethlehem—Handsome Women—Grotto of the Nativity—David's Well—Shepherd's Field—Mar Saba—The Convent—Gorge of the Kedron—A Terrible Storm—View from the Frank Mountain—The Dead Sea—A Pungent Bath—Fords of the Jordan—The Sacred River—Mountains of Moab—A Dilemma—Er-Riha—The Brook Cherith—Elisha's Fountain—Ancient Jericho—Gilgal—Valley of the Jordan—Valley of Achor—Going up to Jerusalem—Falling among Thieves—Bethany—Mount of Olives—Church of the Ascension—Church of Pater Noster—"Climbing up Zion's Hill" 254-293

CHAPTER XII.

An Excellent Guide—Upper Pool of Gihon—Lower Pool—Valley of Hinnom—Field of Blood—The Horrid King—En-Rogel—Pool of Siloam—Fountain of the Virgin—Mount of Offence—Village of Silwan—The King's Dale—Valley of Jehoshaphat—Mohammedan and Jewish Tombs—Tomb of St. James—Tomb of Zechariah—Absalom's Pillar—Three Roads over the Mount of Olives—The Redeemer's Weeping over the City—Mount Scopus—The Quarries—Grotto of Jeremiah—Tombs of the Kings—Russian Possessions 294-314

CHAPTER XIII.

A Sabbath in the Holy City—School for Jewish Boys—Union Service in the Mediterranean Hotel—Ramble over the Mount of Olives—View of the City—Gallop to Jaffa—Port Said—Suez Canal—Ismailia—Baggage Seized—Egyptian Scenes—Goshen—Approaching the Capital—Cairo

Contents.

—A Donkey Ride—The Citadel—Mosques—Tombs of the Caliphs—Bazaars—Museum of Boulak—Palace of Shoobra—Excursion to the Pyramids—The Nile—Ascent of the Great Pyramid—View from the Summit—Interior—King's Chamber and Queen's—Theories of Prof. Smyth and Others—Second and Third Pyramids—The Sphinx—Return to the City 315–349

CHAPTER XIV.

Population of Cairo—Coptic Christians—Missions—Railway Ride to Alexandria—An Oriental Sunset—On the Mediterranean—Sicily—Mount Etna—Stromboli—Bay of Naples—The "Beautiful City"—San Martino—The Museum—Churches—Virgil's Tomb—Sorrento—Pozzuoli—Baja—Capri—Pompeii—The Forum and Temples—Streets and Houses—Villa of Diomedes—Objects in the Museum—Ascent of Vesuvius—A Magnificent Panorama—The Crater—A Weird Memory—Caserta—Casenum—Roma ..350–372

CHAPTER XV.

Old Rome—The Forum—Mamertine Prison—*Via Sacra*—Arch of Titus—Coliseum—Arch of Constantine—Baths of Caracalla—Ruins of Cæsar's Palaces—Forum of Trajan—The Corso—Panorama of the City from the Pincian—St. Peter's—A Climb into the Ball—Interior of the Cathedral—The Vatican—Picture Gallery—Sistine Chapel—Vatican Museum—Library—Famous Statues—Theatre of Marcellus—Protestant Cemetery—St. Paul's—Church of Il Gesu—Santa Maria Sopra Minerva—Pantheon—Other Churches—Scala Santa—Museum of the Capitol—Palace of the Conservatori—Guido's Aurora—Barberini Palace—Dorio—Corsini—Borghese—Ghetto—Appian Way—*Domine Quo Vadis*—Catecombs—Tomb of Cecilia Metella—A Sabbath in Rome—Protestantism in Italy...................... 373–413

xiv   *Contents.*

CHAPTER XVI.

PAGE.

Rome to Florence—Valley of the Arno—The Duomo—Campanile—Baptistery—Ghiberti's Gates—"Sasso di Dante"—Santa Annunziata—Michael Angelo's Bride—Santa Croce—Illustrious Men—San Marco—Savonarola—San Michele—Mansoleum of the Medici—Uffizi and Pitti Palaces—The Tribune—Art in Florence—Pisa—Its "Leaning Miracle"—Genoa—Its Palaces and Campo Santo—Turin—A Day in Milan—The Cathedral—San Ambrogio—"The Last Supper," by Leonardo da Vinci—London—Death of Dr. Punshon—Home Again 414-434

In Memoriam.

REV. WILLIAM MORLEY PUNSHON, LL.D.

A Special Providence—William Morley Punshon—His Early Life—Opening Ministry—Great Popularity—Excessive Labors—His Work in Canada—True Greatness—Bereavements—A Memorable Conversation—Return to England Great Responsibilities and Heavy Sorrows—Failing Health—Continental Tour—Severe Illness at Genoa—Homeward Journey—Sudden Death—Universal Sorrow—Funeral—Affection's Tribute 437-459

TOWARD THE SUNRISE;

OR,

SKETCHES OF TRAVEL IN EUROPE AND THE EAST.

CHAPTER I.

REASONS FOR THE JOURNEY—STARTING.

Reasons for the Journey—Starting—The Dominion Steamship Company—The *Mal de Mer*—Fog Banks—Old Ocean in Winter—Grand Sights—Lessons of the Sea—Chief Occupation on Shipboard—Land Ahead—On English Soil.

IN venturing to give to the world another book of travel to lands invested with the charms of immortal associations, I shall content myself with chronicling the little things, for the great ones have often been written about before. My journey of many thousand miles toward the rising sun seemed providentially ordered. A pastor of the old historic St. James' Street Methodist Church, of Montreal, I was greatly desirous, aside from the intellectual labour of three sermons a week and public duties of some kind every evening, of fully overtaking the immense pastoral demands of a large congregation whose members are scattered over a great city, and was working at the pace of sixteen hours per day, when suddenly I received a peremptory summons from overtasked nature to pause and "be still." As soon as I was able to get out of bed, I started on a visit to the City of Boston.

Two weeks were spent with Doctor Cullis, where I had the opportunity of examining his great Faith Work, in the Consumptives' Home, the Children's Home, Grove Hill Chapel, Faith Chapel and Training College, as well as of observing the spirit of this devoted servant of the Lord in his quiet home on Somerset Street, and of trying to learn the *way of the Lord more perfectly.* Another week in the beautiful household of Mrs. Butters, Union Park, and I began to feel ready to resume work. But my physicians insisting that a longer time was necessary for me to be restored to complete health, my noble officials met together, voted me several months' leave of absence, and procuring tickets, proposed that I should cross the ocean. They said that I had broken down in their service, and should undergo thorough repairs before leaving them. All this was communicated to me by telegraph, as it was desirable that I should start at once. To give up my loved work for two or three months in mid-year went like a stab to my heart; but the question of health was most imperative, and as I dared not step out of what seemed the way of Providence, in a few hours I was whirling away toward Portland. My faithful friend, Mr. John Torrance, a prince among men, a model of recording-stewards, was there to meet me with messages from home and loved ones, and to see me safely on shipboard. My state-room was already secured; and I found that my devoted wife, aided by the Rev. William Hall, M.A., whose skill in these matters is equalled only by his kindness of heart, had anticipated my every want. I was thoroughly equipped for the voyage, and able to send back home a well-filled trunk, having learned by former experiences that one of the greatest inconveniences of travel is to journey with too many conveniences.

On a bright day early in January, 1881, we steamed out of Portland Harbour toward the great open sea. The moment of departure is a trying one. As we hear the rushing and hissing of steam, feel the revolution of the screw and the pulsing of the strong-muscled engine, and know that the vessel is moving away, a feeling of sadness comes over the soul. We wave our farewells to the faithful friends who have come down to the pier to see us off, and we think tenderly of those who in love and self-sacrifice have strengthened their hearts for this separation. Good bye, home, and precious wife and children, and church-work. Your very memories are sweeter far than the music of bells and organs and choirs, that we shall hear in far-famed cathedrals; and we hope to return with renewed strength and zeal for more loving helpfulness and more consecrated service.

And now that our vessel has turned her prow toward the rising sun, let me speak a word for the Dominion Steamship Company.

Our steamer is *The City of Brooklyn*, of three thousand six hundred tons, four hundred feet in length, forty-six feet in breadth, nearly five hundred horsepower, strong and first-class in all its appointments, and for speed the champion of the line. What a marvel of mechanical skill is one of these ocean steamers, so vast, so powerful, so well-proportioned—a living leviathan on the deep. The state-rooms of our good ship are clean and well-ventilated, and large for state-rooms on ship-board, which are generally barely sufficient for a person of moderate tonnage to turn round in, but not ample enough to swing the proverbial cat in without serious injury to the poor animal. The light is not through a bull's eye, but a square window nearly a yard in length. The vessel is nobly officered from the thoughtful, genial commander down to the obliging steward. The table spread is sumptuous—the attendance faithful—everything is that of an elegant and commodious floating palace. All this comfort to Liverpool and return is obtained for ninety dollars, what would cost for best accommodation on other first-class lines at least one hundred and fifty dollars. It is true that we have about three hundred *steerage* passengers, and these *steers* are for the slaughter-market of Liverpool; but unless you were told you would not know that cattle were on board.

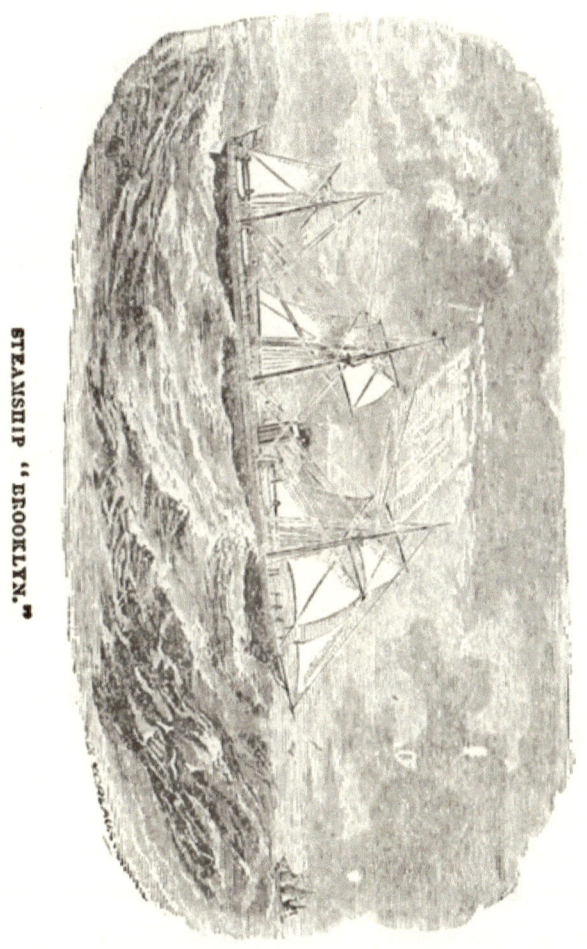

STEAMSHIP "BROOKLYN."

But however elegant the surroundings, old Neptune exacts duty of nearly all "who go down into the sea in ships." "It is a great trial to leave one's country when you have to cross the sea," says Madame de Staël; and it is always a *hardship* to me to embark upon the sea because of the *mal de mer*.

In sailing from Quebec down the broad and beautiful St. Lawrence, one has a chance of getting his sea-legs on, and of becoming accustomed to the odours and movements of the vessel before he encounters the full force of the Atlantic; but in this winter port, like that of New York, you are no sooner out of the quiet harbour than the vessel begins pitching and tossing, and in the cabin a constant warfare is going on between the floor and the ceiling as to which should be uppermost. Oh! then a direful malady breaks out. Your appetite is gone; your pleasures gone; your delight in companionship gone. You throw up books, conversation, amusements, finally your stock of provisions, and then every movable thing within you. What horrid qualms! *Sea-sickness!* "The word is an emetic; while I write it I heave." I am reminded of a Presiding Elder in Washington Territory, who accompanied us on the journey from Victoria, B.C., to Olympia, at the head of that wealth of waters, Puget Sound. Crossing the Straits of *San Juan de Fuca*, it became very rough, when suddenly our garrulous preacher turned pale and observed, "Now some of you will have to do the talking, for I feel *rather sober*." To be compelled to pay homage to old Neptune makes one feel *rather sober*, and one would much rather fling a trident at the head of the old sea-god than what is generally offered. It is an old story, from the days of Cato, who on his death-bed regretted only three things, one of which was, "To have gone by sea when he could have gone by land." Yet what is human experience, in all its heights and depths, but the repetition of an oft-told tale?

After thirty hours' sail, we passed Sable Island, a long stretch of land off the coast of Nova Scotia, and inhabited only by the lighthouse keeper and his family. No more sight of land, henceforth, for seven or eight days, until we reach the shores of the beautiful Emerald Isle. Now we are on the Banks of Newfoundland, which stretch south of the island for two hundred miles, and to the east for two hundred and fifty miles. The Gulf Stream, sweeping up from the tropics, and the polar currents, rushing down from the north, have deposited their sand and sediment at this confluence of ocean currents; and over these Banks the water is from twenty-five to sixty fathoms deep, while as soon as you leave them the soundings are from fifteen to seventeen hundred fathoms. This is the place for fogs. When the warm and cold currents meet, and a breeze is blowing from the south, the cold is overcome and a vapour rises and fills the air; but when a wind from the north is blowing the cold is too strong for the currents from the equator, and there is no fog. When we passed over the Banks a fearful snow-storm was raging, and continued to beat upon us for twenty-four hours. The wind whistled through the cordage of the vessel, or howled surlily amid the machinery, until the roarings of the tempest seemed like the warning whispers of some water-spirit; and the snow fell in blinding, whirling eddies until it lay knee-deep upon the decks. But the sturdy seamen stand to their tasks, and our vessel, battling like a thinking being, struggles bravely through the war of elements.

A sea-voyage in winter is very different from one in summer. The waters are more agitated; the winds more violent; the sky more dark and threatening; the white surges rise above the heaving billows, and the desolation seems more tremendous and terrible. Our passage could not be called a severe one, and yet we have had to make the entire way over the Atlantic, which extends from the Banks of Newfoundland to the chops of the Channel, against strong head-seas washing over the bows, and looking boldly into the very eye of the wind. The Bay of Biscay, that breeder of storms and cauldron of agitation for the northern Atlantic, has given us a steady south-easter.

We have seemed entirely alone upon a waste of waters. Not an object is to be seen on the ocean's horizon. There are no icebergs in winter, for those floating, crystalline islands—those solitary but proud voyagers so magnificent to gaze upon, but so terrible to meet—are not let loose from their Arctic home until the sun of summer has set them free. The sea is full of life, but not a monster or fish or inhabitant of the deep was seen. "The whales," quoth old Chapman, speaking of Neptune, "the whales exulted under him and knew their mighty king." But not a whale spouted or rolled his huge surface above the water. No salutation of friendly steamer. Once, in the far distance, a white-winged ship appeared within our wavering horizon with every sail set, and seemed a "thing of beauty" built of canvas—a many-storied pile of cloud that rose and fell with the waves, but she soon disappeared. On another day the fourth officer came and hurriedly called the captain, saying that he saw what seemed like a boat, but he could not make it out. At once we rushed to the deck, and spy-glasses and marine-glasses were brought into requisition, thinking that some wreck might be discovered and some poor castaways rescued from the hungry deep. But it was only a floating spar; it had no story to tell; it may have been the mast of a wrecked ship; it may have been some drifting, useless timber, or the solitary memento of shipwreck and disaster. And yet the voyage is not monotonous. What a thrill it gives one to stand by day upon the bridge and see the noble ship careering through the waves, the wrathful billows breaking over the bulwarks and rolling white-crested across the decks, while clouds of spray dash high into the air and fall like rain upon your face. Then to see the mammoth waves rolling away from the vessel's sides, and breaking into colours of such brilliancy and delicacy, such splendour and softness, as paint and pencil never dreamed about—the solid colour of the malachite mingling with the transparency of the emerald, or changing into jasper and crystal and amethyst and pearl and opal! Or at night to look through the rustling foam of the ship's bows and try to penetrate that strange darkness, that uncertainty, which lies just ahead. What shall rise over that black rim towards which we sail, but do not overtake? Then to look behind and see the trail of phosphorescent light—the very night-air glittering with a dreamy light disengaged from the ocean.

> "'Twas fire our ship was plunging through;
> Cold fire that o'er the quarter flew,
> And wandering moons of idle flame
> Grew full and waned, and went and came,
> Dappling with light the huge sea-snake
> That slid behind us in the wake."

To one whose heart is not insensible to the beauties of nature there are grand sights at sea.

There is ever-varying grandeur in the wide heavens that stretch themselves above us. A sunrise or sunset in mid-ocean is a magnificent view when in simple grandeur naked sun meets naked sea. The cloud-views, too, are sublime. In the early part of the voyage the clouds were uncoloured and dull; but moving on, the atmosphere became soft and balmy as the south. Then clouds and sea were bathed in crimson, gold, and purple, most beautiful. The sun-dyed garments of the skies piled themselves up into palaces of rosy gold, and argent, and amber, and their massive steps were draped in all the colours of the rainbow.

We have had also the full moon, and this is a vision worth taking a voyage to see, when the silver queen bathes the vast and silent floods with soft and tender light. And the nights—the starlight nights! What a revelation is the sparkling concave of the sky at sea! What hours of ecstacy I have spent watching the shifting groups of stars, and holding converse with these silent but glorious witnesses of the Creator's power! The sky is a poem to me, and to any one who recognizes the constellations and can call the principal stars by name. How I have loved to watch Orion, and Arcturus, and the Pleiades shedding down their sweet influence! To see the steady Pointers looking toward their sovereign, the North Star, and watch how Bootes drives the Great Bear round the pole. King Cepheus sits on his throne of state, and near by his brilliant wife Cassiopeia; and Perseus, with dagger of diamonds and winged sandals of mercury, rescuing the chained Andromeda for his bride. There is the snaky-haired Medusa, and in the eye of that severed head flashes and fades the changeful star Algol. I see Hercules, the mighty hunter; and Pegasus, the winged horse, careering among the stars. The ship Argo sails through the realms of heaven; and there float Aquila, the Dolphin, and the Swan. "Therefore lift up your eyes on high and behold who hath created all these things, that brought out their host by number, that calleth them all by their names in the greatness of His power; for that He is strong in power, not one faileth."

The ocean, too, has an ever-varying, never-ending charm. Now calm and placid—quiet as a sleeping child; now dark and tossing and foam-crested, with its—

> "Yeast of waves which mar
> Alike the Armada's pride, or spoil of Trafalgar."

It is the image of eternity,—

> "Dark, heaving, boundless, endless, and sublime."

How illimitable in extent! Day after day we sail toward that edge which seems to bound it, yet the magic circle stretches forward and we do not overtake it. And should we turn toward the south, our swift-moving steamer could travel for a month before we would come in sight of land. Yet the sea is the Lord's, for He made it. And He measures the waters of the Atlantic, the Pacific, the Indian, the Northern, and Southern Oceans in the hollow of His hand! How safe to be under His care, for, though out alone upon His sea, He watches over me as though the universe were a void and His child the only object of His love! And how one is brought to a sense of his own littleness! Only the other day we felt that we could not be spared from our work; now our vessel, with its freight of living, throbbing hearts, is but a speck upon a dread, fathomless abyss of waters, and should all go down with bubbling groan,—

> "Without a grave, unknelled, unlettered, and unknown,"

the great world would roll on undisturbed. We would simply be, "never heard of more." A few hearts would weep and well-nigh break; but the great, careless world would be no more disturbed than is the forest by the fall of a leaf.

There is the lesson, too, not only of dependence and of littleness, but also of patience. The old saying is, "Light loads carried far grow heavy." What is the use of worry and anxiety out at sea when winds are contrary? We must only learn meekness, patience, and trustfulness. We make the best of our trials when we make the least of them. God embosoms all our anxiety and fears for the future in the hush of the precious promise—"Thou wilt keep him in perfect peace whose mind is stayed on Thee, because he trusteth in Thee."

> "I bring my patient God
> A patient heart."

What a royal opportunity for rest is given by an ocean voyage! No *Herald*, *Gazette*, or *Witness*; no *Globe*, or *Mail* to read; no letters or telegraph messages to receive or despatch. No bills, no visitors, no drudging toils. The great, busy world must go on without us. If it go to ruin, we cannot help it.

The most important operation on shipboard is eating. Taking an early bath one must have a cup of coffee and a cracker; breakfast at eight; luncheon at twelve; dinner at four; tea at seven; supper at ten;

reminding us of the story of a steward who passed through the cabin, ringing the bell and shouting, "All those passengers that have done their breakfast, will please walk down to dinner."

One cannot profess to enjoy a slow passage across the Atlantic. Our steamer has only had in the last two days an opportunity to display her speed, when, with head-wind and waves slightly abated, she bowled along through the surges at the rate of three hundred miles per day. Fancy a poor fellow, whose trouble is *insomnia*, lying in his berth through the long night listening for hours to the revolution of the screw—the whole motion is like riding on a great camel of the desert affected with heart disease, and you do not miss a single throb. And yet out of the salty air and briny spray, and rough tumbling of bed and board, capsized soup-plates and savory contents emptied into your lap; out of these scrambling experiences come health, and refreshment, and strength. The jaded man feels the pulses of a new life throbbing in his veins and cooling the fire of his brain.

Did you ever spend a Sabbath on the sea and join in divine service? How strange, and yet how home-like! What a sense of the presence of the Father-God! My first Sunday was spent in my state-room, for the ocean was piling its frothy hills high in the air, and the most mighty Neptune—

> "Did his dread trident shake
> And make the bold waves tremble."

It was precarious to sit on a chair without being lashed to it, and my untried stomach was not behaving itself with becoming dignity. But on the second Sunday, at the call of the bell, passengers and seamen assembled in the cabin. Appropriate Scripture lessons are read, the form of prayer for those at sea is used, and dear familiar hymns, such as "Jesus, lover of my soul," "Rock of Ages," "Nearer my God to Thee," and "Sun of my soul, Thou Saviour dear," are sung. How hearty is the service! and what a new charm is given to this waiting before the Lord on the bosom of the restless and tossing main!

But what is the matter with our watches? We have been losing half an hour daily, until we have actually lost five hours of our life; and we shall never find these hours again until we pick them up on our return voyage, when we shall no longer go forward to meet the sun, but, advancing with it, shall prolong the day.

Now there is a stir on board. All eyes are turned in one direction, for we are told there is land in sight. Far off, and indistinct, lies the dim, soft outline of the land of Ireland—

> "And well may Erin's sons adore
> Their Isle, which Nature formed so fair."

We do not land at Queenstown or visit the famous city on the spreading Lee. An Irish gentleman once asked Foote, at a dinner, where the wine flowed freely, if he had been to see Cork? "No," was the answer;

"But I've seen many *drawings* of it this evening." We must be content with seeing the drawings of it, for we have *Cork-onians* on board. As we move along the Irish Channel we enjoy splendid views of the coast scenery. All is beauty and freshness. How green the meadows! How charming the sloping hills!

> "When Erin first rose from the dark, swelling flood,
> God blessed the Green Island, He saw it was good;
> The emerald of Europe, it sparkled and shone
> In the ring of the world the most precious stone."

Ireland! famous in story and in song; the little spot that has given to the world more than its share of orators and statesmen, warriors and poets, the sons of genius and of greatness. But unhappy land, its past sad and sorrowful, even to tears and blood; its present clouded and full of agitation and alarm.

While we are musing on Irish questions the Welsh coast attracts our attention—its scenery wild and rugged, and pleasing beyond description. As we pass Holyhead, what exquisite views! The rocky ramparts of the shore, winding bays and harbors; and behind, the mountains, with heavy, massive shadows resting on them!

Now we see the picturesque shores of the Mersey, studded with lovely villas. And there is the great commercial city, with its miles of massive docks, its lofty warehouses and extensive shipping. The voyage is over. There is the clatter of unlading; the breaking up of pleasant friendships formed, and the hurry of departure. And this is English soil! Solid streets are under our feet, carriages and hansoms roll along, a mass of people are hurrying to and fro, and we are in one of the chief centres of the world's commerce. And here we spend a day or two, to rest and see the lions of the city. Meanwhile our hearts go out in gratitude to our heavenly Father, who hath brought us safely to our desired haven.

CHAPTER II.

LIVERPOOL—CHESTER—MANCHESTER—BEDFORD.

Sights of Liverpool—Hotel Life—Chester—Its Walls and Rows—The Cathedral—Dean Howson—Eaton Hall—Railways—English Scenery—Manchester—Bedford—On to London.

LIVERPOOL is a mighty city; but to the majority of travellers from the New World it is only the *doorstep* of England, and they simply stand on it long enough to be let into the "old home." But it is well worth stopping to see. There is nothing in the world like its docks and shipping. Such massive masonry; such length, and breadth, and depth, and solidity, in its seven miles of dock architecture, and such a crowding of steamers and vessels " whose rising masts an endless prospect yields." The streets are thronged with business, and ablaze with light and fashion, while its public buildings and statues are splendid. The equestrian statue of the late Prince Albert is very fine, as well as the colossal monument to Nelson. The hero is represented as falling into the arms of death, while victory descends to crown his brow with the wreath of immortality. St. George's Hall, with its great organ, must not be omitted. The Art Gallery, Library, and Museum are noteworthy structures. I was surprised and delighted with the display of pictures in this Walker Art Gallery. Indeed, the annual autumn exhibition of Fine Arts in Liverpool is the first in the kingdom outside of London. One can never forget such paintings as West's "Death of Nelson," and "Elijah in the Wilderness," by Sir F. Leighton, the President of the Royal Academy. "Eventide," by H. Herkomer, is a scene from a workhouse, where one old body is endeavouring to read, another is drinking her cup of tea, another knitting, and the fourth trying to thread a needle; while each particular face is a study. "Faithful unto Death," by E. J. Poynter, represents the Roman sentinel standing at his post and calmly meeting death, while the other inhabitants are making their escape from the red rain of fire and burning lava. "The Hunted Slave," by Ansdell, where the fugitive turns with axe upon the fierce bloodhounds that are upon him, is another picture which once seen cannot be forgotten.

One's first taste of English hotel life is got in Liverpool. The "Adelphi" is a grand hotel, and is largely patronized by Americans; yet it is intensely English. This is seen especially in the dining-room. Each waiter is dressed in a white tie and swallow-tail coat. When you enter your order is taken for the meal; the number of your room is asked for, and if you have not previously ordered, you must wait till everything you wish is cooked, and then it is served up smoking hot. "Shall I not take mine ease in mine inn?" said Falstaff. Well, one must take his ease, for there is no haste there. One morning I had made an engagement for a certain hour, and descending in what I considered ample time, ordered breakfast. I waited long, and grew impatient; urged haste but all in vain, I had to wait and still wait, until at last the gentleman in swallow-tail leisurely brought my breakfast. I was comforted, in my tribulation, by the afflictions of a fellow-traveller from Australia. He had ordered breakfast, and had come down with a rush to find that there was no breakfast for him. He raised a row. "There is no order on the book," said the clerk. He had certainly ordered it, and was to take the morning train. At length the question was settled by enquiry, "Who did you order it of, the porter or the chambermaid?" "The *chambermaid.*" Ah! that accounted for it. English hotel discipline is thorough; the order had not come through the regularly-appointed channel; and, poor fellow, he had nothing to do but wait for his breakfast and let the train go. When your bill is made up there is a daily charge for "service," and when you depart, the chambermaid is to receive a gratuity, and the porter, and table-waiter, and boots; in fact, all round.

This *feeing* system, imported, I believe, from the Continent, is an abomination. The barber who shaves you is to be *tipped*, and the railway porter, and the restaurant maid, and the church verger, and the porter at the palace gate—any man who renders the smallest service or gives the least information, obsequiously bows for his gratuity. It is said of a Yankee wit, that, as he was leaving the shores of England, he raised his hat to the crowd that was seeing the vessel off, and observed, "Gentlemen, if there is anybody in your country to whom I have not given a shilling, now is the time to speak."

I spent a very delightful Sabbath in Liverpool. In the morning I attended St. Matthias' Church, entered very heartily into the morning service of the Church of England, and heard a capital sermon by a Dr. Harrison, from the text—" Jesus only." He was very earnest and evangelical, and dealt the High Church party some hard blows. In the evening I attended Trinity Wesleyan Church, Grove Street. It is the finest Wesleyan chapel that I have seen in England. The organ and musical service were unusually good. The Rev. Mr. Lambert was the preacher, and gave a carefully-prepared, beautiful, and spiritual discourse on " The eagle stirring up her nest." It was the first Sabbath on land, and the sermons were to me abundant in profit and spiritual consolation.

While near Liverpool, quaint, old-fashioned, red-walled Chester must not be forgotten. I had seen the city before but it well repays a second visit. You will say, with Boswell, of this antique city, whose walls were built by the Romans, when its name was Castra—one of the chief military stations of the Romans, the camp of the Great Legion, the camp *par excellence*, Castral—chester! You will say with the biographer of Dr. Johnson, " I was quite enchanted, so that I could with difficulty quit it." The oldest city in the kingdom; its walls are "grey with the memories of two thousand years." Here the Roman General Suetonius gathered his army in his campaign against the Druids in the Isle of Anglesey. In the year of our Lord 73 it was repaired, walled, and fortified by Marias. In 828 it succumbed to Saxon rule, and in 972, Edgar, the Saxon King, received the homage of his Kings as he was rowed past them on the Dee, sitting in triumph at the prow of his boat. It was the last city in England that held out against William the Conqueror. During the civil wars the city was devoted to the King and was besieged, and taken by the parliamentary forces in 1646. The place is full of antiquities, remains of altars, baths, tesselated pavements, vases, and coins. The walls that girdle the city are from twelve to forty feet high, two miles in circuit, and form a broad footpath. They are very picturesque in their way, crossing over the streets on arches, with towers and gates; below them the windings of the silver stream, once vexed with Cæsar's oarsmen. It is the same Dee, now silted up, of which Kingsley sings—

"O, Mary, call the cattle home
Across the sands of Dee."

It is a delightful promenade of two miles along these historic walls. We ascended them close by the Phœnix Tower, which bears the following inscription:—

KING CHARLES
STOOD ON THIS TOWER,
SEPTEMBER 24TH, 1645, AND SAW
HIS ARMY DEFEATED,
ON ROWTON MOOR.

On this elevated, irregular, uneven footpath, you walk along on a level with the roofs of the old buildings, and look down on crooked streets, churches and abbeys, with towers, ivy and moss-covered; in one place, the venerable defence climbs the hills, in another it stoops into the valleys. Deeply cut in the solid rock, beneath the walls, is the Ellesmere and Chester Canal, the site of the ancient Roman fosse, and out of the crevices of the rock grow great gnarled trees. As you come round to the west, with its fertile meadows, there is a commanding view of the surrounding country; the windings of the Dee, the railway viaduct of forty-seven arches, the camp below, where the Roman legions exercised, now the arena of sports and games; and in the distant background the beautiful range of the Welsh mountains.

The streets of Chester are strange, and so are the houses, with their over-hanging gables and quaintly carved panellings. The old Bishop Lloyd's house has its front divided into squares, and these squares are filled with carved work representing such scenes as Adam and Eve in the Garden, Abel's Sacrifice, Abraham offering up Isaac, etc. "God's Providence House" was the only house on the street which escaped the plague that, in the seventeenth century, devastated the city; and carved on the oaken beam is the inscription and grateful testimony—"God's providence is mine inheritance, 1652."

The rows of Chester are famous and unique. They are half in-door, half out-door sidewalks. Besides the ordinary sidewalk there is a continuous covered gallery through the front of the second story of the houses, caused by the second story being thrust out some fifteen or twenty feet from the front and resting on pillars, so there is an upstairs street and a downstairs street. The front of the lower shops are covered to form a kind of arcade, the roof of which becomes a footpath for the upper and more fashionable row of shops. As some one has said, great is the puzzle of the stranger as to whether the roadway is down in the cellar, or whether he is upstairs on the landing; or whether the houses, by some sudden shock, have turned themselves out of the windows.

Trinity Church invites the stranger's attention because it has in its graveyard the tomb of the distinguished commentator, Matthew Henry. As I stood beside his grave, and observed also in another part of the city a granite monument dedicated to his memory, I felt like thanking God that Matthew Henry had ever lived. But the interest culminates in the Cathedral, which occupies the site of a temple of Apollo, while before that time even the Druids had an older fane. Prince Ethelred, son of Penda, visiting his niece, the holy St. Werburgh, Abbess of Chester, was charged in a vision "To build a church on the spot where he should find a white hind." Engaged in an exciting chase, and coming at once upon a white hind, the pious royal hunter remembered his vision, and founded a Saxon church in the year six hundred and eighty-nine, nearly twelve hundred years ago!

This was the first English Cathedral I had ever seen, and I shall never forget the impression produced by its mouldering massiveness and modern splendor; its weather-worn walls, and tower, and ancient crypt without; its nave, and elaborately-carved stalls, and the oak canopies of the choir within.

Blending the ideal with the real world, how it seemed to recall the words of James Russell Lowell!—

> "With outward senses furloughed and head bowed
> I followed some instinct in my feet,
> Till, to unbend me from the doom of thought,
> Looking up suddenly I found mine eyes
> Confronted with the minster's vast repose,
> Silent and gray as forest-leaguered cliff
> Left inland by the ocean's slow retreat,
> That hears afar the breeze-borne note, and longs.

Remembering shocks of surf that clomb and fell
Spume-sliding down the baffled decuman,
It rose before me, patiently remote,
From the great tides of life it breasted once.
Hearing the noise of men as in a dream
I stood before the triple northern port,
Where dedicated shapes of saints and kings,
Stern faces bleared with immemorial watch,
Looked down benignly grave and seemed to say,
*Ye come and go incessant: we remain
Safe in the hallowed quiets of the past;
Be reverent, ye who flit and are forgot,
Of faith so nobly realized as this.*

I seem to have heard it said by learned folk
Who drench you with æsthetics till you feel
As if all beauty were a ghastly bore,
The faucet to let loose a wash of words,
That Gothic is not Grecian, therefore worse;
But, being convinced by much experiment
How little inventiveness there is in man,
Grave copier of copies, I give thanks
For a new relish, careless to inquire
My pleasure's pedigree, if so it please,
Nobly, I mean, nor renegade to art.
The Grecian gluts me with its perfectness,
Unanswerable as Euclid, self-contained,
The one thing finished in this hasty world,
Forever finished, through the barbarous pit,
Fanatical on hearsay stamp, and shout
As if a miracle could be encored.
But ah! this other, this that never ends,
Still climbing, luring fancy still to climb
As full of morals half-divined as life.
Graceful, grotesque, with ever new surprise
Of hazardous caprices sure to please,
Heavy as nightmare, airy-light as fern,

Imagination's very self in stone!
With one long sigh of infinite release
From pedantries past, present, or to come,
I looked, and owned myself a happy Goth.
Your blood is mine, ye architects of dream,
Builders of aspiration incomplete,
So more consummate, souls self-confident,
Who left your own thought worthy of record
In monumental pomp! No Grecian drop
Rebukes these veins that leap with kindred thrill,
After long exile, to the mother-tongue."

Surely in all the architecture of the world there is nothing finer than the Gothic Cathedral, "imaginations very self in stone." Chester Cathedral consists of a nave with side aisles, a choir, a lady-chapel at the east end, and on the north a cloister, Chapter House, and the King's School. The stones are worn smooth, trodden by the feet of monarchs and martyrs—the great of old. What a place in which to stand and think!

The sacred edifice is sepulchral as well as worshipful, for the main aisles are covered with monumental slabs, and at every step you tread upon a tomb. Almost repellant are these mouldering sepulchres, in aisles with their groined arches overhead, supported by clustered pillars that stand like trunks of trees, tossing their great arms on high, the light falling upon them from windows that blaze in crimson, gold, and emerald.

There is one record on a marble slab, the inscription of which cannot be forgotten :—

HERE REPOSE THE REMAINS OF
ELIZA, WIFE OF WILLIAM MAKEPEACE THACKERAY,
OF THIS CITY,
DIED SEPTEMBER 8TH, 1833.
AGED 64 YEARS.
ALSO
WILLIAM MAKEPEACE THACKERAY, M.D.,
BORN AT CAMBRIDGE, APRIL 15TH, 1770,
EDUCATED AT ETON, AND GRADUATED AT TRINITY COLLEGE,
CAMBRIDGE,
DIED JULY 29TH, 1849.

The Cathedral has been restored by its scholarly Dean, Dr. Howson, and the contrast between the new and old red sandstone is striking and impressive.

The Chapter House is full of interest to every Canadian. It contains the old shot-torn and faded colors of the 22nd, or Cheshire Regiment, carried at the storming and taking of Quebec, and one's patriotism is stirred in the presence of those ragged and blood-stained emblems of heroism. The Lady Chapel is exquisite; the windows have in tracery the principal scenes in the life of the great Apostle, from the work of the Dean and his friend and co-laborer, *Conybeare*, authors of "The Life and Epistles of St. Paul."

I had the honor of meeting Dr. Howson, a name so familiar to Bible students, in the home of that princely man of Montreal, the late Mr. Joseph Mackay, but I was delighted to get a sight of the Dean in his own Cathedral. He is a medium-sized man, in knee-breeches; his hair is gray and curling, his face ruddy, with side-whiskers, and eyes that kindle into a genial glow in conversation. As a preacher he is not a success, his pulpit performances being rather hum-drum, and his voice weak and monotonous; but as a writer his works are always welcomed by Christian students and thinkers.

To crown the enjoyment of the day, we visited Eaton Hall, the seat of the Duke of Westminster, one of the most elegant mansions of England. On the way we passed the old Tower of Cæsar, crossed the famous Grosvenor Bridge, with its magnificent arch spanning two hundred feet—the widest stone arch ever erected—and the Cemetery, charmingly situated on the southern bank of the Dee. The entrance is at the Grosvenor gateway, an elaborate copy of the Abbey gate of St. Augustine at Canterbury. For three miles we rode through a winding avenue shaded with copper birch, elm, and oak; crossed the park of vast extent, full of picturesque scenery and noble vistas; before us the sporting deer; to the right, in the far distance, the mountains of Wales; to the left the Vale Royal of Cheshire, and the Peckforton Hills, on which stands the Peckforton Castle, and near it a bold rock rising perpendicularly five hundred and sixty feet, on which stands, in venerable grandeur, the battered and dismantled towers and walls of the once strong rock and fortress, Beeston Castle, built by that famous crusader, Randle Blundeville, Earl of Chester.

Eaton Hall is one of the most elegant mansions in England. Its owner is the richest nobleman in the kingdom, his annual income being over seven millions of dollars. The grounds are laid out with exquisite taste. The horticultural department is peerless. We were conducted through a corridor six hundred feet long, covered with glass, paved with encaustic tiles, and festooned with climbing roses, giant nasturtiums, climbing fuchsias; double geraniums, one fine specimen covering the wall twenty feet square; passion flowers, and hundreds of other rare beauties beyond our floral knowledge. Off the corridors were conservatories filled with the choicest exotic flowers and fruits, among which we saw the lotus in flower, cocoanut, palm, giant fern, oranges, pine-apples, figs, olives, and other fruits, grown for the nobleman's table. As I walked through this garden of beauty, and in the midst of such magnificence, I wondered if the lordly possessor were happier than the delighted spectator who can truthfully take up the refrain,—

"No foot of land do I possess
No cottage in this wilderness."

Certainly, happiness does not consist in externals. The Duke's father, though he owned an estate of sixty-four square miles, was haunted in his old age with the dread of ending his days in the poor-house, and was so niggardly that rather than pay the toll he would have his carriage drop him at the gate, and he would walk from there into the city. That stately home which has just undergone repairs and improvements to the extent of two millions of pounds, is now shadowed with a great sorrow in the loss of its mistress and lady.

On my first visit to London, I went by the North-Western, stopping at that great manufacturing town, Birmingham—"the toy-shop of Europe"—passing through the *Black Country*, where for miles and miles the earth is honey-combed beneath, and above are nothing but tall chimneys and manufactories, sending out their blasts of flame and smoke. Then I turned aside to see Coventry, wearing in its crown such a Koh-i-noor of legend. Leaving "Peeping Tom" and a hundred reminders of the story of the little dimpled lady, who, for the love she bore the poor,

> Took the tax away,
> And built herself an everlasting name—

we came to Kenilworth, made immortal by the genius of Sir Walter Scott; and Warwick Castle, and Stratford-on-Avon, filled with the vivid, vital image of the myriad-minded, grandly-gifted Shakespeare. From Stratford to Oxford, the famous seat of learning, with its stately palaces and venerable buildings; its many colleges and its chapels and cathedrals, each "dyed in the soft checkerings of a sleepy light;" its shady walks and groves, and grassy quadrangles; its alcoved libraries and museums, filled with treasures of every kind. And from Oxford, after a run of sixty miles, we entered the thunder and rattle of mighty London. But this time I determined to go by the Midland, and get a view of the peaks and hills of Derbyshire.

The English know how to manage railways. The stations are massive and substantial edifices; every officer keeps his place, and moves with the regularity of a chronometer. No one can travel without procuring a ticket, which is got at a booking-office. You are then locked into a carriage—first, second, or third-class in its compartments, and your baggage is committed to the tender mercies of the guard. With us, the baggage is looked after and the man is free; in England, the man is looked after and the baggage is set loose. It does seem as though our checking system would be an improvement, and would certainly relieve the traveller of much trouble and anxiety. The railway carriages are shorter and more plain than ours, and are run on fewer wheels. The difference in the grades lies simply in the upholstering. There is no conductor on board. Tickets are shown the guard on entering the car, examined by station-guards along the route, and taken up by another guard at the end of the journey. The road-bed is perfect; there is no waiting for trains; the tracks are double, and on you go, by what Emerson calls a "cushioned cannon ball," dashing through tunnels, into cuts and out of them, over fields and through cities—away and away!

The Midland carries you through the choicest scenery. The land is gently undulating, and we sweep past hill and valley, river and dale, woodland and field. There is not the rich picture of summer, when the meadows are bright with flowers, the foliage refreshingly green, the hedges beautiful, the whole land adorned as a bride for her husband. O, the charms of Motherland's face, when she looks her best! Hills cultured and of delicious beauty; lawns soft, smooth-shaven, and shadow-flecked; silver waterfalls making delicious music, and gentle streams spanned by perfect little stone bridges of one symmetrical arch; the broad gleam of rivers, woodlands, picturesque lanes and fields covered with luxuriant crops. Now, the fields are smooth, the well-trained hedges of hawthorn are there; parks and mansions of wealth and taste, and antique churches bearded with ivy "creeping where no life is seen," and covering the wrinkles of half a dozen centuries; but there is no fragrance of flowers, no velvety green grass—it is winter. The hills of Derbyshire are very picturesque, and I greatly enjoyed the railway ride along the valley of the Derwent.

The two stopping-places of interest on this trip are Manchester and Bedford. Manchester is like the other great manufacturing centres. You feel the throb and rush of industrial life. Having seen one, you have the pattern of all. Endless rows of brick houses with red-tiled roofs; chimneys standing thick and tall, their thousand lofty columns puffing their foul black breathings into the face and eyes of the sky above. The whole atmosphere laden with the abominations of coal smoke; the whole population grimy and sweltering. Here toil the lineal descendents of Thor. Here sweat and drudge a sturdy set of Tubal Cains; and Vulcans, the sleepless fires of whose mighty manufactories darken the sun at noonday, and illumine the sky at midnight. And in such centres as these the power of Old England couches like a dragon, breathing forth flame and smoke. Bedford is the spot where the immortal dreamer, Bunyan, saw heaven opened, and pointed the whole world to the splendors of the Delectable Mountains. The emotions awakened by the scenes of his waking and dreaming life; Elstow where he was born, Luton, where he preached, and the winding Ouse, along whose banks he so often strayed, need not here be described. An hour's ride and we enter "famous London Town."

CHAPTER III.

THE WORLD'S METROPOLIS.

The World's Metropolis—The People—The Streets—The River—Hyde Park—A Diversion—St. Paul's Cathedral—Westminster Abbey—Jerusalem Chamber—Houses of Parliament—Exciting Debates—Cleopatra's Needle—Her Majesty's Tower.

I REACHED the great metropolis at night, and drove at once to the Devonshire House, Bishopsgate street, a pleasant, comfortable temperance hotel, the headquarters of the Society of Friends, and recommended to me by my dear friends, Mr. and Mrs. Lister, of Hamilton. Everything about the house is quiet and home-like, the bedrooms clean and comfortable, the table service neat and tidy. And they know how to prepare the savory drinks of tea and coffee, so that you have never to repeat the order given in an American hotel: "Waiter, if this is tea bring me coffee; if it is coffee bring me tea." The next morning seemed never to dawn—the mighty city was enveloped in fog. This was my first experience of a London fog. It was hardly so thick that you could push your arm into it, and drawing it back, see the hole you had made ; but it wrapped everything in gloom and darkness. This was followed by two or three dark, muggy, dirty days Indeed all England had just had something unexampled in the way of a "cold snap" and heavy fall of snow. It is estimated that eight million tons of snow fell over the area of London, and the cost to the civic authorities of removing the snow from the city proper exceeded fifty thousand dollars. Now all this snow had melted away, and still there came the constant downpour of rain. At length came the "clear shining," after the rain, and then how I did enjoy the plunge into the stream of life that sweeps along the thoroughfares of this surging metropolis! What a ty !

> "Houses, churches, mixed together,
> Streets crammed full in every weather ;
> Prisons, palaces, contiguous,
> Sinners sad and saints religious,
> Gaudy things enough to tempt ye,
> Outsides showy, insides empty ;
> Baubles, beasts, mechanics, arts,
> Coaches, wheelbarrows, and carts;
> Warrants, bailiffs, bills unpaid,
> Lords, of laundresses afraid ;
> Rogues that nightly prowl and shoot **men,**
> Hangmen, aldermen, and footmen ;
> Lawyers, poets, priests, physicians,
> Nobles, simple, all conditions ;
> Worth beneath a threadbare cover,
> Villainy bedaubed all over.

>Women black, fair, red, and gray,
>Women that can play and pay,
>Handsome, ugly, witty, still,
>Some that *will not*—some that will
>Many a beau without a shilling,
>Many a widow, not unwilling,
>Many a bargain if you strike it—
>This is London if you like it."

And I do like it above all other cities in the world. The first impression is overpowering. Such an endless mass of human life !—the roar of vehicles, the glitter of shops, but especially the streams of people.

>"And he looked upon the city, every side
>   Far and wide ;
>All the mountains topped with steeples, all the glades,
>   Colonnades ;
>All the causeys, bridges, aqueducts, and then,
>   All the men !

Walk along the streets—Cornhill, Cheapside, Fleet, Strand, Piccadilly, Pall Mall, Holborn, Oxford, those traffic-choked, men-crammed thoroughfares, and "the people—O the people !" Where do they come from ? Will the stream never end, that continuous, close black, stream—that living tide, that roaming, surging throng of immortal beings ! No pause, no rest, no stay ! Look into the faces of this teeming sea of humanity, and you see handsome faces, ugly faces, bright faces, dark faces, haggard faces, idle faces, set faces, vacant faces—faces with lines of care, of debt, of anxiety, of crime—faces that tell of laughter and song, faces of pride and pomp, faces of woe and wretchedness. And every one of that countless, hurrying throng redeemed by Christ, and hastening forward to eternal happiness or everlasting wretchedness! One after another dropping out by death, but new-comers filling up continually the gaps in the unbroken line. What a feeling of isolation comes over one, the feeling that you are but a speck on this immense sea of existence, and an unknown speck at that!

London has a greed of growth. Its magnitude overwhelms you. It has swallowed up the surrounding towns, and villages, and intervening meadows smiling with daisies and buttercups. It is a vast concrete of towns and cities. Its extent and population are unlike anything else in the world. It covers within the fifteen miles radius of Charing Cross nearly seven hundred square miles. Take the Metropolitan Railway and sweep around its mighty circumference; or climb to the top of an omnibus and ride along a few of its seven thousand miles of streets, amid the ceaseless tumultuous roar of its busy traffic; or jump into a two-wheeled hansom that whirls you along through narrow, crowded lanes; west-end wealth and splendor, and east-end poverty and want and crime,—and you are more and more bewildered by this great Babylon. Its population comprises more than one hundred thousand foreigners, from every quarter of the globe. It contains more Roman Catholics than Rome; more Jews than all Palestine; more Scotchmen than Aberdeen; more Irish than Belfast; and more Welshmen than Cardiff. Ten thousand new houses are built every year. Let the dwellings in London be placed side by side and they would reach almost to the borders of Scotland; while the beer-shops and gin-palaces are so numerous that their frontages, placed side by side, would extend sixty-five miles:—sixty-five miles of drinking places open every Sunday! Now, take a ride upon the Thames, "the river of ten thousand masts," which divides the city into two unequal parts, and as your little steamer pushes along through the dark waters that have often closed over—

> "One more unfortunate
> Weary of breath;
> Rashly importunate
> Gone to her death—"

passing under bridges, threading its way through barges and vessels of every size, from every land, one thousand of which are in this port every day, look upon the docks and warehouses, factories and markets, and you get another view of—

> "Opulent, enlarged, and still-
> Increasing London."

I love to stand on Westminster Bridge, where you get so fine a view of the Parliament Buildings and Westminster Abbey on one side, and St. Thomas' Hospital on the other; the Thames Embankment, the bridge below, and the throbbing life on the river itself. But London Bridge is the place to see the living stream

The Thames Embankment, London.

of humanity, and the enormous traffic which makes London the commercial metropolis of the world. The first bridge was built A.D. one thousand, and for eight hundred years London managed with only one bridge across its river. On the top of its gates many a trunkless head was stuck upon pikes, and ghastly memories lurk under its arches. This new bridge is about fifty years old, and you get some idea of how it is crowded when it is estimated that eight thousand foot passengers and nine hundred vehicles pass over it every hour —twenty thousand vehicles pass over it every twenty-four hours, which vehicles, averaging five yards each, would extend in close file from Toronto to Hamilton, and fifteen miles beyond towards the Forest City—our new London. The persons passing daily over this bridge, marching in a column of six abreast, would extend fifteen miles up Yonge Street. This is the place to see people—fat men, pretty girls, draymen, sailors, clerks, men of every hue and nationality—carriages, omnibusses, market-carts, waggons loaded with beer, grain, bacon, tea, sugar, tallow, oil, wool, leather, every produce; drays, hansoms, broughams, carriages of the nobility, and trucks of the poor. They say in riding over the bridge you meet an average of seventeen white horses. And the first time I passed over, with Dr. Punshon in early morning, we amused ourselves in counting nineteen white horses that we met on the bridge.

Another favorite resort in the London season is

Rotten Row. This drive, the King's way—"Route de Roi"—in Hyde Park, is thronged by those who make history. Hundreds of carriages—some plain, many coroneted—move slowly up and down between Prince's Gate and that splendid monument, the Albert Memorial. It is a brilliant scene, the rendezvous of beauty, wealth, and fashion, and interesting to watch the handsome carriages with spirited, high-bred horses, driven by liveried and powdered servants, and filled with ladies of hereditary rank and high-born culture, with their fair, fresh faces, and eyes beaming upon their gallant attendants. It is interesting to watch them as they pass and re-pass; but one can hardly see the pleasure there is in driving along at a funereal pace, and coming every five minutes to a dead standstill. Some of these rich dowagers and gaily-dressed women look gloomily grand or stolidly indifferent, and some of the lords and gentlemen seem actually uncomfortable and in need of change. I thought that a little variety would have been given by what I saw on the Brighton Road in Boston. On this brilliant drive, for all Boston, the carriages move slowly up one side of the broad way and down the other; but between this sober stream more daring horsemen dash along, where the swerve of a handbreadth is destructive to equipage and all; and there, one afternoon, I saw two sleighs collide; the lady of one was thrown senseless upon the ice, and the gentleman of the other had his head cut and bleeding by being pitched against an iron lamp-post. The Rotten Row processions need some such *diversion*.

One can give no adequate idea of the museums and picture galleries, the palaces and churches, government and commercial buildings, of this centre of the world. Suppose we commence with St. Paul's Cathedral. The first time I reached London was late one Saturday night. The moon was shining. From my hotel window I looked out, and there, right before me, above the wilderness of buildings, stood a dim gigantic dome. What a bound my heart gave, for I knew it as it towered aloft so mightily.

St. Paul's fully symbolizes the ecclesiastical power of Great Britain. It is built in the form of a cross, and the magnificent nave and transept are five hundred feet in length. The west front entrance is beautiful, its pediment ornamented with statues of the chief apostles, and its entablature with a representation of the miraculous conversion of St. Paul. On entering St. Paul's you are struck with the vastness of the building and the statues of the great which fill its many niches and corners. The afternoon service had just begun, and my distinguished companion, Dr. Punshon, and myself took part, as far as we could, in the devotions of the hour. After service we descended into the crypt, where lie the remains of the illustrious dead. In a sarcophagus of black marble lie the remains of Nelson, and near by, in a porphyry sarcophagus, the body of the Duke of Wellington. Not far from the tomb is his funeral car. Nelson and Wellington are the two idols of England; you see their statues or some memorial of them everywhere. There, also, carved upon simple slabs, were such names as Sir Joshua Reynolds, Lawrence, West, Turner, and Sir Christopher Wren, with the veritable inscription, "*Si quæris monumentum circumspice.*" Surely we are on holy ground. Here are monuments of the great in all professions and pursuits: soldiers, statesmen, seamen, painters, poets, and philosophers. We wandered through the area of the noble structure and gazed upon its various monuments, many of which are not only memorials of the illustrious dead, but remarkable specimens of art. St. Paul's Cathedral is nearly half a mile in circumference, and is said to have cost four millions. It is a vast and venerable pile; but its architecture has not the solemnizing effect, or the power of appeal to the heart—does not speak to the soul, of God, and immortality like the Gothic architecture, with its columns, groined arches and lofty vaultings, that seem to kindle the very spirit of devotion.

Let us make a visit now to Westminster Abbey. This is England's mausoleum of her mighty dead. Its architectural splendor, its transepts and nave and choir, its chapels and cloisters, seem to inspire the spirit of worship; while its monuments and tablets, inscribed with world-famous and familiar names, give a feeling like the sudden meeting of well-known friends.—

"Marble monuments are here displayed
Thronging the walls; and on the floor beneath
Sepulchral stones appear with emblems graven,
And foot-worn epitaphs, and some with small
And shining effigies of brass inlaid."

In this glorious resting-place of kings and heroes, poets and philosophers, we see all that remains of earthly greatness—a tomb amid the dim windows, and fretted pillars, and lofty ceilings, and long colonnades, and many-tinted stones, of Westminster. When one looks at this place of peace and reconciliation, the bones of Romish abbot and Protestant bishop side by side; Elizabeth sleeping in the same vault with her sister, Mary Tudor—"Bloody Mary;" ambitious spirits of every rank of genius content to be there in pure white marble, he is reminded of that old Elizabethan epigram:—

"When I behold, with deep astonishment,
 The famous Westminster, how there resort,
Living in brass or stone monument,
 The princes and the worthies of all sort,
Do I not see reformed nobility,
 Without contempt, or pride, or ostentation,
And look upon offenceless majesty,
 Naked of pomp and earthly domination,
And how a play game of a painted stone,
 Contents the quiet now and silent spirits,
When all the world, which late they stood upon,
 Could not content nor quench their appetites.
Life is a frost of cold felicities,
And death the thaw of all our vanities."

Yet we may not talk of "the play game of a painted stone," or "the worthless honors of a bust;" for even if there were no after-life, it is something to have received a nation's gratitude and to find an immortality even for a few centuries in the hearts of men. What mighty dead are here! Think of such names as Pitt, Wilberforce, Sir Isaac Newton, Cobden, Hastings, Palmerston, Canning, Sir J. Franklin, Wolfe, Wesley, and a host of such worthies. Henry VII.'s Chapel is sown with the richest royalist seed—King Henry, Charles, Edward, William, Mary Queen of Scots, and Queen Elizabeth. In the south transept, called the "Poet's Corner," are Butler, Spenser, Milton, rare Ben. Johnson, Gray, Prior, Chaucer, Campbell, Southey, Shakespeare, Thomson, Goldsmith, and Gay, with the doggerel couplet—

> "Life is a jest, and all things show it;
> I thought so once, but now I know it;"

Thackeray, Addison, Macaulay, Barrow, South, and Taylor.

In the Jerusalem Chamber sits the Committee on the Revision of the Bible, a chamber rendered famous forever, because it is connected with two great events in the history of England. When Henry IV., one early spring, came up to London, covered with a hideous leprosy, and in pain and sickness, the Abbey was cold, and this was the only room which had conveniences for a fire. To it the attendants carried the

King, and laid him upon a pallet before the large fireplace. In a room in the adjoining palace of Westminster, Shakespeare places that affecting scene in which the young prince puts the crown of his sleeping father on his own head; and then he represents Henry, carried at his own request to the Jerusalem Chamber to die,—

> "*King Henry.* Doth any name particular belong
> Unto the lodging where I first did swoon?
>   *Warwick.* 'Tis call'd Jerusalem, my noble lord.
>   *King Henry.* Laud be to God!—even there my life must end.
> It hath been prophesied to me many years,
> I should not die but in Jerusalem;
> Which vainly I suppos'd, the Holy Land:—
> But, bear me to that chamber; there I'll lie;
> In that Jerusalem shall Harry die.

The other event, not so dramatic but not less important, is connected with the origin of one of the largest Protestant denominations of Christendom. Here sat the famous Westminster Assembly. This little chamber, then, is the birth-place of the great Presbyterian Church, and within its walls, with now and then a session in the Chapel of Henry VII., were formed the Longer and Shorter Catechisms, and that famous symbol of theological doctrine, the Westminster Confession of Faith.

Among the curiosities of the Abbey is the coronation chair, an old oak chair in which the kings of England were crowned, and which has in its seat a stone on which the kings of Scotland were crowned, and before that the Irish kings, while tradition has it that this is the stone which Jacob used for a pillow in Bethel.

I would say to my friends, visit Westminster Abbey the first day you enter London; see it every day, and then visit it the last hour you are leaving, lest your eyes may never be blessed with the sight again.

Close to the Abbey are the Houses of Parliament. The entrance is by Westminster Hall, an ancient royal palace, originally built by William Rufus, the scene of many royal feasts and ceremonies. Here Cromwell was inaugurated as Lord Protector; here the great trials of State took place. Warren Hastings was here tried, so also the seven bishops. Here Charles I. was condemned to die. As I stood within those halls and looked up to the carved roof, whose rafters had so often rung with wonderful eloquence, I thought it fitting that this ancient hall should be incorporated with the new and splendid pile—the Houses of Parliament. Entering by Westminster Hall we passed into St. Stephen's Hall, adorned with statues of Hampden, Walpole, Chatham, Fox, and others, and then proceeded into the Grand Central Hall, from which corridors lead to the House of Peers and the House of Lords. These corridors are adorned with fresco paintings, and the halls are richly gilded, and, filled as they were with groups of well-dressed men in conversation, presented a brilliant spectacle. The House of Commons is a room some fifty feet long by forty-five wide; its windows filled with stained glass, its walls panelled with carved oak, and its ceiling richly adorned; the other parts of the room are comparatively plain. The Speaker's chair is in the north end, and on the right of the Speaker is the ministerial side of the House. Over the Speaker's chair is the reporters' gallery, and above that a gallery for ladies, with a screen in front. At the south end of the hall is the gallery for strangers. Through the kindness of friends, I have several times got admission to the House of Lords and of Commons, to hear the debates.

In the House of Peers nothing special seems ever going on, but one has the opportunity of seeing a number of England's distinguished Peers. Near the middle of the room is a seat covered with crimson cloth, the woolsack, and on it the Lord Chancellor sits. Behind him stands the throne used by the Queen at the opening or prorogation of Parliament.

In the House of Commons I have had the fortune to be present during two extraordinary scenes. The first was in connection with Mr. Plimsoll, and the Shipowner's Bill. The House was exceptionally crowded. Several notices of motion had been given and questions asked, and I was busy studying the *personnel* of the House—Sir C. Adderley, Sir G. Jenkinson, Mr. Disraeli, Mr. Gladstone, the Marquis of Hartington, and others —when the then Premier rose and made a statement as to the course of public business. Among other things he said that they would not be able to deal with the Merchants' Shipping Bill this session. When he sat down, Mr. Plimsoll, a representative of the ship-owning community, who seems to have given many years of his life to the effort to improve the condition of sailors of the merchant navy, rose, and, with great emotion, expressed his regret at the withdrawal of the Bill. He was reminded by the Speaker that his remarks were not in order, when he said, with a loud voice, "I beg to move the adjournment of the House." Then, in the most excited tones, he poured forth a torrent of furious invective against certain shipowners and their practices, until the excitement of the House was scarcely less intense than his own; and at the top of his voice cried out, "I am determined to unmask the villains!" At once the Speaker rose, with great calmness and dignity, and said, "The hon. member made use of the word 'villain;' I trust he did not mean to apply the word to any member of this House?" "I did, Sir," shouted Mr. Plimsoll, "and I do not mean to withdraw it." The confusion on both sides of the House was indescribable—it was said to be unparalleled in the annals of the British Parliament. After the tumult had partially subsided, Mr. Disraeli called upon the Speaker to exercise one of his highest duties, and reprimand the honorable member for Derby. The Marquis of Hartington suggested that action might be deferred; and Mr. Sullivan and others pleaded for consideration and indulgence to the hon. member. Mr. Disraeli at once moved that Mr. Plimsoll be requested to attend in his place on that day week. At once the House subsided into quiet calmness, and there seemed not a trace of the fierce hurricane that had swept over it. Afterwards Mr. Plimsoll apologized for violating the rules and regulations of the House, but would not withdraw any statement of facts. His apology was accepted. His outbreak of violence resulted in the Government bringing forward a measure which has helped to remedy the grievous complaints against mercenary shipowners overloading their vessels, and thus imperilling the lives of seamen. The second time I was in the House of Commons I heard the discussion on the famous Protection of Life and Property Bill in Ireland. It is a memorable item in one's experience to have heard Gladstone, Foster, Sir Stafford Northcote, Mr. McCarthy, Dodson, Childers, Sir Wm. Harcourt, the Marquis of Hartington, Mr. Mundella, Sir C. Dilke, and the whole Irish brigade—O'Connor, Sullivan, Biggar, Callan, Cowan, Dr. Cummins, &c. The visitors' galleries were choked, and I could not get out for refreshments till after nine in the evening, when I got the promise that my place would be kept for me for a few minutes. My host, Alex. McArthur, Esq., M.P., led me through the splendid corridors and the sumptuous library into the members' lunch-room; but hardly had we begun eating when a throbbing bell-like sound rang through the rooms, calling for a division. Then there was a rush, and I witnessed the form in which the House divided and registered their "Ayes" and "Nays."

Another of the sights of London is Cleopatra's Needle, one of the great obelisks, named after the beautiful Egyptian Queen, and daughter of Ptolemy, now set up on the Thames Embankment. It is a shaft of rose-colored granite, some seventy feet high, and about eight feet wide at the base. Three of its sides are covered with hieroglyphic inscriptions. I was disappointed in its proportions; but as I stood beneath this monument of the most ancient civilization, I mused upon the past. Joseph very likely had looked upon this column, and the sons of Jacob. It stood in its pride in the days of Moses, of Isaiah, Ezekiel, and Elijah. If stones could speak, how much this obelisk would tell us!

Further down the river is Her Majesty's Tower, the most historic building in Europe. Founded by William the Conqueror, and finished by Henry III., who fortified it with high embattled walls; royal fortress, prison, palace, it is alive with English history. The Middle Tower protects the entrance to the bridge over the moat, which is no longer filled with water. Passing along the outer ward, we notice the gloomy archway of the Traitor's Gate and the Bloody Tower, where the two children of Edward were smothered.

> "The most arch-deed of piteous massacre
> That ever yet this land was guilty of."

The White Tower is a grand specimen of Norman architecture. Here we enter the armories, with their great stores of arms arranged in the form of lilies and passion flowers. We see the heavy suits-of-mail worn in the old days of battle. Gay tournaments were given here when this was the high place of kinghood, and the very suits of armor which we see once glittered and shone on the flower of English nobility and chivalry. Where are they now? The Beauchamp Tower has held many a royal prisoner. What tears have been shed within those thick walls! What memorials are here of Dudley, and Raleigh, and the gentle Lady Jane Grey! We see the Latin inscription of Arundel over the fireplace, the interpretation of which is, "The more suffering with Christ in this world, the more glory with Christ in the next." We peep into the little room where Sir Walter slept— where he wiled away his long imprisonment with writing his "History of the World." The Jewel Room contains the crowns, sceptres, jewels, all the regalia of royalty. What a blaze of splendor! What wealth stored up in gold and jewels, in diadems and coronation plate! The crown of the Sovereign is a purple velvet cap, enclosed in hoops of silver, blazing with over 3,000 diamonds and the "inestimable sapphire." Its value is five millions of dollars. You also see in glass a model of the brilliant "Koh-i-noor." This gem is of great antiquity and of high historic interest, nay every one of the dazzling galaxy of diamond, ruby, emerald, and pearl has its own pedigree and legend. I understand that Her Majesty's Crown has been constructed out of the fragments of half a dozen by-gone insignia of royalty and thus bears a resemblance to the British Constitution which has been patched and mended, enlarged and renovated over and over again. The "Queen's Beef-eaters" are there in their picturesque dress, and velvet hats bright with blue ribbons; but alas! the jolly days of the beef-eating warders are over. Before, they conducted you upstairs and downstairs, and rattled off their story, and got their recompense of reward in a piece of silver dropped in their hand by each visitor. How those old warders compelled you to trail at their heels and listen to their stereotyped stuff!

> "For guide-book prattle when once begun,
> Bequeathed by tedious sire to son,
> Though often told is never done."

But times have changed. Now, the admission is free; much of the red tape is done away with; there is no waiting for a party to gather; each takes his own way. The warders stand solitary and mute, and when I offered one something for a special favor he answered in melancholy mood, "There's no money paid for anything now." O, a rare place is this glorious old structure. What conflicts it has seen! Norman, Saxon, Briton, White Rose, and Red Rose, Revolution, and Rebellion, Protestant, and Papal. It rose with the Conqueror. It welcomed the Lady Plantagenet. It saw the haughty Tudor come and proudly go. It beheld the tyrant Stuart hurled from the throne, and hailed the Hanoverian across the seas. It has heard ten thousand thunderblasts and looked out upon unnumbered storms lashing the rock-bound coasts of the sea-girt isle. What memories it awakens! Its grim and wrinkled lines of wall, work on the senses like a spell.

CHAPTER IV.

THE HEART OF LONDON.

The Heart of London—The Bank—Exchange—Mansion House—National Gallery—Madame Tussaud—Zoölogical Gardens—South Kensington—The British Museum—City Road Chapel—Bunhill Field's Cemetery—The Childrens' Home.

THERE is no end in the exploration of the labyrinths of London. How its streets, and squares, and bridges remind one of Dickens (whose last letter, in his own handwriting, is seen in the British Museum), and the very names of his characters, even to Dombey & Son, are found over shop doors and on street signs.

The real London is inside of Temple Bar. That dark old archway no longer obstructs the streets. But since it served to hold up the heads of so many traitors, that were here exposed, a monument marks the spot where it so long stood. Among the churches after Westminster Abbey and St. Paul's Cathedral, whose mighty dome, noble as St. Peter's at Rome, attracts all eyes and draws all feet toward it, is Bow Church, one of Sir Christopher Wren's handsomest structures

The steeple of this church holds the bells within whose sound the Cockneys are born. The limits of London proper are said be within the sound of Bow Bells. From this point take an omnibus, and climbing to the top, ride along Ludgate Hill, Fleet Street into the Strand, along Pall Mall, Regent Street, and Piccadilly.

In this grand ride if you have made friends with the driver, you will have pointed out to you the collection of buildings so well known in literature, and called the Temple, the centre of the law power with its courts and halls, its lecture-rooms and council-rooms, and church—a beautiful Norman Church—the place where once preached the "Judicious Hooker;" Exeter Hall, the building in which the great May meetings are held; Somerset House, King's College, Charing Cross, where proclamations were wont to be made, and where, in 1837, Victoria was proclaimed Queen; Trafalgar Square, with its column rising up 180 feet, and the granite statue of the hero Nelson on the top, on the four sides the bronze bas-relief, which represent the "Death of Nelson," the "Battle of the Nile," the "Battle of St. Vincent," and the "Battle of Copenhagen," with the couchant Lions of Landseer at the base; Buckingham Palace, the royal residence of the Queen in London; Apsley House, the mansion of the Duke of Wellington, with the Triumphal Arch opposite, surmounted by the equestrian statue of the "Iron Duke;" the mansions of Baron Rothschild and of the good Earl of Shaftesbury; the Royal Albert Hall, and that "perfection of beauty," the memorial to the late Prince Consort, called the Albert Memorial. Its glittering cross, supported by three tiers of emblematic gilt figures, shines from afar, and it seems more like some thing of beauty dropped from the skies than any human workmanship. While you are in the West End amid delightful parks and splendid palaces, return to that grandest site in Europe, Trafalgar Square, and opposite Whitehall, where that brick-faced Bluebeard, Henry VIII., fell in love with the unfortunate Anne Boleyn, and from whose palace window Charles I. stepped to the scaffold, is an uncomely structure, but it is the home of British art, the National Gallery, a place to be ravished with the sight of charming pictures. I am not an artist; perhaps I have not much taste, but I know the pictures that please me. They are those that charm the imagination, and uplift the soul, and purify the heart, and live in the memory. I could mention picture after picture in this gallery that I can never forget. Turner has many choice landscapes. Lingering for hours among the immortal productions of Sir Joshua Reynolds, Sir E. Landseer, Sir David Wilkie, Sir F. Leighton, Gilbert, Leslie, Etty, and other English artists; the Spanish school, represented by Murillo and Velasquez; the Flemish, by Reubens and Vandyck; the Italian by Titian, and others, I could not but notice how art is indebted to revelation for its sublimest conceptions. The two books of the painter are Nature and the Bible. Take such scenes as "Christ Appearing to Mary Magdalene," by Etty; "The Vision of Ezekiel," by Poole; " Christ Lamenting over Jerusalem," by Eastlake; "The Raising of Lazarus," by Hayden; " Marriage of Isaac and Rebecca," by Claude; "The Cave of Adullum ;" " St. John and the Lamb," by Murillo, and they but illustrate what I have just observed. Can any one ever forget "The Remorse of Judas," by Armitage ? The anguish of that face is burned into your heart.

Entering again the busy heart of the city and mingling with the crowds in Leadenhall and Threadneedle Street; the Bank of England, the Exchange, and Mansion House are to be visited. There are no architectural attractions about that wonderful establishment which makes itself felt in every money market in the civilized world, although it covers a quadrangular space of four acres, with a famous street on every side. Close to the Bank is the Royal Exchange, the headquarters of the commerce of this centre of the world. It is a spacious and elegant edifice, with a fine Corinthian portico in front. The pediment is ornamented with allegorical figures, by Westmacott, and in rear of the building is the statue of George Peabody, executed by Story. Close at hand is the official residence of the Lord Mayor, the Mansion House. We passed through the principal room, " Egyptian Hall" as it is called, which is profusely adorned with statues. The next public building we visited was Guildhall.

The chief point of interest here is the great hall where the annual Lord Mayor's dinner is given. At the west end are two grotesque wooden giants called Gog and Magog. Around the hall are marble monuments of Lord Nelson, the Duke of Wellington, the Earl of Chatham, William Pitt, and others. Various courts were being held in Guildhall, and it was a curious spectacle to a Canadian to see judges and lawyers all with powdered wigs on their heads.

I had the honour of dining, in company with Dr. and Mrs. Punshon, and others, at the Lord Mayor's, the Honorable Wm. McArthur, in the Mansion House, so famous for its good dinners; and was shown through the Venetian room, the saloon, and drawing-rooms of this lordly house of the City's Chief Magistrate.

I have also eaten turtle soup in Crosby Hall, the Palace of Richard III. and Henry VIII. Those defunct sovereigns could surely never have dreamed that I, and others of the common crowd, would one day dine in their very Throne-room.

Baker Street must not be forgotten and Madame Tussaud's Wax Figures. This Historical Gallery is justly celebrated, although there are those who pronounce it a fraud. You see the life-like portraits of kings and queens, statesmen, scholars, warriors, reformers, and celebrities of all periods. The faces and forms, the coloring, the attitude, the garments worn, the general appearance, are thoroughly life-like. These life-size forms seem to be real existences, and not mere mouldings of wax. I remember, on one occasion Rev. Dr. Potts and myself amused ourselves for some minutes in trying to decide whether a little dog in the grouping of a queen and her court was a live terrier that had lain down there to rest, and was looking around in complacency, or was only one of the wax group. The turning of the head, the eyes, all were apparently instinct with life, and we waited to see him wag his tail or trot away. In several cases I have been startled, as in the presence of life, for one does feel a little cheap to be found impudently staring in the face of another. The Chamber of Horrors is not so dreadful a place as one would imagine, for some of the most distinguished occupants of this room are rather handsome murderers, and I have heard of visitors being taken for and pointed out as belonging to the show.

The Zoological Gardens are imperative Be sure and spend a day in that most attractive of places,—among reptiles and salamanders, kangaroos and parrots, eagles and lions, kites and vultures, tigers and marsupials, leopards and hyenas, camels and giraffes, elephants and rhinoceroses, antelopes and seals, baboons, apes, and monkeys. It is the largest collection of the kind in the world, and should not on any account be missed. South Kensington Museum is rich in objects of mediæval and modern art. Such a collection of paintings, sculptures, jewels, tapestries, porcelain, pottery, glass, furniture, etc., can nowhere else be seen. This public building, filled with the richest treasures collected from every part of the world, at a cost of ten millions of dollars, is daily open to the public, and free to the poorest citizen of the kingdom.

But if one wishes to get some little conception of the vigor and intellectual life of the British nation let him visit that great National Institution, the *British Museum*. It is a world in its vastness. Here is a collection of antiquities—Egyptian, Assyrian, Greek, Roman, and British—that is unmatched. The building itself is a noble one, and the majestic dome of the Reading-Room is almost a *fac simile* of the Pantheon in Rome. Passing through the court-yard you ascend by twelve steps, each one hundred and twenty-five feet long, a portico formed by a double range of columns, eight on each side, and on the right at east and west angles are projecting wings with columns. Through the portico you enter a magnificent hall, the ceiling enriched with Greek frets and other ornaments in encaustic colors, and around are ranged specimens of famous sculptures.

The Library is one of the most interesting sections of the museum, with its hundreds of thousands of volumes, and its magnificent collection of autographs of the great of all lands and languages. The eyes grow weary with looking at the collection of books, the manuscripts written by kings and queens and great ones—such as Shakespeare, Chaucer, Milton,

Wickliffe, Macaulay, Pope, Knox, and a host of others. Day by day you may roam through the halls, and there is so much that you cannot take it in. *L'embarras des 'richesses* has its fittest illustration here. You can study specimens of birds, beasts, reptiles, and fishes, in the galleries of natural history, or, walking through the avenues of a dead world, the Egyptian and Assyrian antiquities, ancient Roman and Greek art, see more of the great sculptures of Ninevah and Egypt than you can see on the banks of the Euphrates, or the land of the Pharoahs.

Choice specimens of Grecian sculptures are seen in headless and mutilated marble. I remember, among the ancient statuary in the Art Gallery of the Centennial Exhibition, overhearing a young lady remark to her companion, "Noses *has* to suffer here!" Well, noses and other organs of the body have suffered in the marble of the British Museum. London is full of "places to go to," but on no account must one miss the British Museum.

I shall not ask the reader's company in all my rambles about the crowded thoroughfares of the great Metropolis; but I shall ask him to accompany me to a spot dear to the hearts of millions the world over— the Old Mother Church of Methodism.

My memories of *City Road Chapel* are inseparably linked with those of that incomparable man and minister, Rev. Dr. Punshon. A guest of his, and comfortably settled in his delightful home, the kind, great man proposed that I should surrender myself up to him for the first day, and that some of the chief objects of the city should be seen through his eyes. I gladly availed myself of such an honor and privilege. He first introduced me to the Underground Railway system by which sub-London is traversed. Some idea of the extent of this network of lines may be formed when one learns that through the station from which we started—the Addison Road, Kensington—three hundred and sixty-five passenger trains pass daily. We landed at Moorgate, and he led me at once to the *City Road Chapel*, a very simple and unpretending structure it is, and since the fire, has been restored just as it was when first erected. My heart was stirred to see upon the walls the monumental busts of the hero-fathers of the Church—John and Charles Wesley, Fletcher, Watson, Coke, Benson, Clarke, Bunting, Newton, Jackson, and a score of other sacred and familiar names; and to stand in the pulpit from which they preached that Gospel which quickened all England into spiritual life. We entered Mr. Wesley's house and stood in the library where he studied, and in the room where calmly he breathed out his soul into his Redeemer's hands. Then we went into the burial ground and stood by his tomb.

"In the grave-yard of the City Road sleep five thousand dead. They were the early followers and converts of John Wesley. The associations with this place may well touch the hearts of all who revere his teachings, for within its narrow precincts lies the kind reformer, surrounded by nearly all who loved him and whom he loved, by his preachers and assistants, his

CITY ROAD CHAPEL

scholars and teachers, the babes he fondled and the grown men and women whom he cheered and guided, the leaders of his classes, the youths he instructed, the noble women who increased and dispensed his charities, the families over which he watched with a father's care, and the devoted followers who, when he was no more, lived and died with his name ever on their lips. The grave-yard is now closed, and the five thousand rest apart forever. It is not necessary to invoke peace to their ashes, for peace they have attained. They rest well from their labors, and from the graves the voice of love breathes gently over their race. Sweet are the memories of patience and endurance, of joyous hope and calm assurance, of lives given up to the welfare of others, and of hearts that were never cold to human woe, that cluster about this cemetery; and, of whatever sect or creed, he who would learn how to live and how to die would do well to stand reverently before the consecrated tomb where John Wesley sleeps amidst his followers. The ground appropriated to the burial of the dead around City Road Chapel is divided into three portions. In front the court is separated by the path that leads to the chapel into the north and south divisions; the basement under the chapel was used for brick and iron vaults, and the ground in the rear of the building and on its southern side was early devoted by Mr. Wesley and the trustees to the purpose of interment. The first burial took place in 1779: it was closed by the general Act of Parliament in relation to city funerals in 1853. On a memorable day, December 19, 1870, one of its finest monuments was uncovered at noon to the inspection of the public. A fair white shaft of Sicilian marble had been erected, chiefly at the expense of the daughters and mothers of Methodism, to the memory of one who had slept for more than a century in a tomb not far away. The ministers of the city had assembled, a congregation gathered in the open air, and the exercises opened by a stirring hymn, followed by a commemorative address. The December weather was cold, the services short, yet it was with no common interest that the faithful band heard, related anew, the virtuous deeds of Susannah, the mother of the Wesleys. From her lips her sons had learned the elements of the faith they preached so earnestly; from her example they had imbibed order, economy, unselfishness, and a contempt for all that might clog the progress of the spiritual nature. She had broken through the formalism of the Church services, to teach and reform the poor, when John and Charles Wesley were climbing at her knee. But for her rigorous devotion to duty before pleasure, and in contempt of gain, Methodism would have wanted its crowning excellence, and might have sunk into feeble conformity. She had animated and even forced John Wesley into bold and unaccustomed efforts to begin the career of reform. The fair white marble was not more pure than her spotless life, and the monument of Susannah Wesley, the mother of Methodism, raised in the moment of the unbounded prosperity of the cause she had loved, might well recall the simple virtues and the unselfish deeds of those among whom she had labored and died.

"Not far off lies her devoted son. In the grave-yard behind the chapel, in the centre of the ground, and shaded by an elder tree, from which cuttings have been transplanted to many lands, a plain tomb, enclosed by an iron railing, marks the vault where his sarcophagus was reverently laid. The morning was dark. It was at that early hour which he seems ever to have loved. Torches and lanterns glittered around the tomb, a multitude of his followers assembled in the early dawn, and with a burst of tears consecrated his grave. One solemn wail of sobs and weeping swept over the people, and the gray light of morning seldom broke on a more touching scene. It was March, 1791. Four months afterwards, his sister Patty, the admirable and ill-rewarded wife, was placed at his side. She had outlived all her brothers and sisters, and at eighty-five closed the career of the children of Susannah Wesley."

Next we visited, on the opposite side of City Road, Bunhill Fields Burial Ground, the "Campo Santo" of Dissenters, and saw the tombs of Dr. John Owen, John Bunyan, Daniel Defoe, author of *Robinson Crusoe;* George Fox, the Quaker; Dr. Isaac Watts, the hymn writer; Susannah, mother of the Wesleys; John Wilkes, Richard and Henry, the two sons of Cromwell; and others well known to fame. The field does not contain four acres, and yet more than one hundred thousand persons have been buried in this cemetery.

My noble guide next led me to the Wesleyan Book Establishment, and the Centennial Hall and Mission-

House, and then to other noted places of interest, some of which I have already described; historical shrines and memorable places, associated with the great events of the nation's history. That was a red-letter day, and it still lingers with me as a most delightful memory. During my second visit to that Old Land, I was again permitted to sustain most intimate and cherished relations with him.

As soon as I reached London, I made my way to the Mission-House, and there learned with sorrow that he was out of the city, and had just hidden away in Bournemouth, with aching heart, the "beautiful clay" of his first-born son.

But having learned that I was in England, he at once wrote to find my whereabouts, and insisted that as soon as he and Mrs. Punshon returned, I should become their guest during my stay in London; and so I was delightfully homed with him in Tranby, Brixton.

While on these matters I cannot do better than refer to the work of the Rev. T. Bowman Stephenson, M.A., in London. This is "The Children's Home and Refuge," Bonner Road.

While engaged in pastoral work, Mr. Stephenson, a Wesleyan Minister, was strongly impressed with the wretchedness and misery of the poor, and especially with the forlorn condition of little children known as "street Arabs." He established an Orphanage and Refuge for these, which is known as "The Children's Home," Bonner Road. It is one of London's greatest charities—a truly noble and Christian work. In eleven years it has grown from a little cottage to a property worth two hundred thousand dollars. The annual revenue is now about fifty thousand dollars, nearly all of which comes by letter. The system with which the books are kept is perfect. There is a Committee for every branch, and a regular statement is given of the revenue, expenditure, and cost per head of each inmate. There are now two hundred and forty children in the Home. In the institution the family life prevails. In the London head-quarters there are eleven houses. Each house has a mother and sister. The house is divided into sitting-room, dining-room, play-room, bath-room, and bed-room. There is a common kitchen, in which the cooking is done for all. Some of these houses are memorial gifts. I was struck with one inscription—"To the glory of God, and in loving remembrance of Jeanie Walton, this house was erected by her husband, Joseph Walton;" and I thought how much more sensible and Christian than to spend a thousand pounds in erecting a splendid but useless monument over her grave.

These little orphans and waifs are taken up and cared for, and trained for usefulness and for God. The boys are taught useful trades—engineering, printing, book-binding, shoe-making, carpentering, etc., and the girls are drilled in all household work. The principal is a pastor and father, and is greatly beloved by all the children. The services in the chapel are open to the public, and are well attended. The singing is something remarkable; the children are taught by a practical musician. I attended a practice in the chapel, and was surprised to hear those little children sing with perfect accuracy the finest pieces of the great masters; and they sang, at my request, anthem after anthem that I had been accustomed to hear rendered by the choir of St. James Street Church, one of the finest choirs of Montreal. They have also a boys' brass band, one of the best in the kingdom. These little people fill the largest halls in England; and in about six weeks they raised for special purposes connected with the Home, some ten thousand dollars. The boys are all learning trades, and cannot be away long at a time; but when they appear before the public they make a stir. Being connected with the branch in Hamilton, I have taken a special delight in making myself familiar with the details of the home work, and I am more and more persuaded that it is of God.

Besides the London premises there is a Lancashire Branch, a farm consisting of seventy-six acres, with houses, cottages, and extensive farm-buildings; and a Canadian Branch Home, at Hamilton, Ontario, which is not for training, but for distributing the children amongst Christian families in the Dominion.

This is a Christ-like movement, and Mr. Stephenson, in seeking to transform these little waifs of society into industrious, useful, Christian citizens, is performing a work that will endure forever. God bless him and his Home!

CHAPTER V.

LONDON CELEBRITIES.

London Preachers—Charles H. Spurgeon—Archibald G. Brown—Dean Stanley—Cathedral Music—Canon Liddon—The Establishment—Cardinal Manning—Dr. Parker—Dr. Donald Fraser—Dr. Pope—Dr. Rigg—Dr. Wm. Morley Punshon.

I have had the pleasure of spending several Sabbaths in London, and of hearing some of the great preachers of the metropolis. Early the first Sabbath I made my way to the Metropolitan Tabernacle to hear the great Baptist divine, Rev. Charles H. Spurgeon. His chapel is on the Surrey side of the Thames, near the "Elephant and Castle." It is an immense building, with basement floor and two tiers of galleries, and will accommodate an audience of seven thousand. I was early there, but had some difficulty in getting a seat, for the place is always crowded. A minute or two before the hour, Mr. Spurgeon came in and sat down at his table, and with a mild expression of countenance looked over his great congregation, which filled every sitting-place and standing place, aisles, and corners, and nooks, wherever it was possible to pack a human being. In appearance he is short and stout, with a full, square, honest face, little, round, sparkling eyes, a large mouth, shaded by a heavy moustache; the entire appearance and physiognomy giving no indication of the greatness of the orator. Standing up, he began the service with invocation, and led the people in a prayer remarkable for simplicity, directness, and fervor. What a voice! How pleasant and bell-like its tones! How clear in its articulation, how marvellous in its compass, how tender in its modulation! He is leading that vast assembly in a real out-pouring of the soul to God. The prayer concluded, the preacher said, "Now, dear friends, let us sing very heartily the 174th hymn;" and as he announced the hymn he added, "Sing heartily and quickly," and, led by a precentor, the audience did sing heartily—grandly. No pealing organ there, or white-robed singing-boys, giving chaste, sedate, ecclesiastical music, after the Romish style, in which music is employed to add to the splendor of the worship of the Divine Majesty, to awaken in the souls of the faithful the desire of heavenly things; but one grand swelling-up of praise from seven thousand worshipping hearts —a music grander than the most ravishing strains of minster choirs. Mr. Spurgeon keeps the congregation well to time. If any drag he tells them. On one occasion he gave out a hymn which was to be sung to the tune of "China." It seems that there is a tune called "Boston," very much resembling it, and three thousand five hundred people sang the stanza to the tune of "China," and the other three thousand five hundred, in blissful ignorance of what they were doing, poured forth the notes of praise to the tune "Boston." One stanza was enough, and Mr. Spurgeon said, "Friends, we are in a geographical as well as a musical dilemma. China and Boston are a great way apart, and it is useless to attempt to sing them together."

His Scripture lessons were accompanied with brief, running comments, that were truly refreshing. His text was Hebrews xi. 8. Subject; Abraham's prompt obedience to the call of God. The sermon was straightforward, earnest, and practical; and when he came to the second part of his subject: "The peculiarity in Abraham's conduct," he made a moving appeal to Christians. "We Christians," said he, "are to be strangers and foreigners in the land wherein we sojourn. We are not resident traders in this 'Vanity Fair,' we pass through it because it lies on our way home, but we are ill at ease in it. In no tent of all the fair can we rest. O traders in this hubbub of trifles, we have small esteem for your great bargains and tempting cheats! We are not buyers in the Roman-row or French-row. We would give all that we have to leave your polluted streets and be no more annoyed by Beelzebub, the Lord of the fair. Our journey is toward the Celestial City, and when the sons of earth cry to us 'What do ye buy?' we answer

'We buy the truth.' O young man, can you take up in the warehouse the position of being a Christian, though there is no other believer in the house? Come, good woman, dare you serve the Lord, though husband and children ridicule you? Men of business, dare you do the right thing in business: play the Christian, though around you the various methods of trading render it hard for you to be so unflinchingly honest? This singularity is demanded of every brother in Jesus. You cannot be blessed with Abraham, unless, like him, you come out and stand forth as true men:—

> "Dare to be a Daniel;
> Dare to stand alone;
> Dare to have a purpose true;
> Dare to make it known.'"

I have heard him several times, and each time he was fresh, earnest, and practical, and I felt thankful that in this great Babel there was such a champion of the truth. What a racy, instructive, spiritual discourse I heard him give from "A greater than Solomon is here." Speaking of Christ's power to bless, among other things, he said, "I have sometimes wondered if I preach Christ fully and have his power in my heart. I would like to hear myself preach. I hear others now and then, and sometimes when I do, I wish to be at it myself. But not long ago, in one of my enforced rests, I heard an humble man preach. It was a simple discourse, but it touched my heart; the tears came; I laid the dust all around me, and I felt that all I needed was some one to pipe and I would dance to the sound of Jesus' name!" For an hour there was one strong, fresh, full-voiced flow of musical speech. No pause; no hesitation for a word, but plain, rapid, direct, nervous, and luminously transparent language, a perfect mirror of thought. Where is the secret of the power of this greatest and most popular preacher in London? He has been over twenty years in London, and whenever he speaks thousands hang upon his lips. He has had no college training. He commenced, a mere lad, by addressing Sunday-schools and evening meetings. At Waterbeach, in Cambridgeshire, he took charge of an humble little church. But the short chubby youth, with his round, honest face and fervid soul, began to move men's hearts, and the earnest young preacher was called to the charge of the new Park Street Church, in London. The church had sittings for twelve hundred people, with a regular attendance of less than three hundred. But the star of his fame rapidly mounted to the zenith, and it soon became necessary to secure a more capacious building. In the midst of his career of prosperity a great calamity befell him. He was preaching to an audience of ten thousand in the "Music Hall," when two or three persons arose simultaneously and passed out. Almost immediately a cry of fire was given, and in the dreadful panic which followed several were killed and numbers terribly maimed. The young preacher was assailed on every side, and loaded with abuse; many of the papers condemning him as a murderer, and urging that his preaching be stopped. But through it all he passed unharmed, and he has not only succeeded in maintaining his hold upon the public, but is making it daily stronger and more firm than ever. The edifice in which he ministers is a massive stone structure called the "Metropolitan Tabernacle," with a seating capacity for eight thousand people, besides a school-room for accommodating fifteen hundred; parlors, vestries, and library-rooms. His Church numbers nearly five thousand members. More than sixty of his sermons are published every year, and they are eagerly reprinted and read by the inhabitants of two continents. More than twenty millions of discourses have been circulated in the English language, and they have been translated into nearly all the languages of Christendom. His Pastor's College is an institution for the training of evangelists. There are now some two hundred students in attendance, and in the twenty years of its existence it has turned out over three hundred well furnished ministers, who have established some fifty churches in London alone, and one hundred and fifty in England. His Orphan Asylum is composed of *twelve* homes and contains three hundred inmates, and he has ten alms homes for poor old women. His expositions of the Psalms of David are of acknowledged merit; and his "Sword and Trowel," a name suggested from Spurgeon's Coat of

Arms, is a magazine full of force and evangelistic life. His labors are almost incredible. Where is the secret of his power? Not in his culture. He is not a scholar, although he has made himself master of Greek and Latin, and has been a most laborious student in everything connected with the Scriptures, especially drinking deep from the old Puritan divines. It was the fashion once to speak of him as "vulgar," but now the most fashionable and fastidious are drawn to hear him. Not in his appearance. There is nothing to betoken the orator in commanding form, massive brow, or grace of action. Not in his eccentricities. He is not a *sensational* preacher, as the term is commonly understood: there is no trifling or levity in his discourses, though there is often pungent wit. The last time I heard him there was a little *Spurgeonism* at the singing of the second hymn. The coughing in English congregations in winter is something marked. There was in his church a continual *bark*, and he observed that as three-fourths of the congregation were bent on coughing, it might be well for them all to cough at once, for the sake of the few who did not cough. He said, "You can do anything you like while I preach; but, as my brother is going to pray, I hope he will make little pauses for you all to cough." He wound up by reading a verse and saying, "Now cough, but sing."

He overflows with humor, and has a strong sense of the comical. On one occasion when his deacons were taking up a collection one of them called out the name of a donor, "Mr. King, one crown," Spurgeon remarked to his companion, "What a generous king to part with his crown!" Bye-and-bye another deacon shouted, "Mr. Pig, one guinea," "A regular guinea-pig, is'nt he?" said the punster. But in the pulpit, while his sermons are fresh, sparkling, and lighted up with brilliant metaphor, homely illustrations, and quaint and spiritual wit 'there is nothing coarse or profane: he never plays the clown or buffoon. The chief sources of Mr. Spurgeon's power are in his wonderfully original, natural, and impressive delivery; his marvellous command of simple, precise, idiomatic, Saxon language, and his red-hot earnestness and singleness of purpose. He is a man of profound convictions: he "believes, and therefore speaks." He preaches the Gospel because he knows its power, and has a deep inward possession of it. His church is not a place where, as Mrs. Partington observes, "the Gospel is dispensed with." He does not starve his hearers on the dry crusts of philosophy, or the meatless, marrowless bones of scientific speculation, but believing in the old Gospel, he pours upon the people's hearts the overwhelming claims of God; and his success proves that these grand truisms of duty and heaven, the law of God, and eternal judgment, have not lost their hold upon the public heart and mind. Mr. Spurgeon is a great sufferer from rheumatic gout. He seldom speaks without pain. He has undoubtedly worked too hard, and is running the risk of sharing the fate of the "wicked who do not live out half their days." Some think he has too many irons in the fire; preaching, publishing, lecturing, teaching, managing orphans' homes, and all things generally. But he does no drudgery; the pastoral duties and temporal affairs of the church are attended to by his elders and deacons. He writes but little, for his stenographers and secretaries wait upon him. He has not even to attend to his domestic affairs. The deacons have full charge of the entire premises, furniture, horses, carriages; and when anything, great or small, is needed, it is at once supplied. May this richly evangelical and sound expositor of the Word, this earnest and eloquent interpreter of the mind of the Spirit, be long spared to the churches!

One Sabbath morning I went to the Metropolitan Tabernacle, expecting to hear Mr. Spurgeon, but he was unable to preach, and his pulpit was occupied by the Rev. Archibald G. Brown, of the East London Tabernacle. Mr. Brown is one of the best known of Spurgeon's preachers. He has a strong, pleasant voice, an impressive manner, and a large and loving soul. He is a more than ordinary preacher, and has power to attract and hold an audience. His influence is already felt in London, and he has a growing reputation. I was greatly pleased with the sermon he gave us. His text was from Isa. xxxvii. 10: "Let not thy God, in whom thou trustest, deceive thee;" his theme being, "Satanic advice torn up." Some idea of the vigour and style of the sermon may be gathered from the following outline. He said:—

"Faith in God is so noble a grace, and so splendidly equips a man either for patient suffering or bold enterprise, that Satan cannot afford to treat it with indifference. It is attacked from all quarters, but I think I am correct in saying that, generally speaking, the onslaught comes from one of three quarters. Sometimes the attack is made on the very existence of God, and there are moments when it seems to the saint of God as if a dark mist—a very exhalation from hell itself —rolls into his mind, and before ever he is aware he finds himself asking the question, 'After all, is there a God? Is it not a delusion? Is not the whole thing an hallucination—a dream? Is not prayer simply air in action, and nothing more? Is not the idea of God simply an idea?' Modern sceptics, who generally look upon Christians as those who are pre-eminently soft about the head, may well bear this in mind—that there are very few of God's children but have met and passed right through the very doubts, and darker too, which hold them fast. I know that I am not speaking to many present—certainly not to those of us who have been Christians for many years—who have not known at times what it is to have a tremendous assault made upon our very faith in the existence of God, and there have been times when prayer itself appeared almost an absurdity in our eyes, until, perhaps, we happened to see a bird fly across the sky or heard it carol in the branches, or until we saw a fish glide in the deep, or, it may be, until we watched the course of an insect, and, as we looked, we said, 'Oh, fool that I was, ever to doubt the being of a God!' Never surely did the Psalmist pen a truer word than when he said, 'The fool hath said in his heart, there is no God.' The dark nightmare has passed away, and triumphantly we have exclaimed, 'We believe, O God, in thee. Thou the eternal I AM—thou hast become once again the reality of our life.' But when that temptation fails, I think Satan generally brings his power to bear upon the nature of our faith, and then the temptation runs thus: 'Yes, it is quite true there is a God, and it is perfectly true that prayer is a reality, and it is equally true that faith is the mightiest power on earth, but *your* faith is not of the genuine sort. Your faith has something radically wrong about it. If you were only a believer of the right stamp, then you might expect marvels.' And, mark you, if once the tempter can get us to turn our eyes perpetually inward, looking upon our faith, and instead of faith being occupied with God, we become occupied about our faith, then his end is gained. The believer is only strong as his faith goes out towards God, and forgets itself in its object. If my time is spent in analysing my faith—if through life I am always hampered with the thought, 'My faith is not all that it should be. It is not of the right kind. It has not the heavenly brand upon it'—then weakness is certain to come in. But there are some men—

and I think Hezekiah was one of them—whom it would be almost folly on Satan's part to attempt to make disbelieve either the existence of a God or the reality of their faith. Then the temptation assumes this form: 'Yes, there is a God, and you are not fool enough to doubt it, and you have trusted God; perfectly true, and you know it, but will your God help you when you are hard put to it? After all, will not the God in whom you repose your every trust simply be an unmoved spectator of your griefs? Let not thy God, in whom thou trustest, deceive thee. He will not help you. All your praying will do nought for you. You may cry your eyes out, but God will let things go on in their course. He will not intervene to help you.' These were the words that fell upon the ears, and we know from the context they went right down into the soul of Hezekiah. The words are found in the letter sent him by Sennacherib, but think ye not that Satan had to do with the penning of them? The temptation was this, 'O Hezekiah, let not thy God, in whom thou trustest, deceive thee, saying, Jerusalem shall not be given into the hand of the king of Assyria. Have the gods of the nations delivered them which my fathers have destroyed, as Gozan, and Haran, and Rezeph, and the children of Eden? Where is the king of Hamath? Where is the king of Arphad?' and so on 'None of their gods have been able to deliver them, Hezekiah, don't you let your God in whom you trust deceive you. Your trust will do you no good. Your faith in God will avail nothing, he will let me run over you like a mighty torrent, and not concern himself to come to your aid.'

"We shall ask you, first of all, very carefully to weigh a piece of Satanic advice. Then after we have weighed it, God helping us, we will tear it up.

"I. First of all, then, let us weigh this piece of advice—'Let not thy God, in whom thou trustest, deceive thee.' He acts very foolishly who underestimates either the tact or the power of his foes, and we act with great folly if we brush a temptation on one side, and say cavalierly, 'Oh, that is not likely to affect any. There is nothing in it.' Stay a moment. It is a very dangerous temptation, for three reasons. First, because it appeals to the natural pride of the heart. Secondly, there is no disguising the fact that if God did deceive us we are in a hopeless plight, and therefore there is force in the temptation. Why, the very sentence makes one shudder. 'Let not thy God, in whom thou trustest, deceive thee.' My brethren and sisters, suppose he did—suppose he did. What an utter collapse! A child of God is a man who has no two strings to his bow. If God deceive me, then I am altogether, irrevocably ruined, for there is no other trust to fall back on. Yonder is a man who has invested some twenty thousand pounds in different securities, and he says, 'I will not put all my eggs into one basket.' It may be that he has twenty thousand in twenty different investments. Well, if one investment should happen to turn out bad, he comforts himself with the thought, 'The nineteen others are not likely to go.' But yonder is a man who has put his all into one concern, and if when he enters the city to-morrow morning some one were to come to him and say, 'Have you heard the news? Such and such a firm is gone,' he would stagger and gasp, 'Then I am a ruined man, for all I have—everything and every stick—is in it?' And oh, dear brethren and sisters, if God were to deceive us! We acknowledge that when Satan uses this temptation he uses one of awful force and power. The very thought is enough to freeze up the blood within the veins, for our all is in his hands.

"Once again, I think the force of the temptation lies in this; and here I would ask your careful attention. The methods of God's government, being beyond our comprehension, sometimes seem to incline towards the tempter's suggestion, and from appearances one might say, 'God is going to leave us in the lurch.' It was so in Hezekiah's case.

"II. Now, then, let us turn round and just tear the advice up. Hezekiah went and spread it before the Lord, and I have no doubt that after he spread it before the Lord, then he tore it up. If the advice has been given to any of us, God help us now to tear it into fragments, and have done with it from this moment.

"Shall we give you two or three reasons why you may tear it up?

Well, if one may speak on behalf of many, we may as well tear it up, because it comes too late. 'Let not thy God, in whom thou trustest, deceive thee.' It is too late to give us the advice, for if God be a deceiver, we are already so thoroughly deceived, and have been so for years, that it is rather late in the day to come and advise us not to be. Are there not, blessed be God, hundreds, if not thousands, present, who can say, 'Satan, if thou tellest me this morning not to let God deceive me, I can only reply, "Thy counsel comes too late."' For nineteen years the speaker has been deceived, if God be a deceiver. And I think I can hear some grey-haired ones say, 'Certainly the advice is too late for me, for if God be a deceiver, I have been deceived for fifty years.' Ay, and we can add, so delightfully deceived, so blessedly deceived, that we would rather not be undeceived. Oh, if it be a dream, do not wake me! Let me dream on still, for if all that I have thought to be providences have only been a mistake, an hallucination—if all the helps I have received in days that are passed have only been imaginary, all I can say is, they are so much like what is real, that I want nothing better. If that which is past be all ideal, God help me to live perpetually in a realm of imagination, for it is as good as any reality. 'Let not thy God deceive thee.' Tear it up, the advice comes too late.

"But, again, tear it up for this reason. There is not one atom of evidence to support the libel.

"In conclusion, whilst, on the one hand, there is not an atom of evidence to support the libel, there is overwhelming evidence to refute it. Come, Noah. let us hear thy testimony—what is thy experience of God? Noah's testimony is this: 'He said he would drown the world, and he did; and he said that none inside the ark should perish, and I can bear witness that not a sparrow died—that he watched over all, and the rainbow of his covenant shone brightly in the heavens. I know him to be faithful.' I can imagine how Abraham would come forward and say, 'There was a time when I was sorely tempted. God said to me, in Isaac shall thy seed be called, and yet he told me to offer up that only son. My faith almost staggered at that moment, but the Lord brought deliverance at the last moment, and caused me to coin the proverb, "In the mount of the Lord it shall be seen."' But the best witness, after all, is the one most concerned in our text. Let us see what is the testimony of Hezekiah. Turn with me to the 21st verse of this chapter. Hezekiah had laid the message before the Lord. 'Then Isaiah sent unto Hezekiah, saying, Thus saith the Lord God of Israel, whereas thou hast prayed unto me against Sennacherib, king of Assyria, this is the word which the Lord hath spoken concerning him. The virgin, the daughter of Zion hath despised thee, and laughed thee to scorn. The daughter of Jerusalem has shaken her head at thee; whom hast thou reproached and blasphemed? and against whom hast thou exalted thy voice and lifted up thine eyes on high? even against the holy one of Israel.' 'Therefore (in the 33rd verse), thus saith the Lord concerning the king of Assyria, he shall not come into this city, nor shoot an arrow there, nor come before it with shields, nor cast a bank against it. By the way that he came, by the same shall he return, and shall not come into this city, saith the Lord.' And you know how it was accomplished, for,—

> "'The angel of death spread his wings on the blast,
> And breathed in the face of the foe as he passed,
> And the eyes of the sleepers waxed deadly and chill,
> And their breasts but once heaved and for ever grew still.'

"'Let not thy God, O Hezekiah, in whom thou trustest, deceive thee.' Vain taunt! Look at the result:

> "'The widows of Ashur are loud in their wail,
> And the idols are broke in the temple of Baal,
> For the might of the Gentile, unsmote by the sword,
> Hath perished like snow at the glance of the Lord.'

"Never yet did man trust his God and be put to shame. Cheer up, then, dear heart. Thy defenced cities may have been carried. Thou mayest be in thy last stronghold, and the enemy may be saying, 'Let not thy God deceive thee.' Tear up the advice. Thy God is immutably the same. Heaven and earth and hell declare that Jehovah never hath and never can deceive. May the harps now be taken down from the willows, and if we came here despondent, may we leave rejoicing, knowing Hezekiah's God to be our own."

Dean Stanley is another popular London preacher, whom everybody goes to hear. Whenever he occupies the pulpit, Westminster Abbey is crowded to excess with hundreds of living statesmen, scholars, and divines. Standing among the monuments of the illustrious dead, to listen to a sermon within the consecrated precincts of the old Abbey, is itself an event never to be forgotten. A feeling of awe comes over one, a strange inspiration as we turn from the faces of the living to the statues, and busts, and memorial entablatures of the mighty dead, and the life-like marble forms appear to stand in the attitude of listening, until in our imagination the great and powerful of past generations seem to mingle with the services, and by their silence speak to us of the future and immortal existence. The venerable Dean is now approaching seventy, —dignified and handsome in appearance, of courtly and graceful manners, and in the pulpit solemn and impressive. He is a great favorite with royal personages, and has been entertained in many an imperial palace. He is a man of great catholicity of spirit, and broad in his Christian sympathies. He frequently takes part in religious services with dissenters, and his fraternal feeling towards Christians of all sects is a great offence in the eyes of rigid churchmen. When he assisted in the unveiling of a monument of *John Bunyan*, in Bedford, and delivered an address, the extreme churchmen were furious that a Dean of Westminster should pay such homage to a dissenter, and some of them, with bitter sarcasm, recommended the raising of a statue of the devil, expressing their belief that Dean Stanley would be found ready to pronounce the eulogy. The Dean, however, has the courage to stand by his convictions, and can afford to treat with indifference all bigots, high and low, for he is master of the situation, and holds an untrammelled living. His sermons are remarkable for fresh thought and vigorous statement, and they have all the brilliance and polish of his lectures on the Jewish Church. They are always broad enough for the most liberal, and he is by no means restricted in the range of his subjects.

I had the good fortune to hear him one fourth of July, the anniversary of American Independence, and on this occasion the Dean took for his text the 21st and 22nd verses of the fifth chapter of St. Matthew; and, dwelling on the sin of unrighteous anger and the calling of hard names, he held that the precepts of his text applied as well to nations as to individuals, and proceeded to speak of the past and present relations between Great Britain and the United States. Among other noble words, he said: "On such a day [4th of July] may we not feel that the lessons of the text have a peculiar significance and force? The sons of that great country beyond the Atlantic are, indeed, our brothers, in a sense in which no other two great nations on the face of this earth are brethren and sisters to each other,—speaking the same language, inheriting the same traditions, entwined within the same dearest relationships, rejoicing in the same history, in the same faith, in the same hopes. . . . . What American is there who is not proud of that English ancestry, which he then [in the time of the Revolution] spurned behind him? What Englishman is there who is now not proud of the once dreaded name of WASHINGTON?"

Many American travellers were, no doubt, in that crowded audience, and to hear such sentiments of brotherly love, on such a day, from a man occupying so salient and influential a position, must have filled them with delight.

In respect to delivery, the Dean's style is straightforward reading, not preaching. He seldom lifts his eyes from the manuscript, has very little rhetorical action, and still less vocal modulation. He is by no means free from that common vice of Church of England divines—a soporific sameness of sound—one dead level of vocal action without inflection, deflection, or cadence, from the beginning of the discourse to the close; or what is still worse, an artificial and monotonous rise and fall.* These cathedrals, with their naves

* Since writing the above, Arthur Penrhyn Stanley, D.D., has passed away f.om earth to his reward in heaven. Among his latest words were these: "I have labored among many frailties and much weakness to make Westminster Abbey more and more a centre of religious and national life, and I have done this in a truly liberal spirit, without regard to the narrow limitations of creed or dogma." The world will not soon forget his Catholic Christ-like spirit. His

and transepts, and arches and chapels, are singularly unsuited to the preaching of the Gospel; the voice rises and dies away amid the echoes of the ceiling, and those at a little distance off are simply witnesses of a pantomimic exhibition. But we can almost forgive them, because of their marvellously beautiful sound effects in music. How charming to hear the choral service rendered in the mysterious vastness and dim vistas of a Gothic Cathedral!

> "In the great minster's transept,
>   Where lights like glories fall;
> Where the sweet choir sings, and the organ rings
>   Along the emblazoned wall."

The resonance of solid stone walls, the strange acoustic powers of the structure, give a new beauty to cathedral music. Listen to the double organ of Westminster Abbey, giving out its solemn notes:—

> "Now it is like all instruments,
>   Now like a lonely flute;
> And now it is like an angel's song,
>   That makes the heavens be mute."

And when the white-robed choir pour forth their clear airy voices, the echoes take up the words and carry them through the innumerable arches and lofty vault-

---

departure has been deeply and universally mourned throughout both hemispheres; and the Queen, in expressing her profound regret, said, "That in the death of Dean Stanley the Church and the nation had lost one of their noblest and most gifted members."

ings, until an unseen choir seems to answer back, and the old Abbey itself, with its window-painted saints, in their transfiguration robes, and its aisles richly decorated with marble forms, seems to have a soul divine, and breaks forth in anthems of the glorified.

In St. Paul's, with its towering dome and splendid classic architecture, the famous preacher is Canon Liddon. There is always a great throng gathered under the great dome to hear him. His style is perfect, his words are well chosen, his thoughts unexcelled. His delivery is good, his action graceful and impressive; he has a pure and lofty soul, and when he rises to the highest eloquence carries all hearts by storm. The Church of England has not a great number of pre-eminent preachers. I have listened to sermons in large and influential churches, and wondered to hear only average men speaking with no gracefulness of manner, no unction or tenderness, no pathos or power. How is this? Is it because the system of patronage has the rare facility of putting the wrong man in the wrong place? Is it because of the low rank assigned to the sermon in comparison with the liturgical offices; the litany, the creeds, the frequent repetitions of the Lord's Prayer, the chanting and intoning in which the sense is smothered in the harmony of sounds, occupying nearly three-fourths of the time of Sabbath services? How is it that this great Mother Church, in which are so many noble Christian workers, brilliant scholars, and thinkers, has so few great preachers?

Dean Alford says, "The sermons of Dale, and Reynolds, and Raleigh are far above the average of such publications in our Church. Already the Nonconformists have passed us in scholarship and ministerial training." Does not the fact that the Church of England is an establishment cast some light on this question? The Church is upheld by the State and it cannot fall. It is made strong by the laws of the realm. Why, then, should the clergyman labor and toil? He is not dependent upon the people; his public services are all prepared for him beforehand from year to year, except the sermon, which need not exceed in length fifteen or twenty minutes. His very connection with the State gives to him an arrogance, and loftiness, and affected superiority over other ministers to whom he may be immeasurably inferior in ability, and culture, and grace. Under these circumstances it is not strange that so few of the Church of England clergy attain eminence as preachers. Disestablishment would be a boon to the Church herself. Who does not revere the Church of England with her grand history, her splendid ritual, her fervent prayers, her earnest zeal, her saintly and devout bishops, deans, and rectors? "The King's daughter is all glorious within, her raiment is of wrought gold;" but she is bound with golden fetters and crippled by her connection with the State. It is a significant fact that the increase of the Established Church during the past twenty years has been only twenty-five per cent; while that of the great dissenting churches,—the Independents, the Presbyterians, the Baptists, and the Methodists,—was over one hundred per cent. Besides, she is no longer the church of the whole people of England. Not one of the leading dissenting bodies but is doing as great a moral work for the people of the land, in the education of the poor, the relief of the suffering, the advance of knowledge and Gospel light, as that favored Church which professes to be the Church of all. Therefore, she should take her proper place with the other sister churches. In the struggle for dis-establishment there is a curious combination of forces; the dissenters outside, who are evangelical and spiritual, and an inside party consisting of High Churchmen and extreme Ritualists. These latter favor separation from the State because they wish to introduce their Romish practices, and cannot do so while the law of the land regulates the worship of the Church. One instance surely in which establishment seems to be a benefit to the cause of Truth, although the Church herself is a victim to many ills from her connection with the State.

I also heard Cardinal Manning in the Pro-Cathedral, Kensington. His church is always crowded; and on this occasion I was informed that nearly one-half of the congregation were Protestants. After the prayers and choral service, largely given in English, the Director entered the pulpit in his cardinal dress and cap, and took for his text: "Be not conformed to this world, but be ye transformed by the renewing of your mind." The subject was the evidences of the New Birth, or as he expressed it, conformity to the sacred heart of Jesus. The sermon was earnest and evangelical. There was hardly a word in it to which a Protestant could object. The Cardinal is feeble with age and his beautiful sentences were but imperfectly heard, but they dropped like polished diamonds from his lips. Dr. Manning is well known in the religious world. A pervert to the Church of Rome, he has consecrated his distinguished abilities and all the resources of his genius to the endeavor to win his Protestant countrymen back to the fold of the Infallible Pope.

Dr. Parker, of the Temple Church, is another celebrity. He is a well-known Independent divine, and, I should say, as far as metropolitan fame is concerned, next to Spurgeon, one of the most conspicuous Nonconformist ministers in London. His church, the City Temple, stands on Holborn Viaduct, and he has, each Thursday at noon, a service for business men. This Thursday noon service is largely attended, which is a testimony to his extraordinary pulpit ability. On both occasions when I heard him it was very wet, and yet the church was thronged. One of his sermons was on the Parable of the Sower. In his discourse, speaking of the parable being repeated in daily life, he observed there was no such thing as preaching an old sermon, if it was worth calling a sermon. He never hesitated to repeat a sermon; for it was not old if the truth was in it. When we came out I found the sermon for sale in the Fountain, and, expressing my surprise that it should be in print so soon, I was informed that the sermon had been preached before. The Doctor has a singularly impressive voice, and a fervid, eloquent, powerful delivery. He preaches no emasculated gospel, but aims straight at men's hearts and exposes boldly their sins. He is a fine specimen of a man, large-featured, broad-chested, has curly black hair, and a bushy rim of dark whiskers around his face. His mental grip is strong and his style is remarkably fresh and striking. He is not without a consciousness of his own powers. As you listen he makes you feel "this is Dr. Parker;" and the story goes that on one occasion he rose up in the pulpit and announced, "As I am feeling rather indisposed this morning, I shall dispense with my accustomed *action*." This I take as a caricature, for he is a grand, good man, and is doing a noble work. He is the author of *Ecce Deus, The Paraclete,* and *These Sayings of Mine.*

In the Presbyterian Church one of the best pulpit speakers is the Rev. Dr. Frazer, the pastor of Marylebone Presbyterian Church. His congregation is very large and is composed chiefly of Scotch people. He is an old Montrealer, and many a Canadian finds his way to the church on Upper George Street. He has a manner peculiarly his own,—earnest, manly, and striking; his style is exceedingly picturesque; his doctrine richly evangelical, and he has a new and persuasive way of presenting the old gospel.

The English Wesleyans are wide awake, and they have a powerful ministry. The first Sabbath I spent in London, I went to Brixton Hill Wesleyan Chapel, where I enjoyed the liturgical service very much. It was given in such a spirit of devotion. A month before I had attended Phillips Brooks' gorgeous church in Boston. He is a very rapid speaker, and the congregation has caught his gait, and gallops through the responses with unseemly haste. It seemed to me that in this Wesleyan Chapel I never before heard the prayers of the Church of England read with such life, earnestness, and devotion, and the contrast was most marked. The sermon by the pastor, Rev. F. J. Sharr, would do honor to any pulpit in the world.

It was also my privilege to attend the Memorial Service to the late Rev. Dr. Jobson. The sermon was by the Rev. Dr. Pope. It was carefully prepared and closely read, and was just such a discourse as you would expect from so profound a scholar, saintly a man, and earnest a theologian as Dr. Pope. The service was in the City Road Chapel, on a Wednesday afternoon, and the congregation was a representative one, there being present, besides distinguished laymen, many ministers, and, no less than seven ex-Presidents.

I was impressed and delighted beyond measure with a discourse which I had the privilege of hearing from Rev. Dr. James H. Rigg. I was prepared to hear a sermon thoughtful and profound, literary and scholarly; but I did not expect to be thrilled as

I was, with sentence after sentence of brilliant, powerful, and persuasive eloquence. The doctor's face is that of a healthy, temperate Englishman; his form is stalwart; his voice clear and rich; and his manner easy and graceful. As an accomplished man of letters, a master of the educational problems of his country, an experienced and discriminating judge of the philosophic and religious drift and teaching of the day, Dr. Riggs' is, perhaps, the most honored and renowned of all the names in English Methodism. The author of "Modern Anglican Theology" and of "Discourses and Addresses on Leading Truths of Religion and Philosophy," is welcomed throughout the literary and religious world for his remarkably fine, practical sense; clear, subtle, and powerful reasoning; luminous insight into abstruse and difficult questions; and surpassingly noble thoughts, expressed with rare clearness and beauty and with admirable spirit.

But the Apollos of Wesleyan preachers is the Rev. Dr. Wm. Morley Punshon. I heard him in one of the older churches in the heart of the city, and although a week-day evening the edifice was densely thronged, and there SEEMED to be no abatement of his power or popularity. The sermon was of great intellectual force and marvellous rhetorical beauty. What a master of language, and how all hearts are subdued under the spell of his oratory! It is like throwing open the doors of heaven, and getting a glimpse of the glory-land. Dr. Punshon undoubtedly ranks among the foremost preachers of the times, and he never stood so high in the affections and regard of the British people as he does to-day. Always abounding in Gospel labor, his influence is felt from one end of Britain to the other, while, in his responsible position as Chief-Secretary of the Wesleyan Missionary Society, his wisdom, tenderness, and love, his regnant greatness of mind and heart, are felt in the numerous mission-stations on every continent, and in the remotest islands of the sea. Of large physical frame, well-proportioned, and, as to years, in the very prime of life, he is nevertheless weary and seriously exhausted with over-work, and his heart is strained by great anxiety and sorrow.

I had the pleasure also of hearing Dr. Punshon deliver one of his wonderful lectures. It was given in the chapel of Christ Church, of which Dr. Hussey is the genial and learned rector. As I listened to the perfect emphasis, admirable articulation, rich imagery, and torrent of eloquence, carrying the audience into raptures of applause, it seemed but as yesterday since I heard his voice in Canada, and we claimed him as our own. His subject was "The Pilgrim Fathers," and, with overwhelming eloquence, he depicted the struggles of the Puritans, and the fury of their oppressors as they were tracked through wood and wild, "the baying of the fierce sleuth hound breaking upon their sequestered worship." He showed the immense, but scantily acknowledged obligations we owed to those men "of whom the world was not worthy."

And as he traced in golden words their excellence of character, their stern integrity, consistent walking, and heroic endurance, and rebuked in clarion tones the sectarian bitterness, desertion of duty and failure of faith, that belonged to modern, no less than earlier days, he seemed like a brave prophet of old speaking his words to the people. On the way home, I asked him why he had given that lecture to an audience made up almost entirely of Churchmen, who were not accustomed to hear much about the virtues of the Puritans. He answered, that the subject should be of interest to all English people, and that he never faltered in the utterance of his convictions before any congregation. It was a brave thing to do, and no doubt, every hearer thanked him for the noble lessons inculcated. As I think of him now, standing upon that platform, pouring forth a torrent of fervid speech, the audience rapt, spell-bound, electrified, a thousand associations rush upon me, and the tears come into my eyes. This was the last public engagement he ever filled; the last time he ever addressed an audience. How his words and the very tones of his marvellous voice linger in my memory!

CHAPTER VI.

FRANCE.

Alexandra and Crystal Palaces— Kew Gardens — Windsor Castle — Crossing the Channel—France—Paris—First Impressions—French Language—Avenues—Arch of Triumph—Palace of the Tuileries —The Louvre—The Nude in Art—The Luxembourg—Madeleine— Notre Dame—St. Germain l'Auxerrois—Saint Chapelle—Pantheon —Hotel des Invalides—Tomb of Napoleon—Père La Chaise—Les Gobelins—Versailles—Parisian Life—A Sunday in the City.

THERE are many most delightful excursions to be made about London. Alexandra Palace is a very popular place of recreation. Its theatre and its concert-room are very large, its picture gallery fine, and its grounds are beautifully undulating and tastefully laid out. It is quite a rural paradise, on the very borders of the dust and smoke and tumult of the surging metropolis.

But the Crystal Palace still holds its own. The scenery *en route* to Sydenham is enchanting—velvet lawns, circles of stately elms, hawthorn hedges, and superb vistas of parks and villas. The Palace is a mountain of light, and we approach it, by a walk nearly one hundred feet wide, and through a terrace faced with stone-work, and unsparingly adorned with statuary.

RICHMOND BRIDGE.

In the centre, there rises one lofty, trans.ucent vault, intersected three times by transverse arches, the centre one of which, towers majestically above the old structure. You behold, displayed together, wings, façades, towers, domes, and terraces, and the far end of the transept is clearly seen through the shining walls. Entering within, you gaze upon lightsome columns, arches, statues, spiral staircases, while, in the centre, is the great organ and the mighty orchestra. The first impression of the whole is completely overwhelming.

Before the day closed, our feet were worn out wandering through the courts of all the civilized world, ascending staircases and traversing galleries, and our eyes were weary gazing upon the wonders of the scene. We returned in the evening sated with enjoyment and glad to find rest.

I greatly enjoyed a day at Richmond and at Kew. Kew Gardens, with their lakes and fountains, conser-

WINDSOR CASTLE FROM ETON.

vatories and botanic museums, velvet lawns and shady walks, are the finest in the world. Richmond is the seat and home of Walpole. It is a charming spot, full of animated and delightful views of nature, and worthy of being the resting-place of the poet of nature, Thomson, whose spirit seemed to imbibe the freshness and fragrance of the surrounding scenery. One of the Wesleyan Theological Colleges is situated at Richmond. The grounds are large and beautiful, the

NORMAN GATE AND ROUND TOWER.

buildings ample and commodious, and the library large and select. In the chapel of the College is the identical pulpit in which Mr. Wesley preached in the old foundry.

We gave an entire day to Windsor Castle. What a castellated palace! The high place of kinghood and knighthood—the permanent abode of living royalty, adorned and glorified with everything that affection could dictate, wealth procure, and art achieve during eight hundred years of British sovereignty.

Through the kindness of Mr. Michael, of Montreal, who gave us a letter of introduction to his brother, one of the oldest servants in Her Majesty's household, we were favored beyond ordinary visitors to Windsor. This letter opened almost every door in the Palace, and we sauntered leisurely through state chambers and private apartments, adorned with tapestries and paintings, sculpture and art.

We even visited Her Majesty's kitchen, and were admitted to the "silver room" and the "gold room," blazing in the most exquisite services of precious metal. Everything of plate needed for a banquet of three hundred at the Royal Table, all of solid gold! We threaded the towers and climbed to the battlements, surveyed royal gardens and parks, and long avenues of majestic trees. Visited St. George's Chapel and the Albert Chapel, built above the Royal Tomb House—a mausoleum adorned with marble of every kind and color, a worthy monument to the late Prince Consort.

Close to Windsor is Eton College, the training-school of many of England's most illustrious men.

And now we are off for the Continent. We leave London for Paris by the Chatham and Dover Railway, and cross the Channel *via* Dover and Calais, which is the quickest, though not the cheapest route to the metropolis of France. Comfortably seated in a first-

class compartment we are whirled along at a speed of
fifty miles an hour over a fertile and thickly-populated
country, catching glimpses of fine old farm-houses,
lordly mansions, antique churches, and old-fashioned
villages, passing Chatham Barracks and Canterbury

ETON COLLEGE AND CHAPEL.

Cathedral, until we reach Dover, nestled close to the
sea, under the snowy chalk cliffs—the "white cliffs of
Albion." There are the fortifications looking out upon
the old enemy of England, and upon one of the walls,
pointing over the Channel, is still the famous old cannon,
upon whose breech was written:—

"Keep me dry, and keep me clean,
And I'll carry a ball to Calais green."

We at once embark for Calais, and are two hours in crossing the Channel. That "strip of silver sea" was bent on maintaining its famous reputation, and we had a stormy time of it. In one of those miserable steamers, amid the floundering waves, one thinks of the advice of Shakespeare:—

> "Give thanks you have lived so long,
> And make yourself ready in your
> Calm for the mischance of the pour,
> If it so hap."

Though one is ready to take up the words of his hero:

> "The will above be done;
> But I would fain die a dry death."

However, as my stomach preserved its dignity, I was able to bear the misfortunes of others, and was thankful to set foot upon the quay of Calais. Soon we were speeding on over the plains and through the cities of *La belle* France.

Leaving London at 9.30 a.m., by the "Chatham and Dover," you reach the "City of Beauty" at six the same evening, having halted only at Amiens, where, in 1802, the treaty of peace was concluded between England and France. My first work, after securing a room in my hotel, was to sit down to a *table d'hote*. A continental dinner is a formidable affair. There is a great display of clean plates, knives, and forks; and there are at least ten courses. The first is a dish of soup, made who can tell of what; then a portion of fish; next a solitary vegetable; then a mouthful of fowl; a dish of greens, and so on. The summit of the feast is reached in a good piece of roast beef; and then you descend by easy stages through lettuce, cheese, pastry, and fruit to the termination. It is a fine thing in leisure, but a little trying when one has only an hour at his disposal for the repast. After dinner, I sauntered out for a long walk through the splendid Boulevards. After the rush and thunder of busy London, to enter Paris is like going from an active workshop to a lovely drawing-room. The city by night, in the glare of gas and the flash of its electric light, with its population out of doors—the women in slippers and bare-headed, the men chatting and smoking and drinking at little tables before the gay "café,"—is even more brilliant than by day. I passed the magnificent Opera House and Theatres, with their open galleries, crowded with volatile and voluble French ladies and gentlemen making the air ring with their mirth and social glee. You mark at once the contrast between the indoor, quiet home-life of England, and the showy, artificial out-door activity of the Continent. The very emptiness and shallowness of French life and thought seem to strike you. All is luxurious, sensuous evanescent; appearances take the place of reality. The very shops, with their ornaments and finery, their display of jewellery and furniture, everything after the most dazzling and pretentious style, seem to illustrate the character of the people—frivolous, theatric, shallow. And yet, one has to acknowledge their superiority to us, in delicacy and refinement of taste. And this it is that makes Paris, in its wealth and splendor, with all its sins, so dazzling and bewitching to Englishmen and Americans. What an intoxication of pleasure one feels in wandering along her streets, and crossing her squares, and gazing upon her palaces! A former visit had made me perfectly familar with the geography of the city, and I was resolved to make myself so weary that I would have to sleep; and so I wandered along, feasting my eyes, and absorbed in my own reflections, and moralizing on the romance, the mystery, and the tragedy which spot after spot opened up. Some one has said that the art of cultivating pleasant associations is a secret of happiness. I could no more ramble through Paris without thinking of Victor Hugo and *Les Misérables*, than I could tread the streets of London without thinking of Dickens and of Hood. The very gaiety of the passing crowds seemed to deepen the historic musings as I remembered St. Bartholomew, the terrible Revolution, the Commune, the barricaded *places*, and streets made red with human blood. When I could walk no longer, I began to think of riding home to my hotel. The omnibus system of Paris is perfect. All you have to do is to go into a station, tell where you want to go, when a number is given which corresponds with the number of the omnibus that you are to take; you wait until it passes along, jump on board, and, sooner or later, are let down at your own door.

One needs to understand French well to fully enjoy a visit to Paris. I have not so much difficulty in making myself understood as in understanding the answers I get. The people think so rapidly, and their words flow together in one undistinguishable stream. They tell of an Englishman who came over to the French capital, and was greatly disturbed because he could not understand a word. Everybody spoke French —cabmen, hotel-waiters, chamber-maid, all, and he was greatly perplexed and distressed. Early next morning he awoke, and, hearing chanticleer crow, exclaimed, "Thank goodness, there's some English at last!" Another story is told of an inquisitive Yankee, who sauntered along the streets asking all sorts of questions in his own tongue, and only getting in reply a shrug of the shoulders, and "*Je ne sais pas!*" Toward night a funeral procession, with its long train of carriages and horses in mourning passed by, and stopping a stranger he asked, "Who is dead?" "*Je ne sais pas!*" "Is he?" said the prying down-easter. "I am so glad; he has been worrying me all day."

One is sometimes mortified and amused with his own adventures. Coming out of the Louvre, I wished to go to the Palais du Luxembourg, and I asked a gentleman which was the nearest bridge across the Seine. He looked at me, and then said, in perfect English, "Where do you want to go?" I burst into a laugh.

Sketches of Travel.

"Why do you laugh?" he asked. I answered, "To think of my practicing French upon one who knows English as well as I do!" I laugh now every time I think of my own desperate effort, the puzzled, bewildering look of my fellow-countryman, and then his asking in outright English, "What do you want to know?" A fellow-traveller with me on the way to Italy, said he asked a gentleman, "*Parlez vous Anglais?*" and got the answer, "Rather; that is all I can speak."

The magnificent metropolis is a world by itself. I shall not attempt a description of its gay population, its splendid buildings, and matchless boulevards, its palaces, churches, parks, fountains, arches, and columns. The city was entirely reconstructed during the reign of Napoleon III., and made a model of beauty for the world.

The streets and boulevards radiate from numerous points, and range away in majestic perspectives on both sides of the Seine. The business thoroughfares are handsome, the pavement smooth and clean as floors, the buildings of pure bright stone, and the shop windows blazing with jewellery or costly and brilliant wares. The boulevards are broad, and bordered with double rows of shade trees of the rarest foliage. The newer avenues are wider still, with parks and gardens at intervals. The Champs Elysees is, no doubt, the grandest avenue in the world. It is very broad, with rows of trees on either side, patches of woods, beds of rhododendrons and fragrant flowers, flashing fountains, and marble monumental beauties. At the foot of this street is the square or Place de la Concorde, with statues and fountains. In the midst is an obelisk, or monument, 3,300 years old. It stood in the palace of the Kings of Egypt 1,500 years before the Saviour came into the world.

In this spot the guillotine was erected—a terrible instrument of death which cut off the heads of twenty-eight hundred men and women. It began its bloody work with the death of Louis XVI. That dreadful time was rightly called the Reign of Terror, because no one's life was safe.

Marching along under shady trees and passing numerous cafés, you reach the Arch of Triumph, that splendid monument of Napoleon the Great. What was it built for? To keep alive the memory of some good man or of some noble deed? No; but to remind the people of cruel and bloody wars, in which hundreds of thousands perished that one man might be powerful, and the pride of the French pleased. It is sixty feet by twenty at the base, and forty-five feet high, and consists of a central and two smaller lateral arches, intersected by transversal arches of equal height. Eight Corinthian columns of red Languedoc marble support the entablature. The attic is surmounted by a figure of Victory in a triumphal car, and four bronze horses, modelled by Basio, from the original, brought from the Piazza of St. Mark, at Venice. Over each column stands a figure of a

Place de la Concorde.

soldier of Napoleon's army, and over each smaller archway is a marble bas-relief, representing events of the campaign of 1805. It is one of the few public monuments which escaped final destruction by the infuriated Communists.

Near the extreme end of the Champs Elysées is the Palace of the Tuileries. What stirring scenes those blackened walls have witnessed! The Tuileries sprang, as its name indicates, from a tile-yard, which was purchased by Francis I., in 1518. The palace was originally composed merely of what afterwards became the central pavilion, and was a model of elegance and simplicity. Many additions were made to it by Henry IV. and succeeding sovereigns, especially by Louis XIV. before he built Versailles. On the 10th of August, 1791, it was taken by storm and became "the ante-room of the guillotine." Then it became the Palace of the Revolution, and afterwards Robespierre inaugurated the worship of the Goddess of Reason. In 1800 Bonaparte took possession of it. In 1814 the Bourbons returned to the "palace of their fathers," and the Duchesse d'Angoulême, overcome by emotion, fainted. Soon the old palace witnessed another sight when the white flag was replaced by the tri-color, as the people shouted "*A bas les Bourbons! Vive l'Empereur.*" Napoleon arrived in his post-chaise, and amid cries of enthusiasm was carried into the court-yard of the palace. After the Battle of Waterloo, Louis XVIII. and his family once more returned to the Tuileries.

In 1830 the Bourbons were again obliged to fly, and the following year Louis Philippe, the Citizen King, installed himself in the palace, and in his turn was driven out. On the 1st of January, 1852, Louis Napoleon took up his residence at the Tuileries, which he joined to the Louvre. There he was visited by every crowned head in Europe. From this palace he went in 1870 to take command of the army of the Rhine. To it he never returned. Then followed the flight of the Empress Eugénie; the unhappy woman saying, as she left it, "Fatal Palace! Is it then the destiny of all Royalties to leave you thus?" The siege of Paris followed, then the Commune, and the royal edifice was devoted to the flames. Besides the blasted walls of the Tuileries and the Hôtel de Ville, other scars remain to tell of the riot and ruin of the terrible Commune of 1871, when human passions ran wild, and the City of Beauty was under the sway of anarchy, destruction, and death. The Commune was a reckless mob. They carved on churches and public buildings their favorite motto "Liberty, Equality, and Fraternity;" but the meaning underneath these plausible words was license, lust, and ruin. While the soldiers of France were trying to beat back the army of Germany, that was marching in a blaze of triumph to the gates of their capital, these rioters and destroyers, with murder in their heart, and the torch of the incendiary in their hand, were laying waste the marble city. But the day of vengeance came at last, and Paris found relief. The leaders of this deadly order were driven by hundreds into the stately church of the Madeleine, and herded within were shot down and slaughtered like wild beasts. They were literally cut to pieces, and the marble floor ran red with blood.

The Palace of the Louvre is near the Tuileries, and in it you can walk for hours out of one splendid room into another, until you grow weary looking at frescoed ceilings, painted in beautiful colors, floors of smoothly polished inlaid pieces of wood, skilfully put together, gleaming marble pillars, dazzling mirrors, and long halls full of costly paintings and statues. Floors as well as tables are made of different colored marbles and mosaics, while rich cabinets and cases hold many rare and precious things.

It makes one shudder to think that this collection of statuary, paintings, and antiquities would have been destroyed by the furious Communistic mob but for the arrival of the troops. Wandering through the numerous picture galleries, you are surrounded by some of the most famous paintings by masters such as Rubens, Tintoretto, Paul Veronese, Guido Reni, Vandyck, Lorenzo, Titian, Murillo, and a host of masters, ancient and modern, from various schools. Rubens has a great gallery all to himself. Some of these master-pieces speak with great power to the heart.

No picture is placed in this treasure-house of art until the artist has been dead at least ten years. The Louvre is the paradise of cherubs. I must confess, however, I do not like to see such a scarcity of drapery in French art. It gets a little monotonous to see naked Venuses standing alone and stately, and Aphrodites lying in all shapes, naked, upon the sea foam. It is simply old heathenism and not Christian civilization. These modern artists are copying the ancient, it is said. The ancients, however, simply copied the life they saw about them, and took their models from the open day. But it has been well said: "Now-a-days people are as good as born in their clothes, and there is practically not a nude human being in existence." Man is an animal that wears clothes from the cradle to the grave, and the nude figure is not the natural but the unnatural state. To carve and paint the "human form divine," with the clothing stripped off in order to show the perfection of that form, is very much like that famous statue of St. Bartholomew, in Milan Cathedral. The saint is flayed alive, and his skin is thrown over his shoulders. You have a fine display of the muscles and the active circulatory system, but it is scarcely natural. It is, indeed, violently unnatural. The same may be said of a carved or painted nude figure. If clothing is demanded everywhere else, why should they be laid aside in painting and sculpture? The living, actual nakedness would be revolting—why not the representations of nude men and women? Is not high art at variance with nature here? True, the living, breathing warmth of life are absent in the cold stone and glowing canvas, but many an impurity has been perpetuated on marble and immortalized in paint. Compare French art with the ancient. In the ancient, the soul of the artist has clothed the naked Venus with maidenly modesty; but in these imitations, the delicacy and purity are wanting, and we see nothing but the unveiled voluptuousness of the human form. Now, we have written enough to be charged with prudery and over-delicacy, and accused of utter ignorance of high art, which, in depicting winning sweetness and repose, love and tenderness, strength and warmth, demands a stripping off of garments, even though in real life men and women do manage in clothes to take attitudes and positions that are full of dignity, loveliness, and power. Grant that the figure before a pure imagination is just art and nothing more, without suggestiveness and without any evil tendency; but when that figure is without the delicacy and vernal sentiment of womanhood, when the artist has thrown into it a sensuous character, then it becomes a stained and unclean thing. To leave this matter, without trying to discover evil where there is none, we maintain that three-fourths of the Venuses and Aphrodites of the Louvre and Luxembourg, in their wantonness of posture and color, are intolerable and indecent, for they are not goddesses, not women or maidens, but nude female figures.

The Luxembourg Garden has eighty-five acres of trees, flowers, fountains, and statues, and the museum contains the master-pieces of living artists, painters, sculptors, and engravers. What an expanse to wander through! Gorgeously decorated salons, filled with the treasures of art, the galleries crowded with marble forms, and the walls covered with pictures! This museum is devoted to the productions of living painters and sculptors of France. The Louvre and the Luxembourg are altogether too much for one day. Three miles of halls are too much to traverse, aside from the pictures that richly and magnificently adorn them. We have visited these palaces again and again, but instead of exhausting them they have exhausted us.

Among the churches, the first I visited was the Madeleine—the most magnificent and sumptuously decorated of modern churches. It is a majestic structure, in the Corinthian style of architecture. The perfect copy of a Greek temple, it is surrounded by fifty-two immense and exquisitely graceful pillars. I believe it was designed by Napoleon Bonaparte as a temple of glory to the French arms; but it is now the most fashionable place of Roman Catholic worship in the city.

The historic church of France is the venerable Notre Dame. This cathedral was founded in the year 1163, and covers an area of over seven thousand square yards. It is built in the form of a Latin cross, and is four hundred and fifteen feet long, and one hundred and fifty wide. The front is profusely ornamented with scriptural subjects. As we enter and pace the marble floor, or stand before its altars, and admire its columns, and arches, and galleries, and illuminated windows, what associations come crowding upon us! What atrocities have been committed within the walls of this gorgeous cathedral! Here, *Te Deums* were chanted, not only for splendid victories, but also over the cruel murder of Protestants in the St. Bartholomew massacre—place of coronation ceremonies and funereal pomp. Here, during the frenzy of the Revolution, a courtesan was enthroned as the Goddess of Reason. Here, in the presence of the Pope and an assembly, the most brilliant and gorgeous ever witnessed in Paris, Napoleon placed the imperial crown upon his own head, and upon the head of Josephine—that Josephine whom afterwards he divorced and left to pine away, broken-hearted, in the solitude of Malmaison. Within these grand aisles, damaged by many wars, the Communists placed their military stores; and the last desecration was when these destructionists set it on fire, and the flames curled through its arches and gleamed along its vaulted roof. Yet still the historic pile stands in all its magnificence, for it has been re-built, re-modelled, and improved. We cannot recount to you all the treasures and relics of its sacristy. A silver key will open the door to these jewelled splendors—the solid gold and silver utensils used in the great ceremonies of the Church, the splendid robes of the Popes and Bishops. The bullet shown, which killed the Archbishop of Paris, in 1848, is very likely the identical one; but when nails and pieces of wood of the identical cross, and a part of the crown of thorns are presented, we begin to grow dubious.

Behind the Cathedral is that chamber of horrors, the Morgue. We stood opposite a grating and looked into the room upon the sad spectacle of dead bodies, naked and swollen, lying on the slanting stones, placed there for recognition. The room was hung about with garments of men, women, and children that were there, also to be identified by some fond mother, or relative, or friend. Then we visited the Church of St. Germain l'Auxerrois, with its frescoed portico and richly decorated interior, in the tower of which still hangs the bell that sounded out the signal for the bloody massacre of St. Bartholomew. Near by is the Sainte Chapelle, that wonder of Gothic architecture, with its upper and lower chapel, each adorned with a profusion and brilliancy of decorations, the walls interspersed with golden fleurs de lis, the windows filled with painted glass of exquisite and enchanting colors, each tint a gem of purest ray. This church has a history. Built in 1245, it was the place of royal marriages and coronations, as well as the starting point of many crusades to the Holy Land. The front of it was much injured by the Commune, but the radiant beauty of the interior is untarnished. The Pantheon occupies the site of a church built in honor of St. Genevieve, the patron saint of Paris. It is a Græco-Roman edifice, of majestic proportions, and is half church, half temple of fame. The inscription upon the frieze in front is "*Aux grands hommes la patrie reconnaissante.*" In the vaults are the remains of Mirabeau, Murat, Voltaire, and Rousseau.

One of the wonders of Paris is the Tomb of Napoleon, under the magnificent dome of the Hotel des Invalides. This hospital is a refuge for disabled soldiers, and was founded by Louis XIV. in 1670. It has a wide terrace in front laid out as a garden. Five statues in bronze adorn the entrance. There is a large open crypt, the walls of which are of polished granite, and on these are inscribed the names of the hero's great victories. In the middle of the crypt stands the massive sarcophagus, and marble statues keep sentinel about it. Before you is the superb high altar, flooded with golden light from the painted windows, and around are the stately columns which support the lofty dome. The tomb is gorgeous, with everything that marble and gold, sunlight and shade, form and color, can do to dazzle and awe. And this is all that remains of that mightiest Architect of Ruin, Great Napoleon! The remains of the Great Conqueror were transferred from St. Helena, in 1861, to this resting-place of polished porphyry, with awful pomp and solemnity.

> "Glorious tomb o'er glorious sleepers! gallant fellowship to share;
> Paladin and peer and marshal—France, thy noblest dust is here!
> Names that light thy battle annals—names that shock the heart of earth!
> Stars in crimson war's horizon—synonyms for martial worth.

"Room within that shrine of heroes! place, pale spectres of the
    past!
Homage yield, ye battle phantoms! Lo, your mightiest comes at last!
Was his course the woe out-thunder'd from prophetic trumpet's lips
Was his type the ghastly horseman shadow'd in the apocalypse?

"Gray-haired soldiers gather round him. relics of an age of war,
Followers of the Victor-Eagle, when his flight was wild and far;
Men who panted in the death strife on Rodrigo's bloody ridge,
Hearts that sicken'd at the death-shriek from the Russian's shatter'd
    bridge.

"They who loved him—they who feared him—they who in his
    dark hour fled—
Round the mighty burial gather, spell-bound by the awful dead!
Churchmen, princes, statesmen, warriors, all a kingdom's chief array,
And the fox stands—crowned mourner—by the Eagle's hero clay!

"But the last high rite is paid, and the last deep knell is rung—
And the cannons' iron voices have their thunder requiems sung—
And, 'mid banners idly drooping, silent gloom and mouldering state,
Shall the trampler of the world upon the judgment trumpet wait."

The old church is hung with battle-flags, the trophies of French arms. But we were *Englishmen*, and could walk proudly through the place. Among the maimed and worn-out soldiers is the only French survivor of Waterloo. The old man is proud to make the acquaintance of Englishmen, and fares better at their hands than he did in 1815, for few pass him without dropping money into his hands.

Paris is full of places and objects of historical or æsthetic interest; the Musée de Cluny, with its old Roman relics and statues; La Sorbonne, the famous

University of France; the Bourse, where the shouting and excitement is a perfect Bedlam—worse than the warring of the "bulls" and "bears" in Wall-street; the Column Vendome, a mighty shaft, its bronze coating made of pieces of artillery, captured from the enemy in the campaign of 1805, an imitation of Trajan's Column at Rome, one hundred and thirty-five feet high, and though hurled from its base by the Communists, has been reconstructed from the old fragments and stands in its former majesty; the Place de la Bastille where once stood the fearful prison, with its dark, damp dungeons. The prison has been torn down, now there is a monument in the square with the names of more than six hundred killed in one revolution. Of these I dare not more fully write without the risk of becoming tedious. We must not even linger in the crowded cemetery, with its extravagant tombs. Père La Chaise is the national burying-ground, the resting-place of many illustrious Frenchmen. It is thickly filled with the dead, and there are over three thousand magnificent monuments. No tomb is more generally visited than that of Abélard and Héloïse. It is a monument to disappointed affection. Their effigies lie side by side, with hands clasped in prayer. Let my young lady readers, who have had their lives blighted, make a pilgrimage to this tomb; let them offer their tributes and pour out their tears and secure the sympathies of the occupants—" *Sont reunis dans ce tombeau*"—and who can tell how soon the flowers of love will bloom again? In this populous city we found, amid garlands and showy ornaments, the narrow homes of many who have filled the world with the splendors of their achievements,—Fourier, Michelet, Talma, Béranger, Molière, Arago, Laplace, Rothschild, and a host of others.

We visited Les Gobelins, the celebrated carpet and tapestry manufactory belonging to the Government. It was founded in 1450, by Gobelin himself. We passed through the workshops and saw the workmen weaving their magnificent productions, perfect in color and design, unrivalled in beauty and finish, made only for the reigning monarch, or, in the absence of sovereignty, as presents to foreign kings and potentates. These pieces are valued at one hundred pounds sterling to the square foot. In these carpets, which require from five to ten years to be made, we saw imitated, with marvellous delicacy and finish, the finest paintings hung up in the galleries of the Louvre. The work is slow and difficult, and the artist toils patiently on day after day, week after week, month after month, with only the knotty side before him, ever and anon looking at the pattern, until at length, the work completed, he turns it over, and there is some master-picture so beautifully wrought in the tapestry that the costly fabric is fitted only to adorn the palaces of kings. Fit emblem, I thought, of the work of Christian teachers and laborers, who toil on the minds which God has put into their hands, having Christ as the pattern, and trying to impress His dear image there—implanting, instilling, moulding, fashioning, often weary and discouraged, seeing only the earthly side; but, by-and-by, the work shall be completed, and transfigured, glorified, admired by angels and redeemed spirits, the living souls upon which they have wrought, invested with His glory, shining in His splendor—shall adorn the Golden Palace of the King of kings. Such honor have all His saints who serve Him faithfully. Their work endures forever, and shall be found only in the palaces of the Eternal King.

The most interesting excursion from Paris is to Versailles. We made it in one of Cook's four-in-hand carriages. We first passed the pretty village of Anteuil, with its chalets, villas, and summer residences, standing in the midst of gardens and orchards; then on through the exterior line of fortifications to Sèvres, where we visited the porcelain manufactory. The specimens of pottery and porcelain shown are exquisitely beautiful. From Sèvres we drove to the Grand Palace of Versailles. It is a wonderfully brilliant and beautiful place, with its endless avenues, and sparkling fountains, and sylvan lakes, and verdant lawns, and colossal statues, and broad flights of stone steps leading to sumptuous palaces. We wandered through these monuments of prodigality and of royal license—the Grande and Petite Trianon—and were shown the souvenirs of the Great Napoleon—the bed in which he slept—his bath-room—the room in which he dined—the bed of Josephine, the private apartments of Louis XVI., and the boudoir, library, and writing-table of the unhappy Marie Antoinette. Next we were taken to the cumbrous and gold-covered state carriages, and were shown the one in which the Imperial infant rode to be christened. Poor lad! many a heart besides his mother's hoped and dreamed that one day that stately carriage would carry him to be crowned. One thrust of the assegai from Zulu savages has dissipated all these fond anticipations of imperial splendor. We spent hours wandering through the great hall of sculpture and galleries of paintings— all pictures of battle-scenes, in which the fleur-de-lis has waved victorious. There is not a solitary picture of a French defeat. On our return we visited the Prussian cemetery at Ville d'Avray. At St. Cloud we were shown the ruins of the pleasure palace of Louis XIV., as well as the positions of the Prussian batteries, when the proud city was girdled as with fire. Our drive home was through that cultivated, enchanting, endless district, the Bois de Boulogne, with its trees and lakes and sparkling cascades and broad avenues, filled with life, and fashion, and gaiety.

Paris life is one long round of enjoyment. Night is turned into day; theatres and operas are overflowing; out-door concerts crowded, and parks of noble trees, splashing fountains, and gardens bright and fragrant with flowers, are thronged with pleasure-seekers. Family ties and obligations are loosely held. There is little of home life. There is a lack of conjugal fidelity, and out of a population of two millions, it is estimated that one-third of the births are illegitimate. Yet everything outside is fair and well ordered. There is no filth in the streets, nor sights offensive to morality. The masses are neatly and comfortably clad, and the entire appearance is that of a peaceful and orderly community. I spent a Sabbath in the gay city, and attended Protestant service morning and evening. Early in the day we went to the Madeleine to listen to the music. As we stood upon the marble floor, snowy in its whiteness, we thought how completely it is washed of the blood of the seven hundred Communists. We remained throughout the High Mass service; but aside from the deep tones of the noble organ, the well-trained voices of the singers, and the responses of gorgeously-dressed priests at the altar, no one could hear anything save the tinkling of bells, which told the people when they were to stand up, or kneel, or sit down.

After the evening service, in the beautiful little Wesleyan Church, we were invited by the pastor and his accomplished wife to meet a few friends in the parlor of the parsonage; and there were represented, in that little company, the great divisions of the world —Europe, Asia, Africa, and America. There were French Protestants, English, Irish, Scotch, American, a missionary from Spain, and another from West Africa. After tea, an hour was passed in religious communion;

hymns were sung, prayers offered, and the inmost heart was touched more profoundly, than by all else in the brilliant and beautiful capital—the ravishing music of its churches, the resplendent array of its paintings and statuary, or the panorama of its bridges and columns, its palaces and parks of elysian loveliness.

CHAPTER VII.

PARIS TO ALEXANDRIA.

Railway Ride to Turin—Bribing a Guard—Mountain Scenery—Mount Cenis Tunnel—Turin—Marengo—Bologna—A Pleasant Incident—The Shores of the Adriatic—Italians—Brindisi—Scapegraces on the Adriatic—Corfu—Charming Scenery—The People—Greek Church—The Ionian Sea—Classic Lands—Byron's Isles of Greece—Crete and Fair Havens—A Storm—The Mediterranean—Arrival in Alexandria.

IN passing through France and Italy to reach the Austrian Lloyd steamers at Brindisi, it is necessary to make a continuous journey of 500 miles from Paris to Turin. I dreaded this journey. I had travelled once from Geneva to Paris; the ride was through pleasant fields and sunny vineyards, but it was an all-night journey and one of the most tiresome and torturing journeys, I ever made; no Pullman sleeping-car, but compelled to sit bolt upright, with cramped legs and weary body, jolted, joggled and worn out, and able to get sleep only in naps. O deliver me from railway travelling by night on the Continent! But this time, by a little bribing of one of the guards, I got a half compartment to myself, and, by lifting the central arm, was able to lie at full length, and so enjoyed a comfortable night's rest. The only halting-places were at Fontainbleau, Dijon, Macon, and Ambericux. We breakfasted at Culoz, and then began the mountain scenery of Savoy. We crossed the swift and arrowy Rhone near Aix les Bains, and dashed through tunnels and along mountain sides. On one side, rise great snow domes, on the other, naked rocks shoot up hundreds of feet in height. The Alps of Savoy are rich in scenery of the grandest kind—dark crags, pine clad slopes, foaming torrents, each one a glittering sheet, "like a wall of shattered chrysophrase," sweeping down to the depths below, here, purple shadows, and glancing sunbeams there. Mountain scenery gives me intense delight. These giant masses seem, to me, like mighty intelligences. How often and often, I have felt the force of Montgomery's words:—

>"The mountains of this glorious land
>   Are conscious beings to mine eye;
> When at the break of day they stand,
>   Like giants, looking through the sky,
> To hail the sun's unrisen car,
>   That gilds the diadems of snow,
> While, one by one, as star by star,
>   Their peaks, in ether, glow!"

As our road goes twisting and bending among the "everlasting hills," the snowy summits gleam in splendor, while stately pines stand in serried ranks on their steep sides. Here and there nature mingles awe and terror with beauty, where the sides and surfaces of the mountains are seamed and gashed by the sweep of the avalanche. Near Modane, where the Italian road begins, we had a somewhat novel experience. A mighty avalanche had come rushing down the heights, bearing stones, trees, everything before it, and had buried the track for the length of a mile. We were obliged to descend from our carriages and climb over the huge mass of snow and *débris*, to where the track was open on the other side. I had seen the avalanches flashing down the Alps, and heard their distant thunder, but had never before set my foot upon one. I really enjoyed the incident, but was thankful that the awful crash did not come, while we were passing along, otherwise the avalanche would not have been a vivid memory, but a sepulchre, an engulfing tomb.

At Modane, we prepare to enter the tunnel. We see before us the towering mountain, whose heart, we are to pierce. The ascent to the entrance is steep and serpentine, and after a short ride, we see before and below us a charming little town, nestling among the snow-clad hills. What is that place? It is the station we have just left? What a useful language is the French! In our compartment are an Italian, a Frenchman, a Spaniard, and an Englishman, and yet with a smattering of French we carry on conversation and have a pleasant time together. The Englishman speaking

French, like the Duke of Wellington, "with great intrepidity," now and then peppers them with sentences from his own vocabulary which they seem to appreciate, for they respond, "*Oui, oui, monsieur, oui.*" Now we plunge into the darkness, and every one looks at his watch. We are twenty-six minutes in passing through the rock-hewn way, a distance of thirteen kilometres. What an achievement of engineering skill! But at what a sacrifice of life it was accomplished. Four thousand men for ten years working in the heart of a mountain four thousand feet below its highest peak, with every now and then a terrible catastrophe! The tunnel is passed, and as we come out into a burst of sunshine, what a glory is resting upon the mountains, those cathedrals of God, with their gates of rocks and altars of snow! It is one of those pictures of nature, which cannot be described, and which seen once is an inspiration for a lifetime. The view is supremely grand, and romantic beyond description. Immense peaks, and spires, and pinnacles, soaring aloft, awful and inaccessible, and draped in waving folds of snowy vestments; dark scars of crags, between the great white pyramids; blue depths of glacier chasms, magnificent pines, and frozen torrents. Now the verdure of the sunny south comes surging up, more richly wooded are the mountain ranges and more smiling the landscape, for we are descending into the plains of sunny Italia, with the deep blue of its sky, and the soft tinting of its hill-sides. We follow the windings of the Dora, here a little baby stream just leaping from its birthplace among the everlasting hills. We dash through tunnel after tunnel, into rocky cuts and out of them, awaking the slumbering echoes as we pass along. I was reminded of the descent from the Rocky Mountains through Echo and Weber canyons into the pure and perfect landscape of Salt Lake Valley; only the heights here are more imposing, while now and then are castle and tower fortress, each one of which has a history and romance.

At Susa, is an ancient Roman triumphal arch, constructed about the commencement of the Christain era. Passing through the chestnut-clad foot-hills, and sweeping over the vast and fertile plain of Piedmont, we reach the fair City of Turin at six o'clock in the evening. The streets, the plazas, the dress, and manners of the people, all tell of a different civilization. The city has a population of over two hundred thousand, and the places of interest are the Royal Palace and gardens, the armory and picture gallery. Owing to the cloudy weather, however, I missed during this visit the chief attraction—a view of the city and a panorama of the Alps, with Monte Rosa, queen of the Alps, and her coronet of peaks, from the Capuchin Monastery. But as we were leaving the city next day, through a rift the sun shone out, and lo! the snowy bosoms gleamed like the far-off throne of God, and for many a league we had a magnificient view of those Alpine ranges, with their bold serrated outline and fields of everlast-

IN THE HIGH ALPS.

ing snow, along the distant horizon. As we whirled along, an Italian gentleman pointed out to me the Castle Royal de Moncalier, an imposing structure; also Asti, the birth-place of Alfieri, whose genius has invested Turin with immortal interest and associations; and the battle-field of Marengo, where Napoleon gained one of his most splendid victories. This is, indeed, a classic land, the ancient Latium, the nurse of arts and arms, and dear to the hearts of all men. The very ground, we have passed over, was traversed by Hannibal, who, in his descent from the Alps, sacked the ancient City of Turin.

We reach Bologna in time to see the Cathedral, the University made famous by Galvani and his discoveries, and the leaning towers. These towers are not so high as the famous one at Pisa, but they lean toward each other: one is three and a half, the other eight feet and a quarter out of their perpendicular; the soft spongy character of the soil in which they have been built is no doubt, the true explanation of these leaning structures. A very pleasant incident occurred at the table of the Hotel Brun. I sat next a lady and gentleman who were evidently English. We were going through the many courses of a rather sumptuous dinner, when the mere civility of passing a mustard dish started a conversation, and we discovered that we were fellow-Canadians. They were Mr. and Mrs. Charles F. Goodhue, of London, Ontario. They had been up the Nile, had visited Jerusalem, Smyrna, Greece, and were now on their way from Trieste to Rome, thence to Switzerland and the Alps. We were the last at the table that night. I had intended retiring early as I was to make an early start for Brindisi, but we had so many mutual acquaintances to talk about; I had so many inquiries to make concerning my journey, and the lady spoke in such raptures of the lands they had visited, that the evening was charmed away.

Early next morning I was on the road to the south of Italy. The railway from Rimini to Ancona skirts the shores of the Adriatic, whose crystalline blue waters are covered with white sails. The sloping hills, covered with green and crowned with ancient mansions are charming. Over the white stone roads, hot and dusty, trudge women, erect and graceful, carrying their burdens upon their heads. The men are generally riding behind donkeys and milk-white oxen, in little carts. The men seem indolent and listless. The peasant women, with olive complexions and coal-black eyes, drudge in coarse labor, and roughened by toil and weather, blackened by sun and wind, of coarse and slovenly dress, there is nothing very picturesque or passionate-looking about them. Men, women, and children are in the fields at work, digging, planting, and pulling. We on this continent cannot get accustomed to the European system of degrading women to the level of hard-handed tillers of the soil, and making them as coarse, and tough, and nut-browned as men. The Italians are a loyal, vivacious, and cheerful people.

In Bologna, all night, I heard their songs and laughter, and the loud tones of their liquid and beautiful speech. A fellow-traveller in the same compartment, in his light-heartedness, gives a song now and then with air of most exquisite music. The stopping-places are full of chattering, and impassioned gesticulation, until the horn toots and the train is off. But they are desperate cheats: they make most extortionate charges for trifling things. At a railway station, where the train was stopping for a few minutes, a waiter besieged me to bring me something; I ordered hot milk. He brought me a little cup half filled and wanted to charge me a franc. The train was starting, he cried, "Presto! Presto!" The milk was too hot to swallow, and what with my remonstrances for change and the moving of the train I only got a mouthful of my milk. However there is one comfort, they cannot impose upon you more than once in the same place. As we proceed south, the scenery becomes more tropical in appearance; the air is warm, there is a quivering blaze of resplendent sunshine resting on foliage and field; a golden haze is over all; and in the background of blue sea, verdant hills, vales, hamlet, and town, rise the snow-clad ranges of the Appenines. On we go, catching picturesque but momentary glimpses of old Roman remains, and mediæval towers and walls, until Brindisi is reached and the journey by rail adown the Continent of Europe is ended.

Brindisi is the great transit station on the route to

India and the East, by the Mont Cenis Railway and the Suez Canal. It has no interest, save from its classical associations. It is the Brindisium of Horace's mirthful journey; the city in which Pacuvius was born, and in which Virgil died; the termination of the Appian Way. During the conflict between Julius Cæsar and Pompey, "Great Cæsar" endeavored to shut up Pompey's fleet in the inner harbor of Brindisium; and during the eleventh century it was the scene of the chivalrous pageantry of the Court of Tancred.

I, however, associate its crooked and narrow streets with Hamlet's description of midnight :—

> " 'Tis now the witching time of night,
> When churchyards yawn and hell itself breathes out
> Contagion to this world : Now could I drink hot blood,
> And do such bitter business as the day
> Would quake to look on."

Our train, *mirabile dictu*, for an Italian railway, reached its destination ahead of time, and, as there were no carriages at the station, I committed myself and my luggage to the tender mercies of an Italian, and started for the office of the Austrian Lloyds. It was not unpleasant walking down the broad moonlit street toward the shining sea; but when we came to traverse the dark, dismal lanes of the city, with gloomy, clumsy, old dwellings, almost meeting each other, and my guide trudged on, leading me, I knew not where, I must confess that I did not altogether enjoy it, for I thought how easy it would be for

a murder to be committed, and a passing stranger
mysteriously to disappear. However, I put on a
courageous air, and in due time we reached our destination. When we came to the dock, I gave my porter
what I considered a good fee, but, with the consummate
rascality of his race, he demanded more. If I had
planked down a sovereign he would have asked for
another. I settled it by giving him another franc, and
jumping into the boat. The steamer was about two
boat lengths from the wharf, and happily there was a
tariff for rowing this distance. But I had exhausted
all my small change; and when I offered the men
seventy-five centimes, they would not take it. I
showed them that I had nothing but gold. They
wanted to take the piece to get it changed, but I would
not allow that. Then they brought on board a raga-
muffin old Jew to change the money. He brought out
his paper currency and his coppers; but I would take
nothing but silver. He pretended not to have any.
Finally, the matter was wound up by my borrowing
some silver from a fellow-passenger who had just come
on board. Then the old scapegrace wanted a commis-
sion for the service he had volunteered to render; but
I left them all gesticulating passionately and talking
violently as only Italians can, and quickly made my
way into my cabin. This is the land of rascality—
the entire shores of that fair inland sea, the Mediterranean, is given up to chicanery and low trickery.
They say one Spanish Jew puts into his pocket three

German Jews; one Levantine Jew two Spanish Jews; one Greek two Levantines, and one Armenian two Greeks.

Our vessel started at midnight, and I soon forgot, in refreshing sleep, Jew, Greek, and Italian. Next morning I arose and gazed upon a sight of transcendent beauty. Around was a silver sea studded with islands, while to the left were the shores of Turkey and the snow-covered peaks of the Albanian Mountains. We are traversing waters full of haunting memories. This Adriatic Sea was once the centre of worldly traffic, when the Venetian Republic was in the zenith of its power and greatness, admired and honored by all Europe; and the gay Queen of the Adriatic, Venice, sat on her lagoons and marble squares, veined with azure and warmed with gold. Upon what contingencies earthly splendor rests! The discovery of the Cape passage extinguished this dazzling star; the gold and gems and spices of India reached the West through other channels, and seaweed clustered around her marble palaces, now black with age. Thus earthly greatness vanishes; and though the Italian Government may make strenuous efforts to revive the prosperity of Venice, yet the placid dreamy waters shall never again be ploughed, as of old, by fleets of merchantmen from every land. We reached Corfu about three in the afternoon, and spent the evening and following day in that picturesque place.

This Island will repay a visit, for it is one of the

loveliest spots that can be found. The capital itself is very quaint. The streets are narrow, a perfect labyrinth up and down tortuous lanes and passages,

CITADEL, CORFU.

and the tall old houses tower up on either side. Seen from the water the town is very romantic in appearance, but a nearer acquaintance discloses dilapidation, filth, and misery. There are a few houses of architectural merit, being of English or French style, and structures of the Venetian time, with traces of former splendor, but the majority have neither comfort nor beauty.

The view from the Esplanade is most enchanting. On one side, rises the lofty Citadel, built by the Venetians when the Republic, in the 15th century, at the height of its power, held all the coast lands from the mouth of the Pau to Corfu, and had a population of over 8,000,000. On the other side, are the strong battlements built by the English—for this Island was long held by our Government as a military post, and was only a few years ago ceded to the Greeks. Before you, rises the beautiful Albanian shore, with bay, and cape, and point, and headland draped with glory, and the mountains glittering and snow-clad; behind you, are the high, blue-tinged mountains of the Island, of which there are two ranges, the San Salvador or ancient Istone, and Santi Deca or the Ten Saints; around you gardens, castles, groves; below you, the silver, sunlit sea, its glittering surface reflecting mountain, tree, and shore; and down upon all, the firmament sends the ether in rosy reflections of light. The rich, purple haze of the Mediterranean is unlike anything else I ever saw—not like the golden haze of California, or the pure, shimmering light of the Wahsatch Ranges, or the gleaming splendor of Chamounix and Mont Blanc, but a radiance all its own, that produces a magic impression. I am thankful for a happy susceptibility to the beauties of nature. How dull are some before whom pass all these glories of earth and sky!

> "What have you seen?"
> The one, with yawning, made reply,
> 'What have we seen? Not much have 1.
> Trees, meadows, mountains, groves, and streams,
> Blue sky, and clouds, and sunny gleams.'
> The other, smiling, said the same,
> But with face transfigured, and eyes of flame—
> 'Trees, meadows, mountain, groves, and streams,
> Blue sky, and clouds, and sunny gleams.'"

"The works of the Lord are great, sought out of all them that have pleasure therein." The visible creation embodies the thoughts of God, and His autograph is written on the stars, written on the sun, written on the sea, written on the mountain's brow, written everywhere. The Dervish, in the Eastern tale, when he rubbed his eyes with the ointment given to him by the genii, sees flashing diamonds, glowing rubies and emeralds, where before he had seen nothing but bare rocks and dull earth. So when our eyes are anointed with the spiritual eye-salve, we see what others cannot see, and walk through the world as through a home, where the Father's portrait hangs ever upon the walls, and where upon every stairway and in every corridor are memorials of His tender love and care. The heavens above, tapestried with light and fretted with sunbeam and cloud, do but "declare His glory;" and the adorned earth everywhere looks fair in His beauty, with its far-reaching landscapes broken into vales, lifted into islands, heaved into soaring peaks of mountain grandeur, carpeted with emerald and cloth of gold, and girdled by the ancient ocean.

The scenery of Corfu will ever be associated with pleasurable and picturesque recollections. The classic Corcyra, its shape like the sickle or *drepane*, to which it was compared by the ancients, with its undulating surface, its large and wide-spreading olive trees, intermingled with the myrtle, the arbutus, and the bay; its large and luscious oranges, its remains of antiquity, the ruined temple of Neptune,—what a grand place it is to visit! You are amused without fatigue, invigorated without effort. I found an endless charm in walking along its irregular, narrow, and labyrinthine streets that land you in all sorts of unsuspected localities. The atmosphere, too, is so soft and balmy, that to inhale it is a real luxury. No wonder that Napoleon pronounced the climate of Corfu to be the loveliest in the world.

The people, too, are a study. The peasantry are reputed to be the idlest of all the Ionians. They feed on garlic and onions, and grow the olive. It is just the thing for these indolent fellows. The trees once planted, they are allowed to grow unrestrained, and they get the produce of oil with little trouble or expense, beyond the collecting and pressing of the fallen fruit. Good trees yield each about two gallons of oil. Agriculture is entirely neglected. They do not even grow their own vegetables, and it would be difficult now to find the plants such as Homer names adorning the garden of Alcinous,—the wild olive, the oil olive, the pear, pomegranate, apple, fig, and vine. In a population of over seventy thousand, there are many resident foreigners. We met a very intelligent Englishman who had lived there with his family for many years, on account of his health. He had pulmonary trouble, and the climate of Corfu had prolonged his life. He did not care for the society of the place since Great Britain had resigned the protectorate of the Ionian Islands in favor of the Kingdom of Greece. I asked him why he did not return to England, and his significant answer was because he could not *live* in that climate. In the evening, when all the people are out of doors, a varied and unusual life moves before your eyes. What a strange mingling of European with Oriental manners and customs! What an interest in watching the brilliant but many-hued crowds that gather in the public square—Italians, French, English, Spaniards, Portuguese, Greeks, Arabs—a motley collection of every nation, people, and tongue! Men with fiery-red caps, Albanians with short white skirts, like a ballet-dancer's dress, others with raiment indescribable, fancifully dressed children, dashing French and Italian beauties, and women with their gleaming white veils. Listen to the babel of tongues! In a dozen yards you hear as many different languages.

Corfu is now filled with Greek soldiers. The King of Greece is anxious to get possession of Albania, and the Albanian Christians, in sympathy with the movement, have enlisted in considerable numbers. The military movements, the playing of martial music, and the picturesque garb of these courageous Albanians increased the liveliness of the scene. What wonderful inspirations! what acts of devotion and heroism have been inspired by patriotism! The love of country is to nations, what the love of life is to individuals, for a country is the life of a nation. Will the Greeks, animated by the feeling of nationality, extend their boundaries until the scattered members of the Hellenic people linked together, they shall imitate the self-sacrifice, and enthusiasm, and super-human achievements of their forefathers; and Greece, regaining the dignity and grandeur of her ancient days of glory, become again the home of learning, and devotion, of freedom and truth?

On Sabbath morning I attended a Church of England service in what was formerly a Greek church; and also visited some of the Greek churches, the most important of which are the cathedral, dedicated to Our Lady of the Cave, and St. Spiridious, which contains the tomb of the patron saint of the Island. Corfu is the seat of a Roman Catholic as well as of a Greek bishop. The Roman Catholics are mostly descendents of families that immigrated there at the time of the Crusades and during the rule of the Venetians. The great majority of the people, however, belong to the Greek Church, which is independent of the Patriarch of Constantinople—a State Church, and, after the model of the Russian Church, places the management of the affairs of the Church in the hands of a "Holy Synod."

The Greek or Eastern Church calls itself the "Holy Orthodox Catholic and Apostolic Church," and has under its control a population of about seventy millions. Christianity arose in the East, and Greek was not only the language of the Scriptures, but of the early services of the Church. But when the old Roman Empire fell in two, and there came a complete political separation between the East and West, there came also, an ecclesiastical division of the early Church. The Greeks agree with the Roman Catholics in accepting as the rule of faith not only the Bible but also the traditions of the Church; but they differ in the doctrine concerning the procession of the Holy Ghost from the Son, and reject the Papal claim to supremacy. They forbid marriage to bishops, but allow the priests to marry; howbeit they are required to live separate from their wives during the time when they are actually engaged in church service. They do not permit the use of graven images, and there is greater simplicity in their service. Instrumental music is forbidden, but the singing is universal and grand. They have no pews, and the congregation are on their feet from the beginning to the end of the ceremonies, the posture in prayer being the body standing and turned toward the east. They teach that all Christians should receive the bread and the wine, and administer the communion in both kinds, even to children. The creed of the hollow cross is somewhat nearer to Protestantism than that of Popery, and efforts have been made by the Anglican Church to enter into inter-communion with the Greek Church; but the religion of the Eastern Church is more a tradition than a power. It is hard, formal, and intolerant. It has much of the letter that killeth, and little of the spirit which is life-giving. She has had missionary enterprise, but she never conquered her conquerors, and so Christianity did not keep the lands she had once laid hold of. Now her Christianity is more in exhibition than in practice. She reads the New Testament in the original language in her worship, but the Bible is a sealed book. On Sunday afternoon I found the churches vacant and undergoing a general scrubbing out. Soap and water are among the essentials to "pure religion and undefiled;" but there is also an old command "Remember the Sabbath day to keep it holy."

On Sunday evening, we found the vessel that was to take us to Alexandria lying in the harbor before the two castles, waiting for us, and we went on board. It was the good ship *Saturno*, of the Austrian Line, elegant in all its appointments. Dr. Johnson defined a ship as "a prison, with the chance of being drowned." Well, whatever chance there may be of getting drowned, this is surely no prison. Everything clean and comfortable, with excellent fare and accommodation and agreeable society; what can be pleasanter than coasting along the most beautiful and memorable shores in the world!

Next morning we were indeed in classic waters. It is the Ionian Sea, with its haunting memories of the wandering heroes of the "Odyssey" and the "Æneid." The sea is studded with islands, that are invested with immortal associations; and on the mainland every bay and cape and point and headland has been made famous in history and glorious in heroism. There is Ithaca, the home of the wandering Ulysses and his fair Penelope. Yonder is Cephalonia with its antiquities of Roman baths, rock-cut tombs, tesselated pavements, and vast stretches of Cyclopean and Hellenic walls; while rising up five thousand five hundred feet is Mount Ænos, called the Black Mountain, from the darkness of the pines, which constitutes the most striking feature in Cephalonian scenery. There is Zante, "the flower of the Orient," with its picturesque little city and olive gardens, and currant plantations. These islands are all mountainous. The soil is of a reddish brown color and dotted with little white villages in the midst of vineyards and groves of olive trees. Schleimann, the explorer of Troy and Mycene, is here in Ithaca, raking up what remains he can find of the home of the great hero. To our left is the Gulf of Corinth; but the crowded, bustling city is no more. There is Navarino, the scene of a famous fight between the Greeks and Turks in the war for Hellenistic independence. Yon lone mountain, that rises up in such naked majesty, is Parnassus, the home of the Muses. There is Pindus and Mount Athos. Yonder lie the uplands of old Sparta, with its historical reminiscences and marvels of valor in the brave days of old. What a brightness there is in the sun! What beauty in the sea! What classic memories over all! The mind is steeped with thoughts of Agamemnon and Achilles, and the thousand heroes of the elder ages; the glorious deeds of Marathon and Thermopylæ and Salamis. This is the land in which Homer sang, and Socrates taught, and Plato dreamed, and Aristotle studied, and Demosthenes poured forth his fiery philippics; and yet these classical localities are barren, destitute, unpoetical wastes. It is not the Greece of the golden age of glory:—

"'Tis Greece, but living Greece no more."

The ruins, that gleam from the summits of barren hills, are but the symbols of a desolation that has come upon her. Nothing remains of the Greece of two thousand years ago, but her wealthy and imperishable literature.

No wonder Byron, as he looked upon these islands and memorable scenes, sang:—

'The isles of Greece ! the isles of Greece !
  Where burning Sappho loved and sung,—
Where grew the arts of war and peace,—
  Where Delos rose and Phœbus sprung !
Eternal summer gilds them yet,—
But all, except their sun, is set.

'The Scian and the Teian muse,
  The hero's harp, the lover's lute,
Have found the fame your shores refuse ;
  Their place of birth, alone, is mute
To sounds which echo further west
Than your sires' ' Islands of the blest.'

'The mountains look on Marathon,
  And Marathon looks on the sea ;
And musing there an hour alone,
  I dreamed that Greece might still be free ;
For, standing on the Persian's grave,
I could not deem myself a slave.

'A king sat on the rocky brow
  That looks o'er sea-born Salamis ;
And ships by thousands lay below,
  And men in nations ;—all were his !
He counted them at break of day,
And when the sun set, where were they ?

'And where are they ? and where art thou,
  My country ? On thy voiceless shore
Th' heroic lay is tuneless now—
  Th' heroic bosom beats no more !
And must thy lyre, so long divine,
Degenerate into hands like mine ?

''Tis something in the dearth of fame,
  Though linked among a fettered race,
To feel at least a patriot's shame,
  Even as I sing, suffuse my face,

Sketches of Travel.

For what is left the poet here?
For Greeks a blush—for Greece a tear.

'Must we but weep o'er days more blessed?
    Must we but blush? Our Father bled.
Earth! render back from out thy breast
    A remnant of our Spartan dead!
Of the three hundred, grant but three,
    To make a new Thermopylæ!

"What! silent still? and silent all?
    Ah! no;—the voices of the dead
Sound like a distant torrent's fall,
    And answer, 'Let one living head,
But one arise,—we come, we come;'
'Tis but the living who are dumb.

'In vain—in vain; strike other chords;
    Fill high the cup with Samian wine!
Leave battles to the Turkish hordes,
    And shed the blood of Scio's vine!
Hark! rising to the ignoble call—
How answers each bold bacchanal!

'You have the Pyrrhic dance as yet—
    Where is the Pyrrhic phalanx gone?
Of two such lessons, why forget
    The nobler and the manlier one?
You have the letters Cadmus gave—
Think ye he meant them for a slave?

"Fill high the bowl with Samian wine!
    We will not think of themes like these!
It made Anacreon's song divine:
    He served—but served Polycrates—
A tyrant; but our masters then
Were still at least our countrymen.

"The tyrant of the Chersonese
　Was freedom's best and bravest friend;
That tyrant was Miltiades!
　Oh! that the present hour would lend
Another despot of the kind!
Such chains as his were sure to bind.

"Fill high the bowl with Samian wine!
　Our virgins dance beneath the shade,
I see their glorious black eyes shine;
　But, gazing on each glowing maid,
Mine own the burning tear-drop laves
To think such breasts must suckle slaves.

"Place me on Sunium's marbled steep—
　Where nothing save the waves and I
May hear our mutual murmurs weep:
　There swan-like let me sing and die;
A land of slaves shall ne'er be mine—
Dash down yon cup of Samian wine."
　　　　　　　—*The Isles of Greece.*

We passed from the Ionian Sea into the Mediterranean, but a fearful wind from the Archipelago was howling over the tempestuous billows, and our heavily-freighted ship had to put back and find shelter for a night and a day under the heights of Cerigo, and close to Cape Matapan. We had no opportunity to visit the two famous caves of great dimensions and adorned with stalactites of marvellous beauty, nor seek for traces of the shrine of the Venus of Cythera (the ancient classic name of this island) for the Captain was anxious, with the first lull of the terrific storm, to continue his voyage. Again we ventured out, and although the sea ran high, and we had to encounter the violence of the waves, yet we sailed close to Crete and found shelter under Mount Ida, which rises above the sea eight thousand feet. The Apostle, quoting one of their own proverbs, said: "The Cretans are at most liars, evil beasts, slow bellies." If they were on board the *Saturno* just now there would be some activity given to their *slow* bellies. All these islands, decayed, forlorn, almost tenantless and commerceless though they be, have not lost their beauty. You cannot gaze upon them without coming under the spell of their fascination. As a very intelligent young German observed, when we were passing Zante, "De more we gets close, de more it gets picturesque." The coast of Crete, or Candia, is broken and varied in outline. In many places the mountains rise a wall directly from the sea, so that for a day we were well sheltered by that island which claims to be the birthplace of Zeus, father of the Olympian deities, and of Minos, the first monarch who established a naval power and acquired dominion over the sea.

About five miles east of Cape Littinos we passed the port of "Fair Havens," which is mentioned in the voyage of St. Paul, and is still called *Kaloi Limeres*, or the Fair Havens. One is being continually admonished of the uncertainties of Eastern travel. This storm has already robbed me of at least two days in Egypt. Any treacherous weather at Jaffa, in debarkation or embarkation, would delay me at least two weeks in a land where there is no railroad, and where everything is dependent upon steam service, each alternate week. I begin to wonder whether I shall meet my friends in Rome according to appointment, or reach home as soon as I have been anticipating. But I must be patient and hopeful, and trust fully in that Divine Providence whose wonderful unfolding has already turned the bitterest trial of my life into a crowning blessing, enabling me to realize the fascinating dream of my life—a visit to the lands of the Bible. Let there be changes and conditions unexpected, and new events rising up like islands out of the waters of the unknown; yet surely when the Lord has been so good, all doubt should end in satisfaction, and all suffering in patience, when He has a purpose in all, and with infinite love and faithfulness works out the highest and best thing possible in our life. O to live out the life that God appoints, and in complete self-renunciation giving up our selfish, self-appointed, and self-directed ways, realize that His Spirit is shaping all, guiding all, controlling all to the best and most blessed end!

And now that the storm has abated and the waters have again become calm, I begin to realize that I am indeed upon the Mediterranean. Its associations are its chiefest charms! Did ever any other waters lave such shores! Egypt, Canaan, Tyre, Smyrna, Troy, Greece, Carthage, Italy, and Spain. What crafts have sailed over these billows! The ship *Argo*, that sailed out from Iolcus, in Thessaly, to Colchis, in search of the golden fleece in the grove of Mars, the stately ships of Solomon, the merchant vessels of Tyre and Sidon the fleet of Xerxes, Carthaginian and Roman galleys, Genoese and Venetian merchantmen. It has been the highway of all the great nations that have filled the world with their splendor. Over it the great Apostle of the Gentiles sailed on those great missionary tours to which are largely due the enlightenment, and civilization, and proud pre-eminence of Europe to-day. It was on a ship of Alexandria, the port to which we are now sailing, that Paul suffered shipwreck on his way to Italy. It was the *Castor and Pollux*, a ship of Alexandria, that carried him from Malta to Puteoli. A marvellous sea is this that stretches out its blue expanse!

Early on the morning of Friday, February 25th, all was astir on board the good ship *Saturno*. We are looking out for land. There, in the distance, is a long low stretch of coast. It is Egypt—proud and ancient Egypt, with its hoary arts and early civilization. Egypt, the oldest land on earth—mother of civilization—that taught Greece letters, and trained Moses in earthly lore. Egypt, the land of the Pharaohs, of the Ptolemies; the land in which Abraham sojourned, and into which Joseph was sold; the land that gave shelter to the infant Saviour when Joseph arose and took the Young Child and his mother and went down into Egypt. Egypt! there it lies, silent in the morning sunshine wrapping itself in the memories of three thousand years.

The domes and minarets of Alexandria glitter in the sunlight. We enter the famous old harbor and pass the lighthouse where once stood the colossal Pharos, said to have been four hundred feet high; catch a view of that venerable column, Pompey's Pillar, next, the marble Palace of the Khedive, and now, within a magnificent breakwater, our ship comes to anchor. At once we are surrounded by little boats filled with dark-skinned, curiously robed, gesticulating, shouting Arabs. Boats enough to carry the passengers of a *Great Eastern*. We get into one of them, are rowed to shore, and are soon dashing through the streets and bazaars of Alexandria.

CHAPTER VIII

ALEXANDRIA TO THE HOLY LAND.

Alexandria Landing—The Donkey Boys—The Streets and Bazaars—Khedive's Palace—Pompey's Pillar—The Ancient City of the Ptolemies—Library—Arab Quarter—Drives—On Shipboard Again—Aboukir Bay and Nelson's Victory—A Lovely Sunset—Port Said—Landing at Joppa—An Ancient City—The Holy Land.

WE have seen the lions of Alexandria—we have exhausted all its sights, and sounds, and smells. On landing in Egypt, the first thing demanded is your "passport," and the next thing "backsheesh." Having safely got through the hands of the officials, you next have to run the gauntlet of the donkeys. All the donkeys of Egypt—of all colors, white, black, mouse—have come down to meet you; and all the donkey-boys are there to drive them,—shouting, gesticulating, laughing, capering, urging their beasts upon you, if you will not get upon them.

We drove first to the hotel, and then secured a guide and carriage for the day. First, to the bazaars—what views of street life! What a strange commingling of Eastern and Western manners and habits! What a babel of tongues! What a blaze of costumes! What a blending of all colors and nationalities! "Parthians, and Medes, and Elamites, and the dwellers in Mesopotamia, and in Judea, and Cappadocia, in Pontus, and Asia, Phrygia, and Pamphylia, in Egypt, and in the parts of Lybia about Cyrene. Cretes and Arabians:" English, French, Italians, Greeks, Circassians, Chinese, Coolies, Hindoos, Bedouins, black Nubians, high-capped Copts, swarthy Egyptians, veiled women with laughing eyes peering out upon you, and cross-legged Turks smoking their narghilies. The scene is most animated; there is a constant uproar and continual passing of camels, donkeys, and carriages through the surging, heaving, jostling crowd.

Next, to the Palace of the Khedive. It is built of white marble, and the beautiful columns at the entrance were stolen from the Mosque of the Thousand and One Columns, and remind us of the Arabian tales of enchantment. The interior of the palace is in execrable taste—Egyptian, Mohammedan, European treasures and adornments, all arrayed in costly but "Frenchy" display; floors of ebony, divans of silk and knit tapestry, and massive chandeliers, a pair of which alone cost one hundred thousand dollars. The late Khedive had a mania for building palaces, and leaving them unfinished.

The Khedive's Palace stands on a peninsula, what

was formerly the Island of Pharos. The modern city does not occupy the site of the ancient city of the Ptolemies. Pliny tells us that the famous city had a "circumference of fifteen miles. It was built by Alexander the Great, on the African coast, twelve miles from the Canoptic mouth of the Nile, on the Mareotic lake, which was formerly called Arapotes; that Dinochares, an architect of great celebrity, laid down the plan, resembling the shape of a Macedonian mantle, with a circular border full of plaits, and projecting into corners on the right and left; the fifth part of its site being even then dedicated to the palace." Westward, from the Canoptic Gate to the Necropolis, ran a street two hundred feet wide, decorated with magnificent temples, houses, and public buildings, and this street was intersected by another of the same breadth and magnificence, running from south to north. It had three famous stations, the *Regio Judæorum*, or Jews' quarter, in the north-east; the *Rhacotis*, or Egyptian quarter, on the west, with its Serapeum, or Temple of Serapis, containing an image of the god brought from Pontus; and the Brucheum, the Royal or Greek quarter, containing the chief public buildings, the splendid palace, the *Cæsarium* or Temple of the Cæsars, and the Court of Justice. How all this magnificence has vanished! Once, the confluence of eastern and western civilization, the emporium of the commerce of Europe, Asia, and Africa, the only warehouse for receiving the treasures of India, Ethiopia, and Arabia, and for transmitting them to other places; considered by the Romans themselves as inferior only to their own matchless capital, its glory departed with the downfall of the Byzantine Empire, and its commerce was annihilated by the discovery of the Cape of Good Hope.

Under the Turks it sank into utter insignificance, and at the beginning of the present century, it was a small poverty-stricken Arab village of a few hundreds. But when Mahomed Ali rose to power, and became ruler of Egypt, he turned his attention to the restoration of Alexandria. With keen insight, he saw the importance of the ancient mart, and determined that it should fulfil its destinies, not only as the emporium for the rapidly developing trade of Egypt, but become again the magnificent gateway to the East. Up rose a stately city, which now numbers a population of nearly a quarter of a million; and with its canal and railway improvements it is the centre of communication between Europe and India. The Frank quarter of the town, with its streets and squares, shops and hotels, offices and banks, has all the appearance of a European city, and you might fancy yourself to be in the heart of Paris or London, were it not for the motley sights and sounds around you; the donkey-stations, with their pushing, jostling donkey-boys and animals, the strings of ungainly camels stalking solemnly and noiselessly along, with all sorts of bulky and enormous burdens on their backs, surmounted by the driver; vehicles with one or more footmen, with girded loins and swinging staff, who run ahead and cry aloud for room, and clear the way most unceremoniously; while here and there are devout Mussulmans, prostrate in the roadway on their prayer-rugs, and going through their devotions.

The favorite drive, the Rotten Row of Alexandria, is along the Mahmoodieh Canal, which connects with the Rosetta branch of the Nile at Atfeh. This canal was opened in 1820, and was constructed at a cost of a million and a half of dollars, and for want of proper management, a melancholy and awful sacrifice of human life by sickness and privation. It is about fifty miles in length, with an average width of about one hundred feet; and along this canal in the suburbs of the city are numerous handsome villas and charming residences.

The gardens of the Viceroy, which are open to the public, are quite delightful. Here we make the acquaintance, for the first time, of many kinds of tropical trees,—the spreading banyan, sycamore, bamboo, tamarisk, lemon, citron, pepper, and castor-oil; and see shrubs and flowers of great luxuriance and variety. Beyond the city walls to the south, on elevated ground, without a trace of fence or enclosure, is a perfect wilderness of stones. It is the Mohammedan Cemetery, and crowded with the dead. As we stood looking upon the strange scene, two dead bodies passed, borne on the shoulders of men, the priests reading passages from the Koran, and each followed by a crowd of wailing women, making cries and lamentations and piteous outbursts, in proportion to the money paid them for the purpose.

STREET LEADING TO A MOSQUE IN CAIRO.

On this ground rises up that ancient column, styled "Pompey's Pillar," a stately shaft of polished red granite, nearly one hundred feet high, and about thirty feet in circumference. From an inscription, it seems to have been erected in honor of the Emperor Domitian, and it was formerly surmounted by a statue of that monarch. An Arab tradition pretends that this was one of four columns that once supported a dome or other building, while others maintain that it belonged to the Serapeum.

This elevated ground, desolate, unpeopled, save by a filthy Egyptian village, is illustrious ground. It is the site of the ancient city, built by Alexander the Great, the chief city of Eastern commerce, the splendid capital of the Ptolemies, and, under the Cæsars, the granary of Rome; in wealth, luxury, learning, refinement, population, and industry, the second city of that mighty Empire, which stretched from the Euphrates to the Pillars of Hercules, and from the mouth of the Rhine to the Mountains of the Moon; the city in which St. Mark, the Evangelist, preached the Gospel; the city which boasted of its Pharos, one of the seven wonders of the world, and of its famous library of seven hundred thousand volumes.

A word concerning this library. When Greece, losing her national independence, lost also her intellectual supremacy, this city became the new centre of the world's activity and thought. Ptolemy Soter drew around him from various parts of Greece, men eminent in literature and philosophy, and the inspiration of his friend, Demetrius Phalereus, the Athenian orator, laid the foundations of the great library, and started a search for all written works, which resulted in the formation of a collection of books such as the world has seldom seen. The work begun by Ptolemy Soter was carried on vigorously by his successors, and no cost or pains were spared, in adding to the library. Jewish literature was introduced. On the downfall of the Hebrew monarchy, the exiled Jews came pouring into the city, until they formed one-third of the entire population. It was for the use of those Hellenistic Jews that the Septuagint translation was made. A Museum, or Academy of Science, was maintained by royal bounty, and there, men of letters, such as Euclid, Hipparchus, Herôn, Clemens and others, resided, and studied, and taught. Attached to the Museum were four hundred thousand volumes, while the remaining three hundred thousand belonged to the Temple of Serapis. The library of the Museum was destroyed during the war of Julius Cæsar with the Alexandrians, and many of the most valuable works of antiquity were lost forever. During the troublous times of the Roman Empire, the collection in the Serapion was exposed to many dangers and losses; but the ancient volumes were still preserved, until the ruthless vandalism of the Caliph Omar devoted the library to destruction. The story relating to the destruction of the library, is as follows:—"John, the Grammarian, a famous peripatetic philosopher, being in Alexandria at the time of its capture, and in high favor with Amru, begged that he would give him the Royal Library. Amru told him that it was not in his power to grant such a request, but promised to write to the Caliph for his consent. Omar, on hearing the request of his general, is said to have replied that if those books contained the same doctrine with the Koran they could be of no use, since the Koran contained all necessary truths; but if they contained anything contrary to that book, they ought to be destroyed; and, therefore, whatever their contents were, he ordered them to be burnt. Pursuant to this order they were distributed among the public baths, of which there were four thousand in the city, where for six months, they served to supply the fires."

With the library, everything else perished, and as far as the city of Alexander is concerned, we see only the remains and mounds of its probable site; there is scarcely a vestige of its greatness left behind; for, as I have before observed, the present city, with its population of two hundred thousand, its harbor crowded with merchant ships of the Orient and the Occident, is a growth of the present century. Would not those ancient heroes and conquerors and philosophers have a humiliating sense of the vanity of earthly prowess and splendor, could they but behold what we see! But the truth is that ours is a larger experience. As Sidney Smith observes, "there is a confusion of language in the use of the word 'ancient.' We say, the 'ancients,' as if they were older and more experienced men than we are, whereas, the age and experience are entirely on our side. They were the clever children and we only are the white-bearded, silver-headed ancients, who have treasured up and are prepared to profit by all the experience which human life can supply." While cherishing all the results which the past has bequeathed us, let us still reverence, in the midst of these old lands, our own times as the oldest!

The Egyptian and Arab sections of the city are dirty and dingy enough; the people live in filth and extreme wretchedness. Mrs. Partington speaks of her "oil-factories" breathing the "execrations" of coal-smoke, that are so dilatory to health; but what would the old lady say if her "oil-factories" had to take up the aroma of an Egyptian street? Ugh! The odor from bone-factories is the fragrance of roses in comparison. The narrow lanes of streets twist and turn like cow-paths, and the houses are low, wretched hovels, pestiferous dens, in which the father, the mother, and the children are huddled pell-mell, with dogs, cows, goats, and other animals. The children are ragged, squalid, and rickety, blear-eyed and pot-bellied; the women look cowed and dejected, and their long, soiled, and tattered garments scarcely conceal their emaciated forms; while the men are miserable, shabby-looking wretches, undermined by want and blighted by serfdom. In the more respectable native quarters, the houses generally overhang the street in the upper story, and out of the latticed windows peer the eyes of the women of the household—the wives of the often "much-married" husband.

Sketches of Travel. 171

Dust is everywhere and burning sun, and the eyes suffer much from the glare of the light. Ophthalmia is dreadfully prevalent. A traveller tells of landing at Alexandria in a boat in which the pilot was blind of one eye, and so were all the crew, except an old man who had lost both. I did Alexandria pretty thoroughly, but the most interesting scene in the city I witnessed, while sitting in the evening in front of a café in the Great Square, the Place Mehemet Ali. This is the head-quarters of European life. The scene is most novel and entertaining. The street is brilliant with gas; and to watch the curious crowd of all nations,—the dusky natives around you sipping their coffee, playing their games of draughts or smoking and story-telling; the vendors of wares of all sorts, shouting their goods; horses and carriages, with dashing French and Italian belles; donkeys, camels, oriental women veiled up to the eyes, and men in every dress. In every land the most interesting thing you see is man himself. How curiously these Egyptians dress! The women, with their wide trousers and long chooftan with hanging sleeves, and laced from the girdle to the bosom, with a loose shawl round the waist, a head veil of muslin, and a black face-veil reaching often from the eyes to the feet. The men, with wide trousers but tightly-fitting from the knee down, red shoes on their feet, a light, gaily-embroidered jacket, a striped sash round the waist, a small red-tasseled cap, and twisted round it the much-revered turban, carrying under their arms or munching along the way, a flat loaf of poor, black, sour, coarse, barley bread, their principal food, aside from eggs, dates, grasses, and beans.

The Egyptians are a devout people. The chief manifestation of religion is that of Mahomed or El Islam. Our first day in Alexandria was Friday, the Sunday of the Mohammedans, and we heard the muezzins chanting their call to prayers, from the galleries of the mosques and minarets, and, in our drives, saw the places for prayer—a marble floor, under the shadow of some tree, covered with devout Mussulmans turning toward Mecca, going through their prostrations and orisons, attending to their private duties and general devotions. These fellows make first-class Pharisees.

We left Alexandria on Saturday afternoon. The day is charming, and so warm is the sun at this season when Canada is in the depth of winter, that a pocket thermometer placed upon the deck registers nearly 100° Fahrenheit. The sky above is cloudless and radiant, and the warm sunbeams glance and shimmer on the bosom of the waters. Outside the harbor the Mediterranean is like a plain of gold, and around are ships at anchor lying motionless, and others just entering or quitting the port. While the ship is preparing to depart we are highly entertained with the curious rabble of Turks and Arabs in the little boats that swarm around the larger vessels. Such a troop of chattering, wrangling, bargaining, shouting natives, motley in complexion and motley in dress, one never sees, except in the picturesque lands of the Orient.

To Port Said is a delightful sail of fifteen hours. We pass Aboukir Bay, memorable for its great naval engagement, and which at once exalted the name of Nelson to a level with that of the celebrated conqueror, whose success was bringing the entire East under the sway of the French. As the hero, before the battle, made known to his officers his plans and tactics, Captain Berry exclaimed with transport, "If we succeed, what will the world say?" "There is no 'if' in the case," replied the Admiral: "that we shall succeed is certain; who may live to tell the story is a very different question." The French had the advantage in ships, guns, and men; but with all their skill and courage, and all their advantages of number and situation, they were completely vanquished. "Victory," said Nelson, "is not a name strong enough for such a scene." He called it a conquest; and in his success he recognized the God of Battles, for the first words of his despatches on the memorable occasion were "Almighty God has blessed His Majesty's Arms." Four French vessels were all that escaped. Out of thirteen sail of the line, nine were taken and two burnt; of the four frigates, one was sunk, another burnt, and two taken. The ship *Orient* took fire and blew up with a tremendous explosion, and among those who perished were the Commodore, Casa Bianca and his son, a brave lad of only ten, who would not leave the ship. Where is the youthful orator who has not recited—

"The boy stood on the burning deck!"

We sail along amid a perfect revelation of blue seas and blue skies. What a beautiful, tender, warm, indescribably fascinating color is over all! "As," in the language of Egypt, "the golden bark of the sun-god sank below the horizon, the sunset glowed with rubies, and a mass of flaming orange-red clouds piled themselves up until they reached the blue zenith overhead, and, burning with a splendid glory, stretched themselves over the whole heavens until they were lost in the calm, clear gold of the distant horizon." How the waters, too, sparkled and flamed; the quiet sea appearing like a plain of gold, after the departure of Ra, who, as the gray-haired Tum, vanished behind the western horizon, to bestow the blessings of light on the under-world. The stars come out, travelling on silver banks, their endless, unerring, and immeasurable circles through the clear blue vault. How entrancing these Eastern skies by night! What a charm, silently to pace the deck and hear the throbbing of our steamer and look upon the waters with foam and diamonds at the bows, and glints of blue and white at the sides, with here and there a splash of deep, rich green, like the color of Niagara, below the Falls! All night we passed along the low coast-line of Egypt, and early next morning, we reached the junction of the Suez

Canal with the Mediterranean, at Port Said, where we spent the Sabbath.

Port Said is a wretched place, morally and literally, but it seemed to us an oasis in the desert. An active mission among the sailors is prosecuted by Mr. Whytock, a devoted young Scotchman; and we all went ashore and attended service in the little mission-hall, one of our company—Rev. Mr. Scott, a minister from Glasgow—preaching an excellent sermon. At six o'clock, we were off again—this time for Jaffa, the port of Jerusalem. There was not much sleep that night, for we are approaching a land, endeared by associations, linked with our earliest and most hallowed recollections. There is a new charm about the dreamy lapping of the waters, and the clear and lambent light. We are up early in the morning, and amid the pale ethereal colors of the dawn is seen the dim outline of land. Soon the shore is clearly discerned, and in the distance, the rose-purple shoulders of swelling hills. It is Palestine, and we have the strangely-subduing sensation of gazing upon a land, the most sacred on earth. It is the land promised to Abraham, the land of Jacob, the goodly land which Moses in rapt vision saw from the heights of Nebo, the land of Rachel and Ruth, the land of David, the Shepherd-king of Israel and the inspired minstrel of the world, the land of Solomon the Wise, of Elijah and Isaiah, the land of Immanuel, the holy fields—

"O'er whose acres walked those blessed feet,
Which eighteen hundred years ago were nailed
For our advantage on the bitter cross."

Nothing in Egypt, the earliest centre of human thought and culture; in Greece, the mother of philosophy and art; in Rome, the once mighty mistress of the world; in Babylon, Nineveh, or Damascus (the oldest city in the world), can thrill the soul with such feelings, as are inspired by the sight of the Holy Land; and all because of the Nazarene, who wearied along its highways, climbed its hills, trod its valleys, agonized in the Garden of Gethsemane, and died on Calvary.

All steamers and sea-going vessels must anchor outside the ancient harbor of the sole sea-port of Judea, and all passengers and merchandise must be carried in small coasting crafts over the reef of jagged rocks, that most likely formed the pier of Solomon's harbor. We had a delightful morning for landing. Except in the calmest weather the surf breaks with tremendous violence over the long and rugged line of rocks; but for us the sea was quiet and placid, as a molten mirror, and amid the usual clamor and bustle and gesticulation of bare-legged, picturesquely-costumed, yelling, howling Arabs, ourselves and baggage were safely stowed away in boats and rowed to shore through the traditional scene of the classic legend of Andromeda, the beauty, who was chained to a rock to be devoured by the terrible Medusa, when Perseus rescued her for his bride from the monster, and turned him into stone. And there he is to this day, transformed into that ridge of rocks. Jaffa, or Joppa, is a very ancient city. It is said to have been named after Japhet. Pliny declared it to have been standing before the deluge, and it is popularly believed to have been the city where Noah dwelt and built his ark. It is the port from which Jonah started on his whaling expedition; for "fleeing from the presence of the Lord, he went down to Joppa and found a ship going to Tarshish, so he paid the fare thereof, and went down unto Tarshish from the presence of the Lord."—Jonah 1: 3. It was the port to which Hiram sent the cedar-wood for Solomon's magnificent temple, and to which the materials for the rebuilding of the temple were brought. It was the principal landing-place of the Crusaders, when they went forth to rescue the Holy Sepulchre from the infidels; and for a thousand years it has been the spot, on which, pilgrims from every land first set foot, on the sacred soil of Palestine. It looks beautiful from a distance, set as it is upon a hill, with the long bright sweep of the Mediterranean in front, and the dark chain of the Judean Mountains behind; but when you enter the city, you find that the streets are dirty and narrow, the houses wretched, and the people abominable. As soon as you set foot upon the sacred soil, everything about you gives the assurance that you are treading upon Eastern ground. The very moment the boat struck the wet sand we were caught up, by a half-naked Arab and carried up the black, slimy steps, that led to the custom-house. Here we had to wait amid foul sights and smells, surrounded by wretched, chattering creatures, until all the baggage was passed. As we stood amid mud and squalor, the filthy beings of both sexes that squatted around us, clamorously demanded a gift "Backsheesh!" "Backsheesh!" That Arabic word is a very familiar sound in the East, and having once heard it, you will not be allowed to let it slip from your memory.

While we were waiting for these slow Turkish officials to do their work, we had ample opportunity to watch the attitudes, gestures, and occupations of the ever-changing groups about us—a multitudinous mass of men, women, and children—black, brown, white; beasts of burden, camels, horses, and donkeys. The confused noise is overwhelming. We were like children in a toy-shop, where each object caught sight of is hailed with delight, and the most trivial things afford a fund of entertainment. I noticed, in particular, a big, turbaned fellow, with loose flowing robes, baggy trousers, rich dress, and the *distingué* air of a merchant, who got into a quarrel with one of the officials, and such high words, such gestures and bawling, I never witnessed. He was frantic and diabolical. I expected to see bloodshed. Now and then he would pause from sheer exhaustion, and then renew the war of words and demoniac gesticulations. But his passion at length exhausted itself and he became quiet. And this in the "Holy Land!"

At length we were permitted to enter a carriage, and threading our way through the steep, narrow, and unsavory alleys of the old town, we reached wider and cleaner spaces, and drove rapidly through streets and bazaars to the Jerusalem Hotel, which is beautifully located amid gardens and sweet-smelling orange groves. We were in first-class condition for breakfast, but our empty stomachs did not prevent our appreciating the rare beauty of the situation. Before us lay the clear dark-blue of the Mediterranean, north and south stretched the long coast-line of white sand—a noble panorama—the eye sweeping from Gaza to—

"Where Carmel's flowery top perfumes the skies."

Around us, groves of orange, lemon, citron, and fig, vineyards and gardens separated by high, thick, cactus hedges; stretching inland the vast fertile and flower-enamelled plain of Sharon, bounded on the east by the mountains of Judah and Ephraim, which set their blue peaks against the clear and solemn Syrian sky. And, down upon sea and shore, mountain and plain, the sun shimmers its beams, with all the warmth and brilliancy of summer. A lovely picture, but we have not yet satisfied "the keen demands of appetite," and while waiting we look over the hotel register, and have the satisfaction of seeing the familiar Canadian names of Rev. Donald G. Sutherland and his sister, Mrs. Strong, who passed through the Lord's land a few months before.

CHAPTER IX.

THE LORD'S LAND—JOPPA TO JERUSALEM.

First day in the Holy Land—House of Simon the Tanner—Miss Arnott's School—Orange Gardens—A Feast—Getting ready to Start—A Caravan—The Plain of Sharon—The Philistines—Beit Deján—Ludd—Ramleh, or Arimathea—The Tower—A Noble Act—Encampment—Dinner—First Night Under Canvas—A Jackass—Gimzo—Scripture Scenes—Valley of Ajalon—Dr. Tyndall and Joshua's Miracle—Gezer—Amwâs—The Gate of the Valley—The Mountains of Judea—Abu-Gosh—Kirjath Jearim—Val'ey of Elah—A Magnificent View—Valley of Koloniah—The Mountains round about Jerusalem—Arrival in the City.

THE first day in the Holy Land is one of the greatest events and of the grandest memories in a life-time. It is a realization of the dreams and longings of many years. As soon as breakfast was over we sauntered out into the busy life of the town, through the bazaars and along the narrow, irregular, and dirty alleys that are called streets. What tumultuous emotions are awakened as we tread the soil pressed by the feet of God's ancient worthies—the feet of patriarchs, and prophets, and apostles, yea, the feet of God's incarnate Son! Somewhere within the circuit of these walls were the disciples gathered when Tabitha, which by interpretation is called Dorcas, a woman full of good works and alms-deeds, died, and they sent for Peter, who was at Lydda. On his arrival, they brought him into the upper chamber, where her body lay, "and all the widows stood by her weeping, and showing the coats and garments which Dorcas made while she was with them." Acts ix. 39. We visited the traditional house of Simon, the tanner, with whom Peter tarried many days after the raising of Dorcas. The tradition as to the location cannot be far wrong. The house is "by the sea-side," and among tan-pits of great antiquity. An old well of never-failing water is in the outer court-yard, and an ancient stone trough that may have done service from the time of the apostle's visit.

We climbed the rude broken stairs to the flat-roof, and as "the Great Sea" stretched in unbroken expanse before us, we thought how appropriate a spot for the marvellous vision that was here vouchsafed to the apostle. Below is the busy harbor: there, come and go the white-winged ships of Tarshish. It was the point of contact between the Jewish and Gentile world, and from this place the supernatural and symbolic communication is made to Peter, that tne Gentile world, with its diversities of race, "all manner of four-footed beasts and creeping things and fowls of the air," is as admissable to the privileges of Christianity as the Hebrew people; that what the Jew esteemed unclean and profane, is not to be called common; that every ceremonial barrier and partition wall is broken down; that God is no respecter of persons, and that salvation by Christ is for all nations and all men. As we gazed along the shore the spot was pointed out where that most infamous tragedy of modern times occurred, the butchery in cold blood of four thousand Turkish and Albanian prisoners of war by Napoleon Bonaparte. There, on these white sand heaps, on the 10th of March, 1799, was heard for many hours the rattle of musketry and the shrieks and groans of the wounded and the dying. Think of the name of this selfish, ambitious, and blood-thirsty man associated with the scenes and land of the Bible! Yet so it is. Mount Tabor's virgin bosom has been desecrated. From a spot not many miles above us the overturner of thrones and dynasties, pointing to Acre, said to Murat, "The fate of the East depends upon yonder petty town." But under the walls of that petty town he was foiled. Eight times he led his veteran soldiers to the assault; the struggle was desperate, the bravest of his officers fell under the Mameluke sabres; British soldiers, too, were there under Sir Sydney Smith. The French were driven back in defeat. The dream of Constantinople and the Indies, of a new and brilliant empire in the East was shattered forever; and of the English General,

Napoleon bitterly said, "That man made me miss my destiny!"

Plucking a few wild flowers that bloomed on the flat house-top, and a few leaves from a fig-tree that overshadowed it, we descended and made our way to Miss Arnott's school for girls. The building is a very substantial one, and has a commanding view of the town, with its white walls and domed roofs, the groves and gardens of the plain, and the distant mountain summits flushed with soft and rosy light. Miss Arnott, a Scotch lady of indomitable perseverance, started this school in the spring of 1863, with the noble purpose of endeavoring to lift the women of the East from a state of ignorance and degradation. The work has greatly prospered. She has now fifty-six boarders that are under Christian influence, and are being trained as teachers, and nearly one hundred day-scholars. She has a Bible-class on Sunday attended by about three hundred, and the word of God is taught to Jew and Greek and Moslem. The good being done is incalculable. She is teaching the next generation through the girls of the present, and as I looked upon the little ones and heard them sing our Christian hymns, I felt that the work being done was a counterpart of that given to Peter to do when in a vision at Jaffa he saw the great sheet let down from the skies.

But the charming visit of the morning was to an orange garden, of which there are upwards of four hundred in and around Jaffa. What a delight to get into a field crowded with orange trees, each one loaded with the yellow, delicious fruit, and to hear the injunction "Fall to!" How that luscious oval fruit, each as large as your two fists, disappeared before us! The trees were in full leaf and blossom while the branches were bending with the weight of the large luscious fruit. These oranges were three times the size of those we buy at home, and seemed all the more delicious because of the green leaves and beautiful, white, fragrant blossoms that encircled them. The air was loaded with the mingled perfume of orange, lemon, and citron; and to stand in February in an orange orchard and pluck and eat the juicy and richly-flavored fruit is a privilege one can never forget. The wife of the gardener, a dark-eyed, clever woman, stood near us, and gave me as a special favor a loaded branch, and that cluster of fruit served me on the way to Jerusalem. Each was expected when leaving to give in return, for the pleasure and benefit received, a gratuity; and my female friend, who held out her hand for the "backsheesh," made quite a joke. One or two who led the way had given each a piastre, about three cents, and she said in Arabic, "The fruit is very large, but the pieces of money very small." This was a hint to those who came after, who followed with half-francs, much to her delight. She was handsomely rewarded, for oranges here are sold at the rate of eight or ten for a cent.

Returning to our hotel, luncheon is discussed with a relish, for even in the Holy Land poor flesh and blood cannot dispense with creature-comforts. Now we mount and start for the Holy City. The horses are selected according to number, and the steed that fell to me was as bony and lank as Don Quixote's famous Rosinante, But he is not to be judged by first appearances for he turns out to be an excellent walker and an easy trotter. The caravan is in motion. What a spectacle our cavalcade would have presented on St. James Street, Montreal, or King Street, Toronto! Solemn-looking camels, with long, slow, steady stride, neck depressed, head elevated and carrying piles of heterogeneous articles—tents, bedsteads, mattrasses, bedding, linens, carpets, rugs, tables, provisions, dishes, saucepans, baggage; the loaded train stepping to the music of several cowbells; donkeys bearing packs, their rumps bestrided by long-legged Arabs whose toes almost touch the ground; horsemen and women, each with hat or bonnet wrapped in a *pugaree*, of white muslin which covers the head and floats down over the shoulders; each rider wielding a whip and determined " to witch the world with noble horsemanship;" dragomen, on spirited Arab chargers, dashing away; muleteers shouting; and excitable Arab servants shrieking, yelling, scuffling, and scampering along. We force our way along the crowded thoroughfare, jostling busy citizens, foreign pilgrims, camels, mules, donkeys, sheep, and goats; running over women muffled up to the eyes and waddling about "like animated bundles of dirty clothes" as Mrs. Brassey has it. Passing the gate we find a noisy, chattering rabble in squalor, rags, and filth. O the filth of this people! We visited extensive soap factories in Jaffa, but surely every particle made is exported out of Syria. Now, our way is through narrow, shady lanes, bordered by the richest and most beautiful gardens of orange, lemon, citron, quince, apricot, plum, and apple trees. These groves, separated from each other by gigantic cactus hedges, cover an area of many miles and load the air with delicious odors, while here and there—

> "The stately palm-tree lifts its head on high,
> And spreads its feathery plume along the sky"

We pass a fountain with several large sycamore trees in front and a few cypress trees behind. The structure is of Saracenic beauty, and some point out this place as the spot where Dorcas was raised to life. Benevolent woman! How her coats and garments are still needed in Jaffa! Charmed with the fertility and beauty we ride along until we are on the Plains of Sharon. Our party is a large one, and each heart is in high glee. All is new, strange, exhilarating, delightful! We are amid the scenery of the Bible and the customs of the patriarchs.

The Plain of Sharon, upon which we have entered, is one of the most fertile and beautiful in the East. It is larger than the Plain of Esdraelon, and stretches from Jaffa to Carmel in its excellency, and from the shores of the great sea to the central hills of Palestine. It is an undulating table-land, diversified by rolling hills and dales, groves and meadows. Once in its fertility and beauty it was the symbol of prosperity, and the Hebrew people exulted in the glory of Sharon. The excellency of Sharon was proverbial; now that glorious plain is "like a wilderness." The "earth mourneth and languisheth," and no longer is Sharon "a fold for flocks." This magnificent plain, capable of supporting tens of thousands, is almost a solitude. The land is left "void, desolate, and without inhabitants." Here and there a peasant breaking up the clods; a few wretched mud hamlets occupying the sites of once thriving and densely-populated cities. There it is in its amplitude and richness, decked with thousands of gay flowers, scarlet anemones, white and yellow daisies, lovely tulips intermingled with the white cistus, crimson asters, blue iris, and tufts of lilies; an enamelled carpet of many colors that perfumed the air, and offered a scene replete with all that could charm the senses and delight the imagination, and yet solitary and comparatively unpeopled. We are passing over a district made memorable by the exploits of Samson, the son of Manoah. An hour's ride and we reach an elevation which some point out as the spot where the strong man tied the foxes' tails together, and there was such a scampering and spreading flame among the corn-fields of the Philistines. Every step of our journey is full of Scriptural associations. Men are ploughing with a mule and a cow "unequally yoked together," and the plough is two sticks, one in the hand of the farmer and the other in the yoke, and crossing each other where there is a ploughshare, sometimes of iron, often only of wood which, of course, does little more than scratch the ground. The plough is a slender implement indeed, it has only one rude handle, so that the man puts "his hand to the plough," and carries in the other the goad—a sort of spade with which to relieve the choked plough at one end, and a prickly iron prong at the other for the rumps of his lagging cattle; and "it is hard to kick against the pricks." The word of God seems to become more definite and tangible, and less ghostly, amidst the sights and scenes of this land; and I am continually impressed with the saying of my dear friend, the Hon. Senator Ferrier,—"If I had it in my power, I would send every candidate for the ministry to the Holy Land, to complete his Bible studies there.

Béit Deján, with its pine groves, is passed. This is Beth-Dagon of the Philistines; the "house of Dagon," their famous God—the fish-god, which had a man's head, a horse's neck, the body of a fish, and limbs covered with the feathers of different birds. Dr. Thompson thinks that the peasants of Sharon are of

Egyptian origin, and that they have sufficient of the old Philistine blood in their veins to account for their peculiarities of color, contour, and character. His idea is that the Philistines emigrated originally, not from Crete or Cyprus or Cappadocia, but from the neighboring coast of Africa: that they were a roving race of Bedawin—the shepherd kings who conquered Lower Egypt about the time of Abraham, and that when they were at length overcome and expelled, they came north into Palestine, drove out the original inhabitants, took possession of the sea-coast and great plain of Sharon, introduced the civilization which they had acquired from the conquered Egyptians, built their cities, carried on agriculture and trade, and so became a powerful confederacy. We know how enterprising and warlike they were, and how fierce and prolonged was the opposition which they maintained against the chosen people. The very name which the whole country now bears, Palestine, means the land of the Philistines. Overcome by Joshua, they are nevertheless often in the ascendant, until in the days of Eli, houses of Dagon are found far away from the sea-coast even to the very verge of the Jordan valley. Before the triumph of Deborah, "there was not a shield or spear seen among forty thousand in Israel. There was no smith found throughout all the land of Israel; for the Philistines said, 'Lest the Israelites make themselves swords and spears.' But all the Israelites went down to the Philistines to sharpen every one his share, and his coulter, and his axe, and his mattock." 1 Samuel xiii. 19, 20.

On the vast maritime plain stretching as far south as Gerar they founded their royal cities, Gaza, Ashdod, Askelon, Gath, and Ekron, and made their incursions into the heart of Israel, until at length they were absorbed into the splendid kingdom of David and of Solomon. All around us are the traces of their vanished greatness. A short ride beyond Beit-Dejân, and still to the left of the road to Jerusalem, embowered in trees, is a little white-walled village called Ludd, the Lod of the Old Testament, and the Lydda of the New. Here Peter "found a certain man named Æneas, which had kept his bed eight years, and was sick of palsy. And Peter said unto him, 'Æneas, Jesus Christ maketh thee whole; arise and make thy bed,' and he arose immediately. And all that dwelt at Lydda and Saron saw him, and turned to the Lord." Acts ix. 33-35. Here, too, he received the message from the disciples at Joppa, to come to them in their sorrow over the death of Dorcas. This little spot figures conspicuously in history as the birth-place of St. George, the patron saint of England. It contains also his tomb, over which a church has been reared, which incorporates the ruins of a noble church built first by the Emperor Justinian, but destroyed by the Moslems, re-built by Richard Cœur de Lion, destroyed again by the relentless Moslems.

After an hour's ride we reach Ramleh, which has

been identified with the Ramah of the Old Testament and the Arimathæa of the New, the city of "Joseph, an honorable counsellor, a good man, and just," who "went in boldly unto Pilate and craved the body of Jesus." In the middle ages Ramleh was one of the

RAMLEH OR ARIMATHÆA.

chief cities of Palestine, a flourishing and opulent centre of population, but it is now a wretched and dilapidated place.

It is charmingly situated in the midst of orchards of olive, fig, and pomegranate, fields of melons that are celebrated throughout the Levant for their exquisite flavor and refreshing coolness, gardens of vegetables, swelling hills covered with verdure, and cultivated farms luxuriant with wheat, and barley, and corn. The sycamore tree is there and the carob tree, whose fruit is the mealy pod with which the prodigal "would fain have filled his belly," the husks "that the swine did eat." About a quarter of a mile from the town is the Great Tower, an exquisite specimen of Saracenic art. There it stands, a magnificent square tower like the famous Giralda of Seville, built of hewn stone, one hundred and twenty feet high, and standing in the midst of ruins of great extent. Whether it is the minaret of some mosque of the Mameluke period, or the campanile of some noble old Christian church, who can tell? We climbed a flight of narrow and spiral stone steps to the top, and obtained a view of surpassing richness and beauty. All around us stretches the Plain of Sharon, and the eye roams from Cesarœa and Carmel in the north, to Gaza and the Desert of Philistia in the south. Westward, the waters of the Mediterranean gleam and ripple to the verge of the horizon; and to the east are the bare blue mountains of Judea and Samaria, standing in silent and impressive grandeur. All around the tower are immense subterranean vaults or cisterns supported by solid masonry and lighted from above. These may have been used as storehouses for the caravans, or as magazines for the Crusaders, for Ramleh was their rendezvous, and the headquarters of Richard, in 1191. The following incident is related in connection with this Tower: The King of Jerusalem, in 1101, having, with a train of two hundred horses, imprudently attacked an army of several thousand Egyptian invaders, was forced to take refuge with his little band in the castle, the fortifications of which were too weak to enable him to make good his defence on the morrow. The Egyptians had determined to put every soul to death. But an Arab prince, acting with the Egyptian army, stole out of the camp by night, obtained access to the King, and offered to conduct him in safety to the mountains. Why this act? Some months before, Baldwin had made a successful foray beyond Jordan, surprised the tents of the Arabs, seized much booty, and carried off the women and children who had been unable to escape with the men. The Franks immediately recrossed the Jordan, driving the cattle and the captives before them. Among the prisoners was recognized the wife of a powerful prince of the country, with the pangs of child-birth upon her. The moment the King heard of her situation, he commanded a comfortable bed to be provided for her, gave her, out of the spoils, an abundant supply of provisions, and a maiden to wait upon her, and throwing over her his own cloak, sprang on his horse and departed. That very evening the Arab prince, following the track of the invaders, his heart bleeding for the loss of his idolized wife, came unexpectedly to the spot where she lay, with her new-born child. It was the grateful husband and father who now nobly risked his own life to save the man who had performed this rare act of humanity.

Mounting again our horses, we rode between green hedges of enormous cacti, with the scammony in flower twining through their invulnerable armor, into the village, its narrow, crooked lanes, filled with scabby, hairless, howling dogs, blear-eyed men, ragged

CAMP OF THE HOWADJI, RAMLEH.

and dirty children, and rigidly-veiled women. Our camp was pitched to the east of Ramleh on a green hill-side and close to a fountain of water. The tents were already set up, looking bright and cheerful and home-like; and when we dismounted we found everything, as by magic, in complete order.

Messrs. Cook & Son, of London, have brought travelling in the East, as far as it can be done, to perfection. Guides, horses, tents, accommodations, all are the best that can be got. Even such personages as the Crown Prince of Austria, the Emperor of Brazil, Lord Dufferin, and Gladstone, have travelled under them in preference to an independent tour. The tents are placed in a circle, and in the centre of the encampment is the saloon, a spacious tent that serves for parlor, *salle à manger*, and general gathering-place. After a refreshing wash, and a leisurely stretch, the bell rang for dinner. And what a sumptuous repast we enjoy out upon these Syrian wilds—soup, lamb, chicken, vegetables, pudding, pastry, nuts, dates, figs, and oranges! When Sancho Panza was received as governor of the Island of Barataria, he was conducted from the court of justice, over which he had presided, to a sumptuous palace, where a most magnificent entertainment was prepared for him. As he sat down, a certain personage came and stood at his elbow with a whalebone wand in his hand. A dish of fruit was set before the new governor, but hardly had he put one bit into his mouth, before the physician waved his wand, and the dish was taken away by a page in an instant. Another dish with meat was put down, but Sancho had no sooner offered to taste it, than the doctor with the wand conjured it away as fast as the fruit. Sancho was indignant, and demanded why they tantalized people at that rate, feeding their eyes and starving their bellies. He found that this was the physician who took charge of the governor's health, and saw that he ate according to the custom. No wonder he threw up the governorship, when his personal indulgences at table were so provokingly interrupted. Well, we had all the dishes of Sancho's inauguration feast, but they were not whisked away; we ate like hungry travellers, who had accomplished a good day's work, and were well satisfied with themselves and with their surroundings. The day ended, we concluded to retire at once, especially as we had to make an early start in the morning; but there was no sleep for me. The bed was comfortable, but everything was novel, and my mind was excited. Over us was the bright Oriental sky, around us the fragrance of the gardens of Ramleh. Then came strange sounds—the explosive gutturals of our attendants jibbering around the camp-fire, unearthly growls and groanings of the camels, the braying of the donkeys, and, as night deepened, the cry of the jackals. One of our company of three was a little hard of hearing, and as the strange sound, like a wildcat's cry, fell upon his ears, he asked quickly, "What's that?" We answered "a jackal." "A jackass?" he asked incredulously. This raised a laugh. After a while, when all was quiet, I heard stealthy steps approaching. They paused before our tent. My suspicions were aroused. These prowling, thieving Arabs are bent on plunder; they shall find that we are not asleep. Up I got to strike a light   The matches were in an immense box, and in trying to pull one out I set the whole in a blaze. Such a fizzing and flaming surely lucifer matches never made! Then there was real alarm. One of our number screamed and leaped from bed. The sudden flash of light had poured upon his sleeping eyes, the sound seemed like the explosion of a gun, and he told me there rushed upon him the sudden vision of robbers, Bedouins, *murder*. I explained to him what had happened, we laughed and lay down again. Next morning I learned that my alarm had been caused by one of our guides coming to button up the door of our tent.

All was quiet again, but I could not sleep. Upon me crowded the memories of thousands of years. Our tents were pitched on the great crossing-place of the caravan routes, between Jaffa and Jerusalem, Damascus and Egypt. Around us were paths worn by caravans, from the gray dawn of time down to our days. Over this road Joseph went when he was sold into Egypt. What feet had trodden this road through thirty centuries! Jewish, Assyrian, Chaldean, Macedonian, Grecian, Roman, Saracen, Tartar, Turkish, Egyptian, Crusaders, pilgrims. Over it passed Alexander, Titus, Saladin, Richard Cœur de Lion, Napoleon. The interval of centuries is passed over, and the imagination revels in the scenes and historical associations of days long gone by.

Next morning at six, we were roused by the beating of a tattoo, and hastily dressing, and packing our valise at half-past six we went into the large tent for breakfast. When we came out there was not a vestige of tents or baggage. Everything had been silently taken down and folded up by the attendants, while we had been doing justice to tea and coffee, eggs and omelets, cutlets and hot chicken. We mounted and rode away, passing here and there a village with hedges of prickly cacti and pear; the land still retaining its verdure and fertility, but rising in gentle slopes towards the mountains. To the left of us is Jimzû, the ancient Gimzo, which the Philistines took from the Israelites in the time of Ahaz. To the north of us stood Ekron, whither the ark of God was brought from Ashdod. A troublesome possession was that ark to these idolaters. The hand of God lay heavy upon them, and they were anxious to get rid of it. We can trace the path "which the two milch kine, dragging the new cart, which bore the ark and the jewels of gold for a trespass-offering, took, as they went along the highway, lowing as they went, and turning not aside to the right hand or to the left; and the lords of the Philistines went after them unto the border of Beth-shemesh. And they of Beth-shemesh were reaping their wheat harvest in the valley: and they lifted up their eyes, and saw the ark, and rejoiced to see it." 1 Samuel vi. 12, 13. As we ride along the laborers are busy ploughing. There is not the sign of a fence between the farms, only little heaps of stones that could easily be shifted, but "cursed be he that removeth his neighbor's landmarks." Some of the poles which they carry to touch up their oxen are rather formidable, and we remember that "Shamgar, the son of Anath, slew of the Philistines six hundred men with an ox goad." Judges iii. 31.

The village of El Kubab is passed, and we reach the summit of a hill which commands a full view of the Valley of Ajalon, over which Joshua commanded the sun and moon to stand still, on that memorable day when such a complete victory was gained over the five Amorite kings. Our dragoman pointed out to us the two Beth-horons: Beth-horon, the nether, perched on a rocky ridge, and called by the Arabs Beit Ur-el-Tahta, and higher up still, a steep and rough and toilsome ascent of three miles, the upper Beth-horon, or Beit-Ur-el-Foka. Gibeon is to the south-east, at the head of the pass of Beth-Horon. How accurately the topography, after the lapse of three thousand years, illustrates and confirms the inspired narrative! The Amorite chiefs had attacked the Gibeonites, who sent at once to Joshua for relief. The Israelite warrior, by a forced night-march, ascended from Gilgal, took the confederate kings by surprise, and "slew them with a great slaughter at Gibeon, and chased them along the way that goeth up to Beth-horon," then down the precipitous descent, a storm of hail and meteoric stones adding to their confusion and dismay. The discomfited host now reach the valley. Will they escape among the defiles which run in every direction?

Will the day close and the victory be incomplete? "Then spake Joshua to the Lord, and he said in the sight of all Israel, Sun, stand thou still upon Gibeon; and thou, Moon, in the valley of Ajalon." And the sun which had not yet passed the meridian of Gibeon "stood still;" and the moon, the pale, crescent moon, still lingered over Ajalon, "until the people had avenged themselves upon their enemies." The victory was complete. The kings who had hid themselves in yonder cave of Makkedah, at the foot of the rocky declivity, were brought out and slain. Infidels have a terrible time with this miracle. Dr. Tyndall has made the computation, and says: "The energy here involved is equal to six trillions of horses, working for the whole of the time, employed by Joshua in the destruction of his foes." This man of science stands aghast before the six trillion horse-power. He measures the Infinite by himself, and wonders how He can afford to expend such energy, "all for the sake of extinguishing a handful of Amorites." But all difficulties vanish as soon as Almighty God is brought into the calculation; for Dr. Tyndall himself has said, in the application of law in nature, the "terms great and small are unknown." The powers of refraction may have been employed in the miracle, and then the miracle itself would not have needed " the stoppage of an orb fourteen hundred thousand times the earth in size."

Crossing the valley of Ajalon, we behold on the right the extensive ruins of Gezer, a Canaanitish royal city, whose king was defeated by Joshua, and the place given to the Levites of the children of Kohath. Not being dispossessed of its original inhabitants it remained a fortress of the Philistines for long centuries, until Pharaoh conquered it, and gave it "for a present to his daughter, Solomon's wife." 1 Kings ix. 16. After an hour's ride from El-Kubâb, we reach El-Latron, the traditional abode of the penitent thief; but most likely the ancient Modin, the birthplace of the Maccabees. Amwâs, the ancient Nicopolis of Julius Africanus, so often mentioned in the Crusades, is on the right. This site has been regarded as the Emmaus of the New Testament; but it is too far off from Jerusalem to be the village mentioned by Luke, as only three-score furlongs distance from the city. An hour's ride brings us to Bab-el-Wady, or Gate of the Valley, where we stop for rest and refreshment. The lower part of the inn is a stable, but ascending a flight of stone steps we reach an airy, open court, opening upon which is our dining-room. But I am too weary to eat until I have taken a wash, and thrown myself at full length upon one of the hard lounges for rest.

We are called again to the saddle, and at once enter a steep, narrow, rocky defile, with rugged bold, barren, rocky hills on either side. It is the hill-country of Judea, and the stony summits rise in concentric circles one above another, the naked strata of dull-gray limestone looking dreary and monotonous enough. A death-like stillness and impressive wildness reigns in these elevated regions. On we go, over desolate mountains, through silent, rugged wadies, climbing height after height, often fearfully precipitous; descending into narrow and barren defiles until we reach a magnificent grove of olives; pass the village of Sâris, and come to Abu-Gosh, named after that notorious robber chief, that oriental Rob Roy, who made this his hold, striking terror into the hearts of all travellers, and setting at defiance the Turkish Government. But this spot has a worthier fame than that of being the residence of a noted bandit-sheik. It is the ancient Kirjath-Jearim, "the city of woods." Originally one of the four cities of the Gibeonites, it subsequently became a border town between Judah and Benjamin. It is frequently mentioned in the mapping out and division of the land by Joshua; and so accurate are those old records, "The Doomsday Book of the Israelites," that they still afford valuable assistance in settling the topography of the Holy Land. Here the sacred ark rested for twenty years after it had been recovered from the hands of the Philistines. David found it "in the fields of the wood," and gathering all Israel together, with harp and psalteries, cymbal and trumpets, they brought it into the tabernacle on Mount Zion, singing—

> "Arise, O Lord, into thy rest,
> Thou and the ark of thy strength."

In this picturesque little village, now called Kuryet-el-Enab, or town of grapes, is an old Gothic church of the Crusade period, standing well preserved, with its pointed arches and columns; its nave and aisles all chaste and beautiful, but deserted and desolate. Through the midst of this broad and beautiful valley, enclosed by rounded hills, terraced and olive-clad, runs a little brook over its pebbly bed. Some identify this as the valley of Elah, where the stripling David, ruddy and of a fair countenance, met the giant-boaster of Gath, and with his sling and stone smote the tall son of Anak, so that he staggered and fell with the death-moan on his lips. Here, surely, are smooth stones enough for the young champion; and the amphitheatre of hills is bold and well-defined, so that the Philistine hosts could stand, "on a mountain on one side," and Israel, "on a mountain on the other side," and watch the single-handed combat between the uncircumcised Philistine in polished armor, with brazen shield, burnished helmet, powerful sword and spear; and the shepherd-boy with sling and stone, but strong "in the name of the Lord of Hosts, the God of the armies of Israel."

Another tedious climb and we gain the summit of an Apennine ridge where the view is magnificent, sweeping over height after height to the vast plains, far as the gleaming waters of the Mediterranean, and catching holy peaks of the mountains of Judah, Benjamin, and Ephraim. To the north Neby-Samwil is seen, the ancient Mizpah, associated with so many thrilling events in Jewish history, the traditional burial-place of the great prophet, and hence called after the honored son of Hannah. Descending by a zig-zag road into the valley of Koloniah with its olive and fig trees, we pass the little hamlet of Ain Kârim, which tradition makes the birth-place of John the Baptist, whose father's residence is described as "in the hill country in a city of Judah."

Nestling on the hill-side, amid orchards, and groves, and gardens, a little way off the road, so that travellers to the Holy City must turn aside, "as they draw nigh unto it," is Kulon or Kulônia, which many regard as that Emmaus, to which two of the disciples were going, when "Jesus himself drew near and went with them." Luke xxiv. 15.

Now, for an hour and a-half stretch, up steep, and bleak, and desolate hills. We are climbing the mountains "that are round about Jerusalem." Along this road went David and Solomon in the days of Israel's glory; here pressed the feet of David's son and David's Lord; here poured along company after company of Israelites, on their way to the solemn feasts, through a hundred generations; on it trod Roman legions, with eagles high above them; and mailed Crusaders, from every part of Europe, dashed along, eager to catch a glimpse of the sacred city. Now there is no tree or foliage to shield us from the scorching rays of the sun. What barrenness reigns where once was fertility and great productiveness, for "Judah washed his garments in wine and his clothes in the blood of grapes!" Ah! these hills have been stripped of their magnificent olive groves, the terraces have crumbled, and these rough gray stones, so weary to the eye and so painful to the feet, give an aspect as sterile and forbidding as can possibly be conceived! But the outward features of the desolate landscape are forgotten, for we have reached the summit of the last hill, and Olivet is in sight. There is a large monastery and other buildings that obstruct the view. We are impatient to get a glimpse of the Sacred City. A little further on and a line of dim gray, battlemented walls appears; then turrets, and minarets, and domes break upon the tear-filled eyes. It is Jerusalem! The dreams and longings of a life-time are fulfilled. "Our feet shall stand within thy gates, O Jerusalem!" Before us is the Jaffa Gate, and we ride past the citadel of David into the city of the Great King.

CHAPTER X.

THE CITY OF THE GREAT KING.

The Holy City—First Feeling of Disappointment—Topography of the City—The Walls—The Gates—Mount Zion—Tower of Hippicus—Armenian Convent and Church of St. James—House of Caiaphas—Tomb of David—Cœnaculum—Zion "as a Ploughed Field"—Lepers—Jews' Quarter—Wailing Place—An Affecting Scene—Robinson's Arch—Bridge over the Tyropœan Valley—Mosque of Omar—Haram Area—Interior of the Noble Sanctuary—The Sacred Rock—El Aksa—A chance of Heaven—Solomon's Stables—View from the Eastern Wall—Mount Moriah and the Jewish Temple—Christ in the Temple—An angry Sheik—The Tower of Antonia—Pool of Bethesda—St. Stephen's Gate—Outside the City—A Mohammedan Funeral—Climbing the Mount of Olives—View from the Summit—Garden of Gethsemane—The Brook Kedron—Re-entering by the East Gate—Arch of Ecce Homo—Via Dolorosa—Lying Frauds—The Church of the Holy Sepulchre—The Court—Appearance of the Interior—Conflicting Opinions as to the True Site—Weight of testimony in favor of the traditional locale—Calvary—The Holy Sepulchre itself—Chapels of the Latins, Greeks, Armenians, &c.—Chapel of St. Helena—Mediæval legends Impressive Associations—Church of the Holy Sepulchre—The "Holy of Holies" of Jerusalem.

JERUSALEM is the city of cities—the centre of the strongest affections and holiest memories—the true capital of the Christian World! The very sight of it thrills the soul with such feelings as no other spot inspires! It is linked with the grandest and most sacred events in the history of mankind! Not Athens in its splendor, or ancient Rome in the plenitude of her power, or Babylon in her greatness, has so influenced the destinies and held the hearts of men. It was first the ancient Salem, the City of the Priest and King Melchizedek. An old tradition makes Melchizedek to be Shem, so that here one of the sons of Noah built the City of Peace and reigned in righteousness. To this spot Abraham made his sacrificial journey, and in a figure offered up his only son. It was one of the mighty cities of Canaan, the fortress and stronghold of the Jebusites. David stormed the citadel and made it his splendid capital. He had offered the highest prize in his kingdom, the Captainship of the Host, to the soldier that would scale the rocky heights and capture the "stronghold of Zion." The agile Joab made the desperate exploit, clambered up the cliff, smote the garrison down, and was proclaimed Commander-in-chief. As soon as it became the "City of David," it was consecrated as "the Holy City!" "The Lord hath chosen Zion; He hath desired it for His habitation." Solomon enriched and adorned it until it shone in marble and glittered in gold of Ophir. It was the civil and religious centre not only of Palestine but of the world. Hebrew poets and prophets poured forth their most inspired utterances in its praises.

Holy men took pleasure in its stones, and favored even the dust thereof. Thither the tribes went up, even the tribes of the Lord, with music and songs of Zion! There towered the "mountains of Jerusalem," and in the ravines below were Kedron and Siloam, those "flowery brooks beneath that washed their sacred feet!" Encompassing the city was an embattled wall, strongly fortified with towers and bulwarks, the wonder and terror of the nations. On the terraced slopes were the lifted forms of her goodly palaces; and higher, grander than all, arose the Temple, with its golden front and marble thresholds, all the courts glittering with the whiteness of snow, and, over all, the pillared cloud, which rose as the perpetual token of acceptable sacrifice. Pillaged and destroyed by Babylon, it was again re-built under Nehemiah and Ezra. It was adorned with splendor in the days of Herod; through its streets walked the Son of God; over it he shed tears of divine commiseration. Along its pavements he bore his heavy cross, and its hills trembled and shook with the earthquake's power when he gave up the ghost. Then followed the fearful siege and utter destruction of the doomed city, under Titus, when nearly a million and a half perished. Long the city "sat solitary that was full of people," until Hadrian transformed it into a Roman city; then Constantine into a Christian city; and then, in 637, the Khalif Omar into the Mohammedan sacred city. The Crusaders rescued it from the hands of the Turks;

but it again fell under the sway of the Moslems, and Soliman, the Magnificent, built its present walls.

The flag of the Turk still floats over the sacred city. It had existed over two thousand years when destroyed by the Romans. Again and again utterly laid waste, yet ever renewed, Jerusalem is now nearly four thousand years old, and still it has a future before it—a future whose glories who can tell ?

Now for a survey of that city which has been a centre for pilgrimage ever since the days when the Queen of Sheba came up to see the magnificence of Solomon; a city which is sacred to the Jew, the Moslem, and the Christian—the common property of Catholics, Greeks, Armenians, Protestants—and gathers within itself more thought and affection, more profound and reverential interest than any other spot beneath the skies.

One confesses to a feeling of disappointment at first sight of the present city. But the Zion of our solemnities, the city of our earliest and latest associations, our deepest sympathies and present hopes, the city of which Solomon could find no stronger metaphor than "comely as Jerusalem," that is mentioned over eight hundred times in the Bible, and is a type of the heavenly city, the Jerusalem above, is not here but far below. The present city is built upon the accumulated ruins of seven preceding ones, and the excavations carried on through the Palestine Exploration Association, have shown that the foundations of the ancient walls are in many places one hundred and thirty feet below the present surface. The relics of the Jerusalem of the Crusade—the Jerusalem of the Middle Ages—are found at least twenty or twenty-five feet below the present surface; and this gives us some idea of the immense amount of rubbish and *débris* accumulated above the ancient level of the sacred city. But the valleys are here, and the glorious, everlasting hills, "the mountains round about Jerusalem;" all the natural features are unchanged, and we can realize the force of the Psalmist's words when he said, "Jerusalem is builded as a city that is compact together;" or, "Walk about Zion, and go round about her; tell the towers thereof. Mark ye well her bulwarks, consider her palaces: that ye may tell it to the generation following."

Another feeling is that of disgust at the present condition of the city. The streets are narrow, filthy, and wretchedly paved. The walls are gloomy and crumbling; the houses old and miserable, the small domes on the roofs serving not for ornament but to aid in strengthening the otherwise flat roofs, the population squalid. Some quarters are beastly in their abominations, and one does not feel like singing, "Jerusalem the golden," or "Jerusalem, my glorious home!"

But, we remember that we see Zion in her desolation. "Her hymn a dirge; her minstrelsy a moan." She is "trodden down of the Gentiles." "She dwelleth among the heathen; she findeth no rest; and from the daughter of Zion all her beauty is departed." Emphatically are the Saviour's words fulfilled. "Behold, your house is left unto you desolate!" But there is a glory in the very meanness and squalor of her degradation. The first impression of disappointment and disgust are quickly followed by feelings of devoutest reverence and deepest affection. As the localities and sacred sites became familiar, the slippery and rough stones of her wretched streets, become dear. There are Olivet and Kedron, Zion and Moriah, Bethesda and Siloah, Gethsemane and Calvary. To have experienced the throbbing emotions of one glance over the city of which Jehovah said, "This is My rest—here will I dwell," the city in which the Saviour died and where the Holy Ghost was given, is worth all the toil and expense of a journey from the ends of the earth, and I shall give thanks to God all my days for the privilege of having gazed upon those battlements, and towers, and minarets, and domes, toward which the longing hearts of millions upon millions have turned with devout affection through all the Christian centuries. The city is full of inequalities; there are no level streets, and you are continually ascending or descending. It is situated on a mountain platform, elevated nearly two thousand six hundred feet above the level of the Mediterranean. Built on the summits of five hills, the city slopes to the east and south, and is encompassed except on the north by two deep narrow ravines, the one the Valley of Jehoshaphat, running along the eastern side to the south; the other the Valley of Hinnom, sweeping round from the west and uniting with the Valley of Jehoshaphat at the south-east corner.

We learn from Josephus that the ancient city was built upon two parallel ridges with a valley between them, the Tyropæan, or Valley of the Cheesemongers. The eastern ridge was Moriah, the western Mount Zion, and the other hills of which we read—Acra, Bezetha, and Ophel—were most likely considered peaks of these two swelling elevations or ridges.

The walls surrounding the city are about two miles and a half in circuit. They are of grey limestone, and loosely put together, from ten to fifteen feet in thickness and from twenty-five to forty in height, according to the nature of the ground. They have their towers and battlements, and loop-holes, and projections, and are surrounded with a parapet which gives a comparatively safe pathway along the top of these walls. Having been constructed out of every available material, there are blocks of stone that bear marks of very high antiquity, fragments older than the days of Christ, older than the time of Solomon. Very sombre, yet somewhat proudly, stand those old crenelated walls; yet they would prove an idle and useless defence against the mitrailleuse and cannon of modern warfare. The walls are pierced by seven gates. There is the Jaffa Gate, on the west, called also Bethlehem or Hebron Gate. The Damascus Gate, on the north; St. Stephen's Gate, the site of the stoning of Stephen and leading to Olivet, on the east; the Dung Gate, leading to Siloam; and Zion Gate, or the Gate of the prophet David, on the south; Herod's Gate on the north-east, and Golden Gate, in the eastern wall of the Haram, facing Gethsemane, are now walled up. The Golden Gate consists of a double portal spanned by two semicircular arches, richly ornamented. The interior of it is adorned with elegant and elaborate carving in Corinthian style. Some have supposed it to be the "Beautiful Gate" of the Temple, at which the lame man sat begging when Peter and John performed the healing wonder. It is closed up in consequence of Mohammedan tradition, that the Christians will again take possession of the city and that the conquering King will ride triumphantly through this gate. Let us start from Jaffa Gate, a busy spot where the people gather to hear the news, and to engage in traffic of every kind. What the Bourse is to Paris, the Exchange to London, or Wall Street to New York, is the City Gate of the Capital to the Orientals. We are to see the interesting sights of Mount Zion, "the City of David!" Pushing through the crowd of horses, mules, and camels, and the jostling representatives of almost every nation of the habitable globe, let us climb that massive square tower to our right. It is the Tower of David, called by Josephus the Tower of Hippicus. It was most likely standing in the Saviour's time, and, wearying along the "street of David," his shadow may have rested on its wall as he passed along. From the summit you obtain a commanding view of the buildings, public places, and general outline of the city, with its surrounding hills, and ravines. The stones of the lower part are roughly cut and have a deep *bevel* round the edges, and the sheik of the tower told us that the walls were 5,000 years old, but they are not likely older than the time of David. Invested with thrilling associations is the grand old tower that withstood the battering rams of the Romans and has resisted through all the centuries the ravages of time. Opposite the citadel are the Protestant Church Mission Grounds, Christ Church being an English and Prussian Mission, and further on the Armenian Convent, an immense establishment, having dormitories capable of accommodating eight thousand pilgrims. Within the Convent is the Church of St. James, a rich, splendid church, being next in size to the Church of the Holy Sepulchre, and one of the most gorgeous and elaborately adorned structures in the East. The tesselated floor is inlaid with rich Mosaics, and the walls are ornamented with pictures of the Byzantine School. The church stands on the traditional site of the martyrdom of St. James the Apostle, and the chair in which the first Bishop of Jerusalem sat is preserved; while within a little cloister of the main room, richly adorned with marble and gold, coral and pearl, is the Sepulchral Chapel, which marks the place where he was beheaded and where his ashes lie. Close at hand is Zion Gate or Bab-en-Neby David, and just outside on Zion Gate is the House of Caiaphas.

This was the palace to which the Blessed Saviour was taken from the house of Annas, and where He was condemned before the Sanhedrim. A small cell adorned with porcelain and pearl is shown as the prison in which our Lord was kept the night before His crucifixion. Other relics these Armenians show: as the legendary stone which closed the door of our Lord's tomb, stolen from the Church of the Holy Sepulchre; the spot where Peter stood when he denied his Master; and even the stone where the cock was roosting when he crowed three times while Peter was blushing before the damsel, and with cursing denying his Lord. A little south of the house of Caiaphas is a Mussulman mosque with a graceful minaret, formerly a Christian Church, erected over the Tomb of David, the illustrious King of Israel. The identity of this burial-place is pretty satisfactorily established. We know that he was buried in "the city of David," the city which he had made his own; and in Nehemiah we read, "After him repaired Nehemiah, the son of Azbuk, ... unto the place over against the sepulchres of David." Neh. iii. 16. It was one of the landmarks of the city in the time of the Apostles, for Peter in his sermon on the Day of Pentecost says, "Men and brethren, let me freely speak unto you of the patriarch David, that he is both dead and buried, and his sepulchre is with us unto this day." Acts ii. 29. That the dust of Israel's renowned singer and saintly shepherd king is sleeping somewhere near this spot is conclusive. Josephus tells us that Solomon interred his father, who died at the age of seventy, with great magnificence, and buried a vast treasure within the tomb, which remained undisturbed until Hyrcanus broke open and plundered one of its chambers. Afterwards Herod the Great also opened and plundered the royal vault. It is said to have fallen into ruin in the time of Hadrian, and its present dilapidated appearance is not at all in keeping with the dignity of David's sepulchre. What a pity this reputed tomb should be in the hands of the fanatical Moslems, who guard it with such superstitious jealousy, that no Jew or Christian is permitted to enter it! From an elevated recess, we were permitted to look through a screen upon a sarcophagus, covered with green tapestry, embroidered with gold. Before a door, said to be the entrance to the cave, stand two massive silver candlesticks, and in this cave repose the royal ashes. Of this vault, hewn most likely out of the solid rock, with proportions and grandeur becoming royalty, the world must remain in ignorance until the Moslem authorities relax their restrictions and remove their bars of exclusion, or the Holy City pass into Christian hands, when the impenetrable mysteries about these sacred and interesting spots shall be laid open, and every locality thoroughly explored. Then we shall see whether this cave answers to the glowing description given by Benjamin, of Tudela, in the twelfth century. He tells us that hired laborers, engaged in repairing the foundation of the walls of Zion, uncovered the mouth of a cavern, and on exploring it in search of treasure they reached a large hall supported by marble pillars incrusted with gold and silver, and in this hall were two tables on each of which lay a golden sceptre and crown. This proved to be the sepulchre of David and of the Kings of Israel who were buried there. They were hindered from penetrating by a blast of wind which issued from the cavern, and threw them almost lifeless to the ground. On reporting their adventure to the patriarch of the city, the palace was "walled up so as to hide it effectually from any one to the present day."

Under the roof of this building is the Cœnaculum, a large and desolate looking "upper room," some fifty or sixty feet in length by thirty feet in width. Tradition has it that this is the "guest chamber," where the Saviour celebrated His last Passover with His sorrow-stricken disciples, and at the close of it instituted the "Supper."

It is stated that among the few buildings that survived the destruction by Titus was this old house, and that the earliest Christians identified it as the "upper room" where the Master ate the Passover with His disciples, and where He gave the touching lesson of humility by laying aside His garments and washing their feet; where after His resurrection He appeared in the midst of His disciples and said, "Peace be unto you," and where on the day of Pentecost "suddenly there came a sound from heaven as of a rushing mighty wind, and it filled all the house where they were sitting. And there appeared unto them cloven tongues like as of fire, and it sat upon each of them. And they were all filled with the Holy Ghost, and began to speak with other tongues, as the Spirit gave them utterance."—Acts ii. 2-4. On the bare supposition that this is the scene of the Last Supper, and of the grand inauguration of the dispensation of the Spirit, the head is bent, the heart filled with reverential love. And the prayer ascends that we too may receive "the Promise of the Father," even the "Baptism of the Holy Ghost."

More than one-half of the hill of Zion lies outside the present walls, and as we wandered through gardens of vegetables and fields of growing grain, we were struck with the wonderful fulfilment of Divine predictions uttered twenty-five hundred years ago. "Therefore, shall Zion for your sake be ploughed as a field, and Jerusalem shall become heaps, and the mountain of the house as the high places of the forest." —Micah iii. 12. Where is now the springing corn and wheat once stood the matchless edifices and stately palaces of the Holy City. Spot of unrivalled wealth and glory, where Solomon the Wise held his court, and surrounded himself with the luxuries and pleasures of an unequalled regal greatness; hallowed even by the sojourn of the sacred ark! How the glory has departed! Yet with Zion in her "shame" and in the dust, we see how eminently adapted was this site for David's kingly home, Solomon's palace, "the House of the Forest of Lebanon," and of those great historic events that have gone rolling in music down the centuries! Entering the city again by the Zion Gate, just within the wall, we come upon the "quarters of the Lepers." Formerly excluded from the city, they are now suffered to build their miserable hovels along the wall. Whether this disease is the leprosy of Scripture is a question not yet settled. But most pitiable objects are these lepers, and a sickening and loathsome spectacle is the sight of these wretched outcasts from society, holding up their maimed or handless arms, "*sans* eyes, *sans* nose, *sans* hair," exposing their disfigured bodies, corroded with ulcers, and begging in husky and piteous tones, "Pilgrim, give me; for Allah's sake, give me." They live together and inter-marry only with each other. We met them frequently between the Zion and the Jaffa Gates, and the horrid forms of such a beggar crowd, and the unearthly sounds that gurgle through their throats, almost make one cry out in terror and fly from them. It is a significant commentary on the Government of the country, not only that they are permitted to perpetuate their fearful malady by making marriage alliances, but also left to expose their loathsome misery to the public, as wayside beggars. Having seen the principal places of interest on Mount Zion let us visit the Jews' Quarter along the eastern declivities of Zion, extending down into the Tyropean Valley. Somehow we expected to find this section of the city clean and comfortable, but it is the foulest and most wretched part of Jerusalem. There dwell in poverty the most squalid, and in filth the most indescribable, about eight thousand of the sons of Abraham. They have fifteen synagogues and four schools. They are chiefly paupers, and have come up from all parts of the earth whither the Lord hath driven them, to weep over the desolations of Zion, to bemoan their wickedness, and die, and be buried near the sepulchres of their fathers. They nearly all look aged, dilapidated, and woe-begone. They love to dwell in their filth and rags in the heart of the city, for although Sir Moses Montefiore, of London, has built rows of home-like cottages for their accommodation in the suburbs, yet they prefer their execrable lane-like streets and wretched hovels within the walls. Only a few of the Jewish community are thrifty, industrious, and enterprising. They have not come to Jerusalem to trade, amass wealth, or live in a well-to-do style, but to purge away the guilt of their past lives, pour out their lamentations at the foot of their ancient sanctuary, die and be buried in the Valley of Jehoshaphat. A very touching and sadly suggestive scene is the wailing of the Jews when, from week to week, these poor, despised, down-trodden people gather to sigh, and mourn, and sob over the ruins of their temple.

The Jews' Wailing Place is a little quadrangular area, about one hundred feet long and thirty feet wide, an exposed part of the outer western wall of the Haram, between the gates of the Chain and of the Strangers. It is a fragment of the old wall of the Temple, as shown by the five courses of large bevelled stones, and here on Friday afternoons the Jews gather together to weep over the ruins of the Holy City, and mourn for their "holy and beautiful house" defiled by infidels. There are old Jews with black caps and dingy dress, sitting on the ground, reading out of old, greasy books; and Jewesses, draped in their white izars, sitting in sorrow, their cheeks bathed in tears, or kissing passionately the stones which formed part of the foundations of the holy house. Unhappy ones, they can get no nearer the place of their fallen temple, for to cross the threshold of the sacred inclosure, on Mount Moriah, is instant death to a Jew. There they are, engaged in their devotions; some standing, some sitting, some kneeling, others lying prostrate upon the ground. They read lamentation after lamentation: "Be not wrath very sore, O Lord; neither remember iniquity forever; behold, see, we beseech thee, we are all thy people. Thy holy cities are a wilderness; Zion is a wilderness, Jerusalem a desolation. Our holy and our beautiful house, where our fathers praised thee, is burned up with fire, and all our pleasant things are laid waste."—Isa. lxiv. 9, 11. "O God, the heathen are come unto thine inheritance; thy holy temple have they defiled; they have laid Jerusalem on heaps. We are become a reproach to our neighbors, a scorn and derision to them that are around about us." —Ps. lxxix. 1-4.

One of their wailing chants is in words like these:—

> "Because of the palace which is deserted,
> We sit alone and weep;
> Because of the temple which is destroyed,
> We sit alone and weep;
> Because of the walls that are broken down,
> We sit alone and weep;
> Because of our greatness which is departed,
> We sit alone and weep;
> Because of the precious stones of the Temple ground to powder,
> We sit alone and weep."

South of the "Wailing Place" is the famous "Robinson's Arch," consisting of three courses of huge stones, projecting one over the other so as to form the segment of an arch. Viewed casually, these stones appear to have been pushed out from their places, by some convulsion, and Dr. Robinson, when he first saw them, supposed that they were merely a bulge in the wall; but on a more careful examination they were found to form the first courses of an arch. Further explorations have established the fact that this wall is a part of the wall of the Ancient Temple, and that this arch is a part of that magnificent bridge, which, Josephus tells us, spanned the valley, and connected the temple with the Palace on Mount Zion. This gigantic work belongs to the age of Solomon, and the colossal bridge, with its massive piers and arches, could not have been less than three hundred and fifty feet in length. Over this arched bridge often passed "Solomon in all his glory," in the midst of a gorgeous array of princes, his guards around him, his sceptre in his hand, the crown on his head, his royal robes one blaze of glory, and scented with the perfumes of India or Arabia! Before this wonderful work—the climax of all the wonders which she had seen—the Queen of Sheba sank overpowered, for when she beheld the "ascent by which he went up into the house of the Lord, there was no more spirit in her."—1 Kings x. 5. Over this structure of undoubted antiquity, the Blessed Saviour often passed from the Temple to the "Upper City;" and on it Titus stood to address the Jews in the Temple, in order to urge them to stop the dreadful carnage, by submitting to the Roman Power. The spot is now deserted enough, and the entire valley and hillside are covered with a vast growth of cacti. Let us retrace our steps, and following the Sanctuary Walls, past "Wilson's Arch," a part of the "Gate of the Chain," let us enter by the Bab-on-Nazir, "Gate of the Inspector," the precincts of el-Haram es Shereif, or Noble Sanctuary. We obtained permission from the British Consul, and, accompanied by a Turkish escort, we stood upon the site of Solomon's Temple, the area of what is known as the Mosque of Omar, " next after Mecca, the most sacred, next after Cordova, the most beautiful of all Moslem shrines." We have entered the North-west corner of the Temple area, and the first thing that strikes us is the magnitude of the sacred enclosure. It is an oblong quadrangle, extending about fifteen hundred feet on the east and west sides, and about a thousand feet at the northern and southern ends. Within this area are many shrines, marked by graceful minarets, and small domes, columns, and oratories, airy arches, and carved niches; but the larger portion of the Court is covered with grass in vernal beauty, enamelled with flowers, and dotted over with trees: the sombre olive, the stately palm, the graceful cypress, the spreading cedar, just as of old, for we read: "In Salem is his Tabernacle," or leafy covert. We walked in our ordinary shoes toward the centre of the area, and ascended the marble platform from which rises the Mosque, with its many-coloured marbles, and tiling, and surmounted with that most exquisite of domes, glittering in the sunlight. Then we took our shoes from off our feet, and we put on red morocco slippers furnished us, and while making the change, our attention was called to a gem of Arab architecture, situated only about twenty yards from the Great Mosque—the "Dome of the Chain," erected over the spot where Mohammed obtained his first glimpse of the enchanting maidens of Paradise. Now we enter the Noble Sanctuary, an octagonal edifice,

Mosque of Omar—Distant View

one hundred and seventy feet in diameter, each of the eight sides being sixty-seven feet long. There are four doors pointing to four points of the compass. Two corridors encircle the interior, an outer formed of eight massive piers, and sixteen Corinthian columns, exceedingly graceful, and an inner, formed of four piers, and twelve columns of polished porphyry, purple in color. These four piers sustain the dome, which is sixty feet in diameter, is highly ornamented, and rising over one hundred and fifty feet in height. The dome is surmounted by a slender spire, which supports a gilded crescent. The walls of the interior are covered with mosaics, marbles, and gilt stucco, on which are traced, in Arabic characters, quotations from the Koran. The stained glass windows are gorgeously rich, and the soft, subdued light passing through them is changed into ruby tints, heaven's blue, golden yellow, and every intermediate color.

But the great attraction is the immense mass of native rock, the remnant of the summit ridge of Moriah, some sixty feet in length, fifty-five in width, and rising five or six feet above the marble floor. This is unquestionably a part of that sacred rock which David bought from Araunah, the Jebusite, on the day when the pestilence was stayed. All the rest of this rocky, irregular threshing-floor was cut away when levelling off the platform for the Temple, and its Courts. No mark of any tool of iron is upon this bare rugged rock. It is surrounded with an iron railing, and over it hangs the crimson war-banner of the Caliph Omar. The Mohammedans regard this rock with peculiar sanctity, and their tradition is that it descended from heaven, when the spirit of prophecy was withdrawn from earth; but that when Mohammed took his flight to Paradise, he ascended from this rock, which attempted to return with him to its native glory, and was only restrained by the powerful hand of the Angel Gabriel. In proof of this they show us on the rock the footprints of the Prophet, and also the prints of the Angel's huge fingers on the stone. The rock, although its ascension was prevented, refused to touch the earth again, and there it remains suspended in mid-air. In proof of this they take you into the "Noble Cave" below, and strike the sides of the vault, which emit a hollow sound, thus indicating a vacant space beyond. But this ringing sound altogether likely comes from a plastered wall, enclosing the sides of the cavern. Turning from these idle tales, this Sakhrah of the Arabs has an undying interest to any Christian. On this rock, perhaps, Abraham offered his only son, Isaac; here stood the destroying angel, "having a drawn sword in his hand, stretched out over Jerusalem;" here was the threshing-floor of Ornan or Araunah,—the heathen Prince—which David bought for six hundred shekels of gold, by weight, that he might offer thereon burnt-offerings unto the Lord; and here, most likely, was the great altar of the first and second Temples, from which the

Sacred fire of the burnt-offerings went up spire-like to the sky. In the cavern below is the Well of the Spirits, in which, the Moslems believe, all departed souls are confined by the Great Prophet, until the Judgment. This well is, no doubt, the cesspool of the altar, into which the sacrificial blood and washings were conveyed into the sewers underneath the Temple area.

I will not weary you with all the legends as to the praying places of Abraham, Elijah, David, and Solomon. Near the dome of the rock is a stone slab which originally had nineteen nails in it, now there are only three-and-a-half; when they disappear the end of the world will come. You put backsheeh right over one of these nails and you are sure to get to heaven. "Sure," said I to the big turbaned fellow that knelt over the stone, as I deposited my coin right upon one of the nails. "Sure to get to heaven?" He looked into my face, and without faltering, answered: "Yes, sure."

Leaving the Mosque of Omar, by its southern door, and traversing a wide tesselated avenue, lined with palms and tall graceful cypresses, we reach the porch of *El-Aksa*. This mosque is two hundred and sixty feet in length, by one hundred and sixty feet in width, and was undoubtedly a temple of Christian worship, and probably the one built by Justinian in the sixth century. It consists of a noble nave, six aisles, and a transept, over which rises a dome one hundred and thirty feet in height. The interior bears a striking resemblance to some of the basilicas of the Eternal City. The pavement was once adorned with

AT THE DOOR OF THE MOSQUE.

beautiful mosaics, and in the southern side of the church are some of the most exquisite mosaics.

Beneath the dome is the pulpit of Saladin, elaborately carved in wood, inlaid with ivory. Near by is an infallible test as to whether you are a fit subject for Paradise. Here is a polished marble column, in the wall across the aisle is a black marble slab, and with your face to the column and your back to the stone, shutting your eyes, put your hand upon the pillar, turn around and walking across the floor, place your hand upon the black marble slab! It was quite a gratification to the company that I was the only parson that stood a chance of heaven, for I was the only one that succeeded. I did not try the "passage of the columns," not because I was already sure of Paradise, but for fear I should not succeed in the attempt, leaving it for some of the "leaner kine" of our party to squeeze themselves between the columns. From *El-Aksa* we enter a subterranean passage and descend to what are commonly called "Solomon's stables." The vaults with their arches and columns, and mysterious passages, are of extraordinary workmanship, and are supposed to have belonged to Solomonic times. But why are these subterranean apartments called "Solomon's stables?" We know that this magnificent monarch was the first to introduce horses into the domestic establishment. His stables were on the most splendid scale. Four thousand stalls were attached to the royal palace; and from holes found, seemingly for fastening horses, it has been conjectured, that these sub-structures were erected for that purpose.

These vaults may have been used by the crusaders for stabling their horses; but if they are coeval with the temple, they would most likely be the store-houses of the Holy Place. How massive and grand they are! These enormous arches and piers may have been built up from beneath to enlarge the level area of Mount

MODERN JERUSALEM.

Moriah, which sloped downward on the east, and west, and south. When these underground apartments are cleared of their piles of rubbish, and thoroughly explored by scientific architects, we shall know something more of their real design, and whether they were built prior to the Christian era. Ascending from these sub-structures to the summit of the east wall we have a magnificent view of the Mount of Olives,

Mount Scopus, the Hill of Offence, the Jericho Road, the Valley of Kedron, and the Garden of Gethsemane. Mohammed's Judgment Seat, a stone projecting on the outside wall, is within straddling distance, and near by the Golden Gate which we have already described. The Haram enclosure itself is uncommonly beautiful, and with its minarets and domes, mosques and columns, oratories and arches, trees and fountains, forms a never-to-be-forgotten picture. As I gazed long upon this suggestive spot and its surroundings, endeared by hallowed memories and associations, I thought of the House "exceeding magnificent, of fame, and of glory throughout all countries," which it was in the heart of David to build, and toward which he had given such preparatory toil. Before my vision rose the temple in its beauty and completeness. The architects of Israel, and the best workmen of Tyre have expended their skill upon it, and there it stands gleaming in the sunlight, fragrant with cedar of Lebanon, and costly with gold. Then came the dedication day,—day of national triumph and gladness—as the white-robed king stands on the scaffold of burnished brass, and lifts up his voice in the consecration prayer. Then when innumerable offerings had been laid upon the heaped altars, and the kingly builder stood before the altar of the Lord, with the nobles and princes of Israel; around him the Levites, with cymbals and psalteries, and one hundred and twenty priests sounding with trumpets; then as the great choral hymn burst from the lips of the assembled thousands, suddenly "the fire came down from heaven and consumed the burnt-offerings and the sacrifices," and the cloud of glory descended and filled the place with such a brightness that the priests shrank back in dismay and could not minister at the altar. I thought of the long days of splendor for this Shekinahed Temple, with its ministering priests, its bleeding and smoking propitiations, its odorous clouds of incense, and its throngs of worshippers. Then came the destruction of this temple by the Chaldæans, when its sacred vessels and ornaments were taken away to adorn the temples and tables of the Babylonian court, and the enemies of Judah, the fierce Ammonite, the cold-blooded Moabite, the hateful Philistine, and the wild Edomite rejoiced, and indulged their heathen revels on this sacred hill. Next rose the humbler structure of Nehemiah, which was superseded by the Temple of Herod, with its long and lofty marble arcades, its courts paved with costliest stones, and rising terrace above terrace, its spaces built up with incredible labor from the valley below, a solid mass of masonry, six hundred feet in length, and hundreds of feet in height; while "on the top of an erection so unequalled, rose the magnificent Royal Porch, a building larger and higher than York Cathedral"; its sanctuary ablaze with gold; its wonderful gates, the pride of the nation, and famous for their magnificence throughout the world, and over all the marble walls and glittering roof, reflecting a dazzling brightness. I thought of the greater glory of Jesus, the Divine Teacher, walking and teaching in these courts and amid these marble colonnades, cleansing His Father's House, and uttering His predictions concerning the destruction of this building, revered with such a zealous idolatry, the hope and pride of the nation!

In less than forty years His terrible denunciations were fulfilled by the Romans, who fired the holy fane and left it a blasted and smouldering heap of ruins. For seventy years this spot lay desolate until the Emperor Hadrian rebuilt Jerusalem, and called it Ælia Capitolina. Ploughing up the surface of Mount Zion, he erected on this consecrated site a temple to Jupiter. In the year 636, A.D., the Khalif Omar captured Jerusalem, and on entering the city he inquired for the site of Solomon's Temple. He was led by the patriarch Sophronius first to the Church of the Holy Sepulchre, and then to the Church on Mount Zion. To each of these he replied: "Thou liest!" When led to the sacred rock, he paused, and looking around said, "This is that which the Apostle of God described to me." The place had been turned into a dunghill in contempt of the Jews, but with his own hands he cleared away the filth and rubbish and ordered the erection of a mosque upon the spot. When the brave Crusaders held the city this mosque became a Christian Church, but when Saladin re-took Jerusalem, the cross was taken down, and the gilt crescent of Islam, again hung over Moriah. Still that symbol of the False Prophet is in the ascendant, and " how long, O Lord, how long ? "

On leaving the mosque an incident occurred which might have proved of a serious character. Until recently the mosque was an inaccessible sanctuary to the Christian traveller. Even now the difficulties and expense are so great that visitors form themselves into parties and go under military protection. Our shoes had been brought to the door of this most sacred fane from which we made our exit, and we were putting them on again and paying for the use of the slippers. One of our party, an American from the West, something of an invalid, and worried by the constant and unreasonable demands of these insatiable Arabs, did not pay quite the price of the slippers, and when the man demanded more he pushed him away with his cane. It proved to be the Sheik of the Mosque; he was greatly enraged and began to foam at the mouth, and with difficulty could our guide quiet him down. Had his rage become ungovernable, and had he uttered the word, a thousand fanatics would have rushed upon us, and our double guard of Turkish soldiers and the consul's permit would have been of no avail. The inflamed zealots would have torn us in pieces. But soft words, a humble apology from the guide, and backsheesh prevailed.

We traversed the entire bounds of the area, which

occupies one-eighth of the city, and as we passd along from point to point we said, "What a platform for the erection of the grandest temple that ever stood upon the earth!" At the north-west corner a tapering minaret rises from the wall. It is called the Tower of Antonia, as marking a part of the ground occupied by that ancient tower, one of the grandest human structures. Constructed first by Judas Maccabeus, it was enlarged by Herod the Great, who called it Antonia, and combined in it the strength of a fortress, with the splendors and luxuries of a palace. It was reared for the protection of the temple. Hence, when it yielded to the conquering arms of Titus at once, the temple was pillaged and laid waste. Coming out of one of the three gates of the northern wall of the enclosure, we are at a pool, the traditional Pool of Bethesda. "Now there is at Jerusalem by the Sheep Gate a pool which is called in the Hebrew tongue Bethesda, having five porches. In these lay a great multitude of impotent folk, of blind, halt, withered, waiting for the moving of the water.—John v. 2-3. The pool is about three hundred and fifty feet in length, and about one hundred and thirty in breadth. It is choked with filth, but it is still quite deep in places; about its side are the remains of cement and undoubted traces of the five porches. Dr. Robinson thinks that the identification is doubtful, and is of opinion that the Pool of the Virgin under Mount Ophel was the Pool of Bethesda. But the size of this pool, its five porches, its position, for the Sheep Gate was near the north-east angle of the temple area, the name of the adjacent hill *Bezetha*, which means *washing*, all point to this traditional pool as the real Bethesda. We were informed that an English gentleman had offered, at his own expense, to clean out and restore the pool, but the jealous and bigoted authorities will not allow him to do so an illustration of the difficulties under which the Palestine Exploration Society pursue their work. There is another pool in the city close to the Mediterranean Hotel, the Pool of Hezekiah. This old fountain is two hundred and fifty feet in length by one hundred and fifty broad. It is no doubt the construction of that prudent Monarch who foreseeing that the waters of the fountain called Gihon might be cut off from his capital by the enemy in time of assault, stopped " the upper water-course of Gihon," and conducted it by a secret aqueduct " down to the west side of the city of David."—2 Chron. xxxii. 30. Of Hezekiah, is said, " He made a pool and a conduit, and brought water into the city." 2 Kings xx. 20. These two pools are the only ones we noticed in the city, although all under the temple area we heard the sound of water, and saw the traces of the genius of Solomon in supplying the city and temple with crystal water, brought from his pools at Etham, seven miles south of Jerusalem. We are at St. Stephen's Gate, and as we wander outside the wall, on the left is the Pool of the Tribes. There the entire slope of the hill is covered with Moslem tombs, and as we are seated on a grassy knoll, looking over the valley upon the slopes of Olivet and Scopus, and observing the water girls that come down to the pool to fill their pitchers, and then walk away erect as queens with these great water urns for crowns, a funeral procession advances. A Mohammedan is being borne to his grave, attended with great lamentation and unearthly screaming. The crowd was orderly; the bier was borne by men, and the women followed, dressed in white, howling and weeping. They were the mourning women, hired to do this feigned lamentation. From this gate the road leads down the hill and across the brook Kedron. Let us follow it, and take one of the three roads over the Mount of Olives. We climb to the top of Olivet to get a view from this "Mount of Ascension." And what a panorama! This view is, in many respects, the most impressive and interesting in all the world. Far to the East we trace the course of the sacred Jordan, and beyond the distant Mountains of Moab, brought near, so near by the wondrous purity of the atmosphere, that you mark every cleft and undulation in their many outlines. Through the opening cliffs are seen the glittering waters of the Salt Dead Sea. Between us and the Jordan Valley is the Wilderness of Judea, a perfect picture of sterility and desolation. These doleful hills, with their savage grandeur, their worn and haggard features powerfully impress the mind, and strangely fascinate our eyes, for

JERUSALEM—FROM THE MOUNT OF OLIVES.

we know that somewhere in this wilderness was the suffering Son of God led after his baptism to encounter the fiercest temptations of the power of darkness. Southward the hill country has a greener and fresher aspect, and the most conspicuous object is the truncated Frank Mountain, so called from the tradition that the Franks or Crusaders here made their last stand where driven out of the Holy City. There is the Hill of Offence, the fertile Plain of Rephaim, where David " heard the sound of a going in the tops of the mulberry trees," and farther on the white domes of Bethlehem. On the western horizon, beyond the city, the Mountains of Judah shut in the view. Northward is a succession of gray rocky, rounded hills, with the Mountains of Ephraim beyond. High above the whole region, the eye rests on Neby-Samwêl, the ancient Mizpah, where the great prophet held his court. Hard by are Gibeon and Ajalon, and farther northward Michmash, the scene of Jonathan's exploits. But the charm of all is at your feet, the *entourage* of the Holy City, the surrounding valleys and hills, dotted with hamlets and olive groves, the deep ravines of Kedron and Hinnom, the terrible walls, with their gates, and towers, and frowning battlements, Zion, Moriah, Calvary, the Haram area, with the white and colored marbles of its beautiful structures, contrasting with the brilliant green of its grassy surface, dotted over with noble cypresses, olive and carob trees, the synagogues of the Jews, the two domes of the Church of the Sepulchre, the compact mass of cupolas and flat roofs of the city; and dominating over all, on the western wall, the Tower of David. No wonder that with the sacred and tender associations of the spot the eye is fascinated, and the soul entranced! Descending again to the junction of the three roads which lead to Bethany, we enter an enclosed spot, about eighty yards square. It is the Garden of Gethsemane. An aged monk of the Franciscan order admits us, and we find the ground laid out in flower-beds, and blooming with roses, carnations, marigolds, heliotropes, and fragrant plants. The bitter wormwood is there, and the beautiful passion-flower. A few palms and cypress trees are there; but the feature of the garden is the eight ancient olive trees. These venerable trees, their trunks gnarled and hollow, their roots far above the ground, and their spreading branches, covered with a scanty foliage, are pointed out as witnesses of the mysterious agony. In such a place, with what vivid reality came before me the whole scene of the Redeemer's suffering, when the red blood oozed from his every pore, and fell in beaded drops upon the ground. Here he lay prostrate on the ground, and prayed, "O my Father, if it be possible let this cup pass from me!" Here descended an angel and strengthened him. Along yon path, lighted by the full paschal moon, "with lanterns, and torches, and weapons," came Judas, the betrayer, "leading a band of men and officers." Here the shepherd was smitten and the flock scattered.

Here the disciples fled, and the meek Sufferer surrendered Himself to His murderers. Gethsemane, the place of the wine-press; "I have trodden the winepress alone;" how near it brings us to Him who was bowed in agony and crushed in spirit for our sins.

> "Can I Gethsemane forget,
> Or there thy conflict see,
> Thine agony and bloody sweat
> And not remember Thee?"

Now let us cross the Kedron and climbing the hill re-enter St. Stephen's Gate. We follow the street leading directly west, called the street of Jehoshaphat, and come to the Church of St. Anne, built on the hill Bezetha, and said to mark the dwelling-place of the mother of Mary, the Virgin. Passing along the walls, enclosing the Barracks, we come to where a stone arch spans the street. This is the *Ecce Homo* arch. The Barracks, it is thought, occupy the site of the northwest angle of the Tower of Antonia, where was stationed the military guard, and where was the seat of public justice. Here then was Pilate's Judgment Hall, and the spot is shown from which was taken the *Scala Santa*, or Pilate's Staircase, removed by Constantine to Rome, and placed in the Basilica of St. John Lateran. The staircase is accounted holy because Jesus ascended it to the Judgment Hall. Opposite is the Church of Flagellation, marking the spot where He was scourged. And this arch across the street marks the place where He, wearing a crown of thorns and a purple robe, was exposed to the infuriated mob, while Pilate exclaimed, "Behold the man." From this place begins the *Via Doloroso*, the "Street of Grief," that lane-like crooked street, which marks the footsteps of the suffering Son of God, as He bore His cross from the Pavement to Golgotha. It runs through the heart of the present city and terminates at the Church of the Holy Sepulchre. From this fact that it is now a thronged street, many conclude that this could not possibly be the dreary walk which He pursued, for the rulers "feared an uproar among the people," and they would not risk a disturbance and a rescue in a populous part of the city. But the side of the natural rock has been traced under the houses of this irregular street by the Palestine Exploration Fund, "and it is found to be beyond the first, possibly the second wall of the city." So that there its winding would probably be close along the wall inside the city. There are several stations on this narrow zig-zag street that have been wet with the tears of long generations of pilgrims who have sought to follow the footsteps of the Master as He bore the heavy cross. A deep impression in the solid stone wall of a house is shown as the place where Christ sunk under the cross. The house of St. Veronica, the holy woman who wiped the Saviour's sweaty brow and had His features left impressed upon her handkerchief, is also pointed out; and broken columns mark the places where Simon was compelled to bear His cross, and where the Saviour addressed the weeping daughters of Jerusalem.

These "stations" these sacred points and places are mere "inventions," pure fiction. This is one of the things that sadden us, and arouse our indignation, the lying legends and cheats and impostures, that are mixed up with these venerable, revered, tremendous associations. Moslem, Greek, Latin, Armenian, Copt, all are involved in these lying frauds and shams. Each tries to out-do the other, and so the Holy City, the city which witnessed the wondrous scenes and sights involved in the Redemption of humanity, is crowded with relics, myths, fictions, and clumsy figments enough to make infidels of thinking men if they do not learn to separate the chaff from the wheat, the false from the true. For illustration: Along this way is shown one of the stones with a mouth in it which would have cried out if the children had held their peace; also the house of Dives, and opposite the house of Lazarus, the beggar, looking quite as substantial. In the Mosque of Omar is shown a footprint of Christ when, as a lad, He stood in the Temple; also on the Mount of Olives, a foot-print of the Saviour on the rock, made before His Ascension. On the Hill of Evil Counsel is pointed out the tree on which Judas hanged himself. Nay, in the Church of the Holy Sepulchre are shown the Stone of Unction, where the body of our Lord was laid for anointing; the column of the scourging, the place of the division of the vestments—the centre of the earth—the tomb of Melchizedek; nay, the very place where Adam was buried!

And now we come to the most interesting religious edifice in the world, the Church of the Holy Sepulchre, which covers all the scenes made memorable by the crucifixion, entombment, and resurrection of our Lord and Saviour Jesus Christ. The Church itself is a venerable structure, the joint property of the Greeks, the Roman Catholics, the Armenians, and the Copts. The open court in front, paved with common flagstone, presents a novel and most extraordinary scene. It is the gathering place of pilgrims from every land. There they are in their different costumes, Latin, Armenian, Russian, Greek, and Coptic priests and friars. Turks with their flowing robes and white turbans, wild Bedouins of the Desert, ragged Arab women, and beggars, halt and blind—a motley throng presenting a motley appearance. It is the market-place for the sale of trinkets, rosaries, amulets, pictures, and curiosities. There sit the vendors of holy merchandise, reminding you of the money-changers in the court of Herod's Temple, offering you models of the Holy Sepulchre in wood, inlaid with mother of pearl. Mother of pearl shells brought from the Red Sea, with religious subjects engraved upon them by the Bethlehemites, sandal-wood beads from Mecca, and drinking cups from the shores of the Jordan. The venerable structure of Romanesque architecture, with its grand old façade—dilapidated through it be—its stones timeworn and dingy with the dust of ages, nevertheless, presents a pleasing appearance. The two wide doorways are elaborately ornamented with mouldings and richly-sculptured architraves, representing Christ's triumphal entry into Jerusalem. Just inside the principal entrance are stationed Turkish soldiers to keep the peace between the rival sects and nationalities that visit the sacred shrine and prevent the Christians from devouring each other over the very scene of the death and burial of the Prince of Peace. And now we stand upon the very spot, around which have centered the hopes and affections of millions of hearts through all the Christian centuries. We have little to say on the vexed questions of identity and genuineness. This is no place for cold, hard, critical inquiry, for the soul is absorbed with other thoughts. The church stands in a crowded part of the city, while we know that our Lord was crucified and buried, outside the city. Yet it is quite possible that the modern Calvary should have lain without the limits of the second wall, which was probably older than the time of Hezekiah, and standing at the time of Christ, which began at the Gate of Gennath, in the Castle of David, and ran to the fortress of Antonia. If this wall had been in a straight line between these points, it would certainly have left the Church of the Holy Sepulchre without the city. But Josephus tells us that it it ran in a curve; yet even with the curve the course of the wall might easily exclude the present traditional site from the ancient city, and leave it outside the inhabited district. So much on the topographical part of the question. Now for the traditional evidences in favor of the genuineness of the present site. We know that before the destruction of the Holy City by Titus, the Christians fled to Pella beyond the Jordan, and after the tempest of war had subsided, they again gathered about the sacred places of the city of their affection.

It is scarcely possible that they could have forgotten the place of the Saviour's execution and of his interment, and when the Empress Helena, the mother of Constantine, in her zeal and piety, visited the sacred places of Jerusalem early in the fourth century, the Christians led her to the site of Calvary. This locality was accepted by Constantine, and while clearing the ground, a cave cut out in the rock, " the venerable and hallowed monument of our Saviour's resurrection was discovered." The present renowned church stands upon the same spot, and although such great authorities as Robinson, Ferguson, Burckhardt, and others, throw doubt upon the tradition, yet I accept the spot, covered by this pile of ecclesiastical buildings, as the *locale* of the most stupendous events that ever occurred on the face of the earth. The church, or rather cluster of churches, may be said to consist of a nave three hundred feet in length and a transept extending nearly two hundred feet.

Turning at once to the right of the entrance and ascending a marble staircase of eighteen steps we enter the Chapel of Calvary, a room about fifteen feet square, paved with marble in Mosaic, and hung on every side with silken tapestry and costly lamps. At the extremity is an altar, blazing in gold and silver and decorated censers, and a splendid crucifix; under the altar is a circular plate, which covers a hole in the limestone rock below. In this the Saviour's cross was fixed and near by on the same marble platform is a crevice several inches wide, the *rent* in the rock made by the earthquake at His death. I could not but surrender myself to the impressions of the place. I noticed not the picture of the Virgin, flashing with pearls, the tawdry tinsel and ornamentation, but gave myself up to devout and reverent meditation of the Redeemer's mysterious and awful passion. This place stands in direct relation to the dark, appalling mystery of sin, and hence His cross is the overshadowing tragedy of time. *Here* He dies "the just for the unjust" to bring us to God. Here He moans and sobs in agony, and wails out the most bitter cry that ever broke from human heart: "My God! my God! why hast Thou forsaken me?" Here His sacred heart, rent by the pressure of intolerable woe, broke for us. If not standing on the precise spot, I am standing near the ground on which dropped the precious blood which can alone give peace to the conscience; for it is only when we place the death of Christ between us and our sins, in their multitude and mass of guilt and weight of punishment, that the conscience finds peace, and we experience the joys of salvation. O the light and warmth, and healing and salvation, that flow from Calvary! How near, and real, and definite, and tangible His love becomes, while standing at the foot of His cross. Blessed Saviour—

> "Thine the sharp thorns, and mine the golden crown;
> Mine the life won, and Thine the life laid down."

Descending the staircase and returning to the transept we pass a long flat stone, the legendary stone of Unction on which the body of our Lord was laid, when taken down from the cross, and anointed in preparation for the burial. In part of this is the magnificent chapel of the Greeks with its gorgeous high altar and profuse decorations. Turning a little to the left, we enter the great rotunda, a circular space one hundred feet in diameter, with eighteen massive piers, above which springs a majestic dome, with an opening at the top for light and ventilation like that of the Pantheon at Rome. In the very centre of this rotunda, and immediately below the dome rises a small oblong building of yellowish marble, twenty feet in length, twelve feet in breadth, and about fifteen in height, surrounded by a small cupola. Within this is the reputed sepulchre of our Lord. The entrance is decorated with gold and silver lamps set with precious stones. The interior is divided into two small chapels.

the Chapel of the Angel, which contains the stone on which he sat (?) and the sepulchre itself a vault seven feet long and six wide. The tomb itself is elevated about three feet above the floor, and faced with white marble, worn smooth by the passionate kisses from the lips of pilgrims from every clime, who, with prostrations and streaming tears, advance upon their knees along the marble floor, until they reach the sepulchral couch, which they clasp and embrace with tearful joy and devout reverence. It is maintained that the four-sided room is a genuine rock tomb merely cased in marble. Forty-two gold lamps burn continually before this revered shrine. Whether this be in reality our Lord's sepulchre or not, no one can stand in that little apartment without the profoundest emotions. It illustrates the power of the outward over the imaginations and passions of men, when for fifteen centuries it has been guarded with the most tender solicitude; when to save it from dishonor, army after army of the Crusaders went forth from western and southern Europe, and kings and princes, nobles and bishops, gave their treasure and their blood to rescue it from the hands of the infidel. It is the symbol of victory over Death and the Grave, for if Christ be not risen, if death holds Him still, and the Syrian stars look down upon His sleeping dust, then is He a deceiver and a blasphemer, the scandal of the Cross is not wiped away, there is no forgivness, the world is desolate, the grave is dark, sin abides, and death is an eternal sleep. But this truth, this central miracle of our whole belief stands as the mountain of God. There is not only this empty, open tomb, with its loud question where is His body; but the Christian Sabbath, a perpetual celebration of the first Easter victory, the Christian Church founded and growing on the rock of her belief in a crucified and risen Saviour, and the experimental proof of His resurrection power and working in the hearts and lives of all true believers. The critic who does not believe the resurrection of Christ must believe in a still greater prodigy and "has not merely the faith which can remove mountains, but the credulity that can swallow them."

The Sepulchre itself, over which floats the banner of the Cross, is the common ground of all the Christian sects, and in the arcades round are the various Chapels. The largest, and most imposing of these is the Greek Chapel, which we have already described, whose galleries afford a fine view of the scenes and orgies to be witnessed on the great festival days. Nearly in range of the front of the sepulchre is a large opening, forming a court to the entrance of the Latin Chapel, The little room in which the organ stands, is called the Chapel of the Apparition—where Christ appeared to Mary. In a little enclosure, entirely hidden from view, is the pillar of flagellation. A monk stands near, and giving you a long stick, which has a piece of leather at the end of it, you are allowed to touch the pillar. The

Armenian Chapel, too, is of goodly size; but the Chapels for the Syrians, and Maronites, are very small, while the poor Copts have nothing but a nook a few feet square. One of the most picturesque of these Chapels, is the half-subterranean Church of St. Helena. It is reached by a descent of thirty steps, and it contains among other things the marble chair, in which the pious Queen is said to have sat and watched the workmen digging for the true Cross. A descent of twelve steps, still eastward, leads to the cave, where the Church tells us she found the three Crosses, This shrine, with its altar and crucifix, is very sacred to the pilgrims. We will not detain you with an account of all the aisles, and stairways, vaults, tombs, altars, concealed relics, and holy "inventions," from the real centre of the earth, in the Greek Chapel, to the place where the earth was taken, out of which Adam was formed. Within this vast and confused mass of buildings, are no less than seventy "stations," and the air is laden with the legends and wonders of Monkish and Mediæval days. But all these myths and frauds cannot destroy the deeper significance and impressive associations of this venerable temple. We condemn the superstitions, and regret the bad taste of tawdry finery and gaudy ornamentation; we are indignant at the frauds and lying abominations; yet, still, the Church of the Holy Sepulchre awakens the most thrilling and affecting interest, of any structure in the world, for it covers the spot where the Saviour was crucified, and "the place where the Lord lay." It is the "holy of holies," among the holy places in the City of Jerusalem—City of Mystery and of Miracles, and still to be the scene of wonders!

Sakieh

CHAPTER XI.

BETHLEHEM, THE DEAD SEA, AND THE JORDAN.

Bethlehem—the Dead Sea and the Jordan—an Oriental Salutation—Journey to Bethlehem—"Through Hell"—Plains of Rephaim—Rachel's Tomb—Zelzal—Solomon's Pools—Hebron—Cave of Machpelah—Etham—Bethlehem—Handsome Women—Grotto of the Nativity—David's Well—Shepherd's Field—Mar Saba—The Convent—Gorge of the Kedron—A Terrible Storm—View from the Frank Mountain—The Dead Sea—A Pungent Bath—Fords of the Jordan—The Sacred River—Mountains of Moab—A Dilemma—Er-Riha—The Brook Cherith—Elisha's Fountain—Ancient Jericho—Gilgal—Valley of the Jordan—Valley of Achor—Going up to Jerusalem—Falling Among Thieves—Bethany—Mount of Olives—Church of the Ascension—Church of Pater Noster—"Climbing up Zion's Hill."

ONE evening, as we came out of the Jaffa Gate, we noticed an Arab encampment, and a tall, princely-looking man advanced to meet our guide. The salutation was in true Oriental style; first they embraced, next they kissed first the right cheek and then the left; then they touched their foreheads together gently; then followed the flow of Arabic speech. After a little conversation, they parted, and the guide said to us "That is the sheik, the robber-chief of the Jordan; he has come to be our escort through the country of his wild and lawless people."

The journey from Jerusalem to Bethlehem, thence to Mat Saba, the Dead Sea, the Jordan, and back to the city by Bethany, and over the Mount of Olives, occupies three days.

Our party started in high spirits. We crossed the Valley of Hinnom, within whose steep and rocky sides Solomon built the high places to Moloch, and Ahaz and Manasseh made their own sons pass through the fire, according to the abominations of the heathen. The place became so polluted that it was in later times called Ge Hinnom, or Gehenna, and was made to signify the place of everlasting torment. It was the common sink of all the filth and corruption of the city; and as a place of defilement and perpetual fire, it became to the Jewish mind the emblem and the name of the place of final punishment in the world to come. The word,—originally the name of the valley,—contracted and changed, was employed by the Jews concerning hell and its torments, so that long before the Christian era, the only sense of the Greek *Geenna*, was hell—the place of torment for the wicked. One of our party said, as we reached the other side, "Now, we have gone through hell." Yes, if this valley were the only hell, and yet not strictly, for we have rather crossed the Valley of Gihon, before it deepens into Hinnom. On the southern side is Aceldama, the traditionary Field of Blood of Judas. There are many tombs and caverns hewn in the rock, and the scene is desolate enough. On our left is also the Hill of Evil Counsel, so called because it is the supposed site of the country palace of Caiaphas, the high priest, who declared that it was expedient that Christ should die for the nation. Now, we are upon the Plain of Rephaim, which was the boundary between Judah and Benjamin, once a most fertile plain, but now covered with a sparse population. This was the camp of the Philistines, in the days of Saul, and contained a mulberry grove. The "sound of a going" in the tree-tops, was to David the signal of attack, and the pæan of triumph over the enemies of Israel. After an hour's ride, we reach the gloomy, prison-like Convent of Elijah, called Mâr Elîas, from the tradition that on this spot, the Prophet rested, when he fled for his life from the wicked Jezebel. A little beyond, we reach a place of absorbing interest and sanctity to Moslem, Jew, and Christian. It is a little Mosque, on the road-side, a square, white-washed building, surmounted by a dome. It is the birthplace of Benjamin, and the tomb of Rachel. Here the Patriarch laid away his beautiful wife, whom he loved with so strong and tender an affection; for "Rachel died and was buried in the way to Ephrath, which is Bethlehem, and Jacob set a pillar upon her grave; that is the pillar of Rachel's grave to this day."—Gen.

xxxv. 19-20. The identity of the site has never been questioned; standing by the side of the great road, between Jerusalem and Hebron—and the roads in the East never vary, but continue to follow the same course from generation to generation; then it is on the roadside "in the way to Ephrath, which is Bethlehem." The spot is wild and uncultured; the pillar has given place to a simple dome; and yet this humble sepulchre excites a deeper interest than other more splendid mausoleums. How comes it that the memory of the very spot, where rest the ashes of this devoted wife and mother of Israel, has been preserved for three thousand six hundred years; while the most splendid Queens of the East have died and been forgotten? Where is Zenobia? and Cleopatra, daughter of the Ptolemies, with the rich genius of Greece, and the hot blood of Africa in her veins; at once, poetess, sovereign, enchantress; wonderful in her grand and dazzling loveliness; brilliant and imperial, even in her vices, the very majesty of voluptuousness; assuming divine honors, as Isis, and making herself Queen of Egypt, Cyprus, Libya and Cœlo-Syria; where is she? She sleeps in an unknown grave, while pilgrim feet are thronging to the last resting-place of a quiet Hebrew woman. Why is this? Simply because of the high domestic virtues and qualities which belonged to Rachel. These are more imperishable than any wisdom, greatness, or loveliness which belongs to earth. Long ages after the Patriarch had buried his loved and

s

faithful wife, her motherly rest is represented by the prophet as being disturbed by the slaughter of the innocents, in and around Bethlehem, by Herod. "Rachel weeping for her children, and would not be comforted, because they are not.'—Matt. ii. 18.

A little beyond is Zelah, the ancient Zelzal, where Saul, after his anointing by Samuel, was met by the messengers, who told him " that the asses were found, and that his father had left the care of the asses, and was sorrowing for his son."—1 Sam. x. 2. At this point we made a *detour* to Solomon's Pools, an hour's ride further on. These pools are enormous basins of marble masonry, in an almost perfect state of preservation; and from these reservoirs the wealthy and wise monarch supplied his capital with pure water, through an aqueduct twelve or fourteen miles in length. I had formed no conception of the magnificence of these remarkable cisterns. Their extent and massiveness are really worthy of the great king of Israel. The dimensions are truly royal, the upper pool being three hundred and eighty feet long by two hundred and thirty broad, and twenty-five deep; the middle four hundred and twenty-three feet long by two hundred and thirty broad and forty deep; and the lower pool nearly six hundred feet long by two hundred wide and fifty deep. They are located at convenient distances apart, and are so constructed that when the water in the upper cistern has reached a certain height, it flows into the second and thence into the third. They are fed by perennial springs, one of which, rising from the south-west corner of a dilapidated old castle, is pointed out by tradition as the sealed fountain to which the "beloved" is compared. A spring shut up, a fountain sealed.—Song iv. 12.

A few hours' ride south of these pools stands the ancient Hebron. Of this most interesting city, ranking with Damascus in age, says the Hon. James Ferrier: "Here Abraham lived and fed his flocks, even where our tents were pitched; here he dwelt when the news of Sodom plundered and of Lot's captivity reached him; hence he set out to the rescue with his three hundred and eighteen servants; and here he sat in his tent door and received the angels of the Lord, who came and promised him a son and informed him that the Cities of the Plain, Sodom and Gomorrah, would be destroyed. Sarah died in this place; and Abraham bought from Ephron, the Hittite, the only portion of the land of promise he could ever call his own—the cave and field of Machpelah for his family tomb. This burial place received the remains of Sarah, Abraham, Isaac, Rebekah, and Leah, and subsequently the embalmed body of Jacob. For no less than three thousand seven hundred years, Jews, Christians, and Moslems have honoured this sepulchre of the great Patriarch, the friend of God; a large mosque covers the cave, which is two hundred feet long, one hundred and fifteen feet wide, and sixty feet high." In Hebron David established his throne, and here he reigned for "seven years and six months." There are two large tanks just outside the city, which supply the inhabitants with water. And from their great antiquity it is quite certain that over one of these David hanged the murderers of Ish-bosheth, the son of Saul.—2 Sam. iv. 12. The town now contains a few hundred Arab families. The cave of Machpelah cannot be entered, and aside from the magnificent tree called Abraham's Oak, and the Valley of Eschol, with its grapes, there is little to detain the traveller. We rode along the hill-side over the Wady-Urtâs, following the long-covered aqueduct from Solomon's Pools as far as Bethlehem. This aqueduct runs along the hill-side from Bethlehem, past the Convent of Elijah, and descends around the southern declivity of Zion, where, in Solomon's time, it entered the south-western corner of the temple area, and was employed in the various services of the sanctuary. This was the crystal stream which "made glad the city of God;" and as we followed its windings amongst the rocky knolls of Judea, we thought the Psalmist's description, "The little hills rejoice on every side; the pastures are clothed with flocks; the valleys also are covered over with corn; they shout for joy, they also sing."—Ps. lxv. 12-13. The road was stony, and in some places dangerous, but the views were picturesque, and the valley charming and well cultivated. It is the site of Solomon's Gardens. The wise man says, "I made me great works; I builded me houses; I planted me vineyards; I made me gardens and orchards, and I planted in them all kinds of fruits; I made me pools of water."—Ecc. ii. 4-6. This was "Etham," and thither, according to Jewish tradition, the King, clothed in white, "would drive out from Jerusalem in one of his numerous chariots, drawn by horses of unparalleled swiftness and beauty, followed by a train of mounted archers, all splendid youths of magnificent stature, dressed in purple, their long black hair flowing behind them, powdered with gold dust, which glittered in the sun as they galloped along after their master."

The Songs of Solomon were laid amid these exquisite scenes of pleasant fruits and fragrant spices and playing fountains. One has to reproduce in imagination these scenes of fruits and flowers, groves and orchards, and climbing vines, terraced slopes, and lovely villas, for Palestine is now a land of rocks and barrenness. The curse is on it, and thorns and briars it bringeth forth. Yet, all it needs is proper cultivation to make the wilderness like Eden, and the desert like a garden of the Lord. The very hills between Jerusalem and the Dead Sea, even where the grass does not grow, are covered with many-tinted flowers, or if they are not flowers they are *weeds* as "beautiful as flowers." That there is any special curse upon the Holy Land I do not believe. It is contrary to His word who has promised: "I will not again curse the ground any more for man's sake." The curse is miserable husbandry, the destruction of trees and forests, the crumbling away of artificial terraces, which once supported the soil upon steep declivities where is now naked rock. A little European or American enterprise would change the entire face of the country, and make it as of old, a fruitful and blessed land, and what many are expecting for it soon in that happy time "when the Lord shall bring again Zion."

BETHLEHEM.

We reached Bethlehem in a pelting rain, and rode through its steep and slippery and narrow streets to the Khan. Here we had ample time for rest and thought; and as the Bethlehemites gathered around us, how there came rushing upon us the sacred associations of the place. The handsome faces of the women, who are remarkable for personal beauty, reminded us of Ruth, the beautiful Moabitess, and the well-developed forms and noble bearing of the young men called to mind her illustrious great-grandson, whose ancestral home was here. On these surrounding and picturesque hills the youth, "ruddy, blue-eyed, and of a beautiful countenance," tended his father's flocks, and displayed his prowess by struggling with a lion and a bear, destroying them both. From this place he went to see his brothers in the army, met the Philistine champion, and, with shepherd sling and pebble, full of spirit and faith, struck down the insolent giant that had insulted the whole army of Israel. Here he acquired his skill in music, so that with harp and song he was able "to minister to a mind diseased," and banish the evil spirit from the moody Saul. Here, as the inspired minstrel of the world, he composed his earliest Psalms, and passed through spiritual exercises and experiences which made him the master and interpreter of the heart's deepest and highest emotions, up to the very rapture of heaven, down to the lowest depths of despair. Above all, it was here that the Redeemer of men displayed his amazing condescension, when he stooped to become a little child. "But thou, Bethlehem Ephratah—though thou be little among the thousands of Judah, yet out of thee shall He come forth unto me that is to be Ruler in Israel, whose goings forth have been from old, from everlasting."—Micah v. 2.

What a household word is this little Judean village, perched upon its limestone hills! Wherever the name of Jesus is loved and revered, Bethlehem is known. At every Christmastide, over the mountains and valleys of Europe, along the shores of Asia and Africa, over America, with its cities and its prairies, and amid the isles of the sea, the hearts of old men and matrons, young men and maidens, and little lisping children, turn to Bethlehem and to the manger cradle. Here the King of Glory is found as a babe, born amid the lowing of herds and the radiant minstrelsy of angels. In this little "City of David" a Light shone and a King was born whom we call Lord and Christ. We descend at once a flight of marble steps, and traversing a subterranean corridor enter the rock-hewn Chapel of the Nativity. The sacred grotto is thirty-eight feet long, eleven wide, and two deep. Near the eastern end is a white marble slab, with a large silver star in the centre, encircled with a Latin inscription, which no one can read without emotion, "*Hic de Virgine Maria Jesus Christus natus est.*" "Here Jesus Christ was born of the Virgin Mary." Do we, then, actually stand on the very spot where the Virgin "brought forth her first-born son, and called his name Jesus"? There is scarcely a doubt about it. The grotto has all the appearance of having been the cellar of a house or khan, which, according to a custom still prevalent in the East, serves as a stable. In the very beginning of the second century Justin Martyr, who was born in

Nablus, described our Lord's birth-place as "a cave at Bethlehem." And Jerome, a native of Syria, took up his abode in a cave adjacent that he might be near his Lord's birth-place. Here occurred the most stupendous event that ever took place in the universe. How near one is brought to the Child Jesus while standing on the spot reverenced as His birth-place! And at this very cradle of the Christian faith I pledged my heart and life anew to Him who passed by the thrones and palaces of kings and descended to the lowest level of humanity, that he might lift me and all the race to the radiant glory which He had with the Father before the world was. This spot, like the place of the Holy Sepulchre, is disfigured by trumpery lamps, golden censers, gorgeous embroidery, and tawdry ornaments. How much better to have left it undefiled by church or chapel, gaudy trappings and gewgaws in execrable taste. Every sacred locality is so transformed and mystified that we are often robbed of the sweet and hallowed reflections and emotions which the sight of them is calculated to awaken. And yet one has to confess that amid the changes and revolutions of time the only way to have preserved these sacred rites was to have marked them as they have been marked by the convent and basilica and other cherished tokens in accord with the sentiments of the age. To preserve them just as they were from age to age, amid war and tumult and fierce fanaticism would have been impossible, so let us be thankful for the traditions and the mementos while we regret, the superstitious and artificial distractions that surround the actual scenes.

In a corner, to the south of the Cave of the Nativity, is the Chapel of the Manger. This is a substituted crib of colored marble, for the wooden manger, exhibited in earlier times; as the real cradle of the Saviour was carried to Rome, in 1486, by Pope Sixtus V., and deposited in the Church of Santa Maria Maggiore. A painting of the Adoration of the Shepherds, by Murillo, covers the rock, and opposite is the Station of the Wise Men. You are also shown the "Chapel of St. Joseph," and the "Altar of the Innocents." There are also the Altar of Eusebius, and the tombs of St. Paula, and her daughter, Eustochia, two eminently holy Roman ladies, friends of Jerome, who spent their days here in charity and devotion.

We traversed the long, winding subterranean gallery until we reached a rough-hewn rocky chamber, about twenty feet square, and nine feet high, where that great theologian and preacher, St. Jerome, for thirty years fasted, and prayed, and studied, and made his famous translation of the Holy Scriptures into the Latin Vulgate, and then, from that rocky cell, the "Father of the Church,"—as the Latins denominate him,—passed to his reward.

Re-ascending the marble staircase, we entered the Church of the Nativity proper, the oldest monument of Christian architecture in the world. It is built in the form of the cross, is of imposing size, but the nave is desolate and cheerless, with its forty-four pillars, in seven rows, taken, according to tradition, from the porches of the Temple at Jerusalem. Originally, the roof and rafters were of cedar, from the forests of Lebanon; but at present they are of oak, the gift of Edward IV., of England, and they look dreary enough. This noble edifice, one of the grandest of Basilicas, is sadly in need of repair, as well as the old, and half-decayed convent, which crowns the hill, and looks, in its extent, and buttressed strength, like a mediæval castle.

Outside the village, a little to the north-east, is a well of cold, clear, sparkling water, called "David's Well." David never forgot the flavor of the water of the well of his birth-place, as shown in the heroic incident recorded in 1 Chron. xi. 15-20:—" Now three of the thirty captains went down to the rock to David, into the cave of Adullam; and the host of the Philistines encamped in the Valley of Rephaim. And David was then in the hold, and the Philistines' garrison was then at Bethlehem. And David longed, and said, Oh that one would give me drink of the water of the well of Bethlehem, that is at the gate! And the three brake through the host of the Philistines, and drew water out of the well of Bethlehem, that was by the gate, and took it, and brought it to David: but David refused to drink of it, but poured it out to the Lord, and said, My God forbid it me, that I should do this thing: shall I drink the blood of these men that have put their lives in jeopardy? for with the jeopardy of their lives they brought it, Therefore he would not drink it." That longed-for draught of water had been won by the lives of his three valiant young chiefs; it was too sacred and too costly to touch his famished lips, and on that very account worthy to be consecrated in sacrifice to God; so he poured the cherished water on the ground, "as an offering to the Lord."

Toward the south and east, is the fertile plain, where Ruth gleaned, and where the glory of the Lord shone around the shepherds, as they watched their flocks on that night when the Redeemer of the world was born.

A ride of fifteen minutes brought us to the Shepherd's Field. It is a kind of plain, and we thought of that night, surpassing all other nights in wonders, when, as the peaceful shepherds watch their flocks, that lie on the hill-sides, like snow drifts in the late spring, suddenly the whole heavens are filled with splendor; a supernatural glory bursts upon them; the light grows brighter, until it takes the form of a shining angel, and there is wafted to them the celestial strain:—" Fear not, for, behold, I bring you glad tidings of great joy, which shall be to all people. For unto you is born this day in the City of David, a Saviour, which is Christ the Lord." Then, as if the heavens must burst to disclose their joyous minstrelsy, a mighty orchestra—" a multitude of the heavenly host"—pour forth the *Gloria in*

Excelsis, until through all the balconies of light, and the galleries of the skies, from rock to rock, from throne

ORIENTAL SHEPHERDS.

to throne, from the hills of earth to the gateways of pearl, from cherubim to seraphim, is heard the rapturous refrain, "Glory to God in the highest, and on earth peace, good will toward men!"—Luke ii. 10-14.

The ride to Mar Saba is over hill and dale, and through wild and barren scenery. The dominion of sterility and weird desolation is complete and undisputed; lonely mountains and dark ravines, rough, bleak spurs of rocks, sharp ridges, and awful chasms, with now and then a glimpse of the Dead Sea, with the purple cliffs of the Moab mountains looming up in the distant background. After three hours' ride from Bethlehem, the Convent of Mar Saba is reached. This convent stands on the west side of a deep gorge of the Kedron, whose precipitous rock walls rise hundreds of feet in height, and the Monastery is one of the weirdest, most curious structures one was ever in. This lofty, and extraordinary pile rises in terraces, on the sides of the precipice, which here takes the form of an ampitheatre, and, amid the bewildering labyrinths of caves and cells, winding stairs, corridors, natural cavities and constructed chambers, you can scarcely tell which is rock and which is dwelling. There is such a getting up and down stairs, such a winding through labyrinths and chapels, and through cells and hanging gardens—in one of which a solitary palm tree is shown that was planted by St. Saba, in the fourth century, and is now nearly one thousand five hundred years old. We first make a descent by vague and wild passages and stairs, down this Convent castle, into a queer open court, in front of the church. The church, after the Byzantine order, is most splendid—blazing with gold and silver, and ornamental lamps, and covered with pictures, sacred banners, and Greek inscriptions. The founder of the convent was a native of Cappadocia, a man of great sanctity, who came to this spot of wild, weird grandeur,—so perfectly adapted to the tastes of an anchorite—founded his establishment about A. D, 483, drew around him thousands of followers, and lived and ruled within these walls for half a century. The tomb of the miracle-working saint is shown, and the cave from which he bade the lion of the Kedron leave him, when he found that they could not live together in peace and harmony. The magnanimous beast evacuated his premises, and left his noble lair to its famous destiny. Here is also a chapel, in which are shown the skulls and bones of thousands of the monks of this order, who were slain by the Persian hordes. A ghastly array of skeletons are these bones of fourteen thousand martyrs. The seventy monks now here seem "jolly good fellows," but they must have a lonely time of it, burrowing in their holes, never eating meat, and subjecting themselves to the severest austerities. No woman is allowed ever to enter the Convent. No female has ever seen the inside of these walls Miss Martineau says: "The monks are too holy to be hospitable;" but they have an outside building constructed for special emergencies, and when there is a woman in the party wishing to spend the night in the Convent, she, poor creature, is forced to mount a high ladder into an upper window, when the ladder is taken away, and she is secure and secured for the night.

Passing out of the ponderous gates of the Convent, we mounted our horses and rode a mile or two along the Valley of the Kedron, to our camping-place. Its deep and rocky sides are burrowed with holes and caverns, once filled with hermits, who were wont to retire from the world to fast and pray in imitation of Christ. No choicer spot for monks and hermits could be imagined, than around the stupendous cliffs of this wild, deep gorge; and these abounding caverns—now the homes of owls and bats—were once alive with anchorites, who sought to escape the pollutions and degradations of the world around them, in a life of seclusion and poverty, simplicity and piety. The entire course of the Valley of the Kedron—from its starting-point, where the declivity of Moriah breaks away from the brow on which the glittering Temple stood, until it reaches the borders of the Dead Sea— is through a barren, verdureless, waterless waste, the scene of the prophetic vision of Ezekiel: "He brought me again unto the door of the house; and, behold, waters issued out from under the threshold of the house eastward: for the forefront of the house stood toward the east, and the waters came down from under from the right side of the house, at the south side of the altar. Then brought he me out of the way of the

gate northward, and led me about the way without
unto the utter gate by the way that looketh eastward;
and, behold there ran out waters on the right side.
And when the man that had the line in his hand went
forth eastward, he measured a thousand cubits, and he
brought me through the waters; the waters were to
the ankles. Again he measured a thousand, and
brought me through the waters; the waters were to
the knees. Again he measured a thousand, and
brought me through; the waters were to the loins.
Afterward he measured a thousand; and it was a
river that I could not pass over; for the waters were
risen, waters to swim in, a river that could not be
passed over. And he said unto me, Son of man, hast
thou seen this? Then he brought me, and caused me
to return to the brink of the river. Now, when I had
returned, behold, at the bank of the river were very
many trees on the one side and on the other. Then
said he unto me, These waters issue out toward the
east country, and go down into the desert, and go into the
sea: which being brought forth into the sea, the
waters shall be healed. And it shall come to pass,
that every thing that liveth, which moveth, whither-
soever the rivers shall come, shall live; and there
shall be a very great multitude of fish, because these
waters shall come thither: for they shall be healed;
and every thing shall live whither the river cometh.
And it shall come to pass, that the fishers shall stand
upon it from Engedi even unto Eneglaim; they shall

T

be a place to spread forth nets; their fish shall be according to their kinds, as the fish of the great sea, exceeding many."—Ezekiel xlvii. 1–10.

That fertilizing river—representing the origin, progress, and life-giving results of the Gospel—at first a few drops, then ankle-deep, then to the knees, then to the loins, then waters to swim in, "a river that could not be passed over," goes on, widening and deepening, until its waters fully reach to the Dead Sea, and fill it to the surrounding hills. Before the stream had issued, all was barren. It was one monotonous, ashen-gray wilderness; no tree, no shrub was there, but burning sand, dancing mirage, and weary desert, stretching away, and away! Now, tall trees grow on either side, their trunks spread out, their fruit is in beauty and plenty, and their leaves are for the healing of the nations. The river itself is full of life; verdure and vegetation everywhere line its banks, and where death and desolation reigned, are motion, verdure, thanksgiving, and the voice of melody. Gazing upon this desolate, sterile landscape—a fit emblem of the world's condition without the Gospel, we long for the flow of this blessed River, when the weary desert and wilderness of the world shall be "a fruitful field," and every dead sea of error be transformed into a receptacle of purity and life.

We encamped in this desolate and wonderful gorge —the Wady-en-Nar, or Valley of Fire, as the Kedron is here called—and that night a terrible storm burst upon us. The lightning flashed, and lit up the wild landscape; the thunder rolled, and shook the hills; the rain fell in torrents; the winds were let loose, and swept the canvas tents. Our poor Arab attendants fled terrified towards the caves, crying, "Allah! Allah!" and the dragomen could with difficulty keep them at their post. The order went round that none were to undress. There was a running from tent to tent, and a strengthening of the stakes; but the storm passed, leaving us unharmed; and though during the night the rain descended, we were perfectly dry and secure.

Next morning we made a long and tedious ascent to the summit of the mountains, and there burst upon us one of the grandest views in all Palestine. Below us, the mountainous undulations we had passed, with their wild and desolate ravines and ridges. Before us the blue and rugged chain of the Moab Mountains, their feet washed by that "great and melancholy marvel," the Dead Sea; far away the Jordan Valley, with its line of verdure; and, in the distance, rose notable peak after peak, until the eye rested on snowy Hermon, its white, glittering summit set against the distant sky. The entire length and breadth of the land was clearly discerned, and we were filled with wonder that a country so small and circumscribed should have exercised so potent and imperishable an influence on the destinies of humanity. Yet here it is—the land of patriarchs and of prophets, the land of Immanuel!

Now we descend into the valley of the Jordan to

THE DEAD SEA.

the northern shore of the Dead Sea, passing here and there in our windings down the hills and through the pasture land the tents of Kedar, which, in the distance, look like black, circular rings. The sea, usually calm and placid, was disturbed by the wind, and the great waves lashed the shore. But we were all eager for a dip, and plunged in. The waves rolled over us. How the water made the eyes smart, and the whole body tingle! It filled our mouth. Ugh! What a taste of potassium, sodium, magnesium, asphaltum, and the decayed sinners of Sodom and Gomorrah! That pungently acrid, nauseous, detestable taste, salt, bitter, sulphurous; that unpleasant, sticky, glutinous stuff, making the body burn and smart, inflaming the eyes, stiffening the hair and setting "each particular hair on end!" We were not able to ascertain the buoyant property of the waters, for swimming was impossible, but we noticed the great specific gravity by the weight and violence of the waves. It has been ascertained by careful analysis that while sea-water contains less than four per cent. of salts, fully twenty-five per cent. of this water consists of various salts. Most mysterious of seas! Covering a superficial area of two hundred and fifty miles, its surface thirteen hundred feet below the level of the Mediterranean; its deepest bed is at least twenty-six hundred below the sea-level, a phenomenon without parallel. It has no outlet, and though receiving the waters of the Jordan and other smaller mountain torrents, its mighty cauldron is never filled to overflowing, and it never rises more than a few feet above its average level. The sea lies in a deep trough and shut in by lofty cliffs of barren limestone; exposed to the unclouded beams of the sun the evaporation is so rapid that the supply of water never exceeds the demand. It is destitute of all animal and piscine life. The beach is strewn with branches and trunks of trees brought down by the streams into the sea, and then, after tossing on the bitter waters, driven by the violence of the waves on the shore; but not a tree, or flower, or blade of grass, or shell can be found along this northern shore. A strange gloom seems to hang over this land of saltness and sea of death. How awful the associations connected with it! We cannot keep out of mind that fearful catastrophe, when the dark clouds of Divine indignation gathered, and "the Lord rained upon Sodom and Gomorrah brimstone and fire." The whole plain, once fertile and "well watered everywhere, even as the garden of the Lord," is turned into a "burning, fiery furnace," all because of the wickedness of those guilty cities; and "the smoke of the country went up like the smoke of a furnace."—Gen. xix. 29. The instruments of destruction were close at hand in the beds of sulphur and bitumen upon which they rested, and when the hour of judgment came the flames from beneath leaped up to meet the fiery rain from above, and amid earthquake and conflagration they were completely overwhelmed. Where is the exact site of these destroyed cities? Most likely somewhere near this northern shore, although it is generally supposed that the Dead Sea covers the spot. We have spoken of the shore as being most desolate and sterile, a naked, blasted waste, and yet the view southward, down the "Salt Sea," is one of striking beauty and grandeur. The sky was clear and placid, the sun was shining brilliantly, the waves, lashed by the storm of the preceding night, were crested with dazzling white foam, which contrasted beautifully with the deep blue of the clear crystal water, while the long unbroken mountain walls on either side, their ridges and precipices, draped in that marvellous coloring, that richness of tinting so peculiar to these localities, green and blue, pink and white, crimson and purple, blending in magical beauty, gave to the entire landscape an appearance striking and unique beyond description. I was reminded of the scenery of the Great Salt Lake in Utah, where the vapory gold of the atmosphere as it floats over the valley in a languid dream, contrasts beautifully with the cloudless azure of the sky, the intense blue of sea and the rosy surfaces of the encircling hills.

We rode another hour over the hot, bare plain, with its white sulphurous crust, before we reached the Fords of the Jordan. The heat was intense; our body was smarting from the bath as if it had been rubbed with caustic; our lips were parched with thirst, and we toiled painfully along, every step of the horse breaking through the nitrous crust of soft bare soil, and now

The Valley of the Jordan.

and then plunging knee-deep into a morass, overgrown with reeds and rushes. A few stunted trees, their leaves crusted with salt, are seen, among them the *osher* or apple of Sodom, that fruit—

> "Which grows
> Near that bituminous lake where Sodom stood."

I had no relish to examine that deceitful fruit, which plucked, turns to ashes in the hand. A thicket of poplars, willows, and sycamores hid the sacred stream from our view. But soon we got a glimpse of Jordan, and leaping from our horse we stood on the banks of that river so sacred with historical associations. What a muddy little, turbulent, treacherous torrent, and how it runs, whirling and eddying along between its steep banks that are scarcely one hundred feet apart. But for its associations it would be one of the most uninteresting streams. But our halting place is at the ancient Ford, the pilgrims' bathing-place, the traditional spot where the Israelites "passed over, nigh against Jericho;" where Elijah smote the Jordan with his mantle, when its waters rolled back to give a passage for the prophets; where Jesus was baptised, "when the heavens opened and the Spirit descended like a dove and rested upon Him." Standing on such a consecrated spot could we forget the passage of the mysterious river where the priests stood on the edge of the swollen stream with the Ark on their shoulders, and suddenly high up the river, far as Admah, thirty miles away, the waters stood as if in a barrier or heap; and those that "descended toward the sea of the plain even the salt sea failed and were cut off!"—Josh. iii. 16. The whole river-bed, through all its windings, was left dry; and over it, dry-shod, passed the army, the women and the children, the exulting millions rejoicing to set foot on Canaan. Five hundred years after this rapid torrent was here twice divided, once for Elijah and Elisha's crossing, "when the Lord would take Elijah up into heaven," and again for the return of Elisha from Moab to Jericho. As we looked at the muddy stream rushing on with precipitous fury we wondered not that Naaman, the Syrian, should say in disappointment and scorn, "Are not Abana and Pharpar, rivers of Damascus, better than all the waters of Israel?"—2 Kings v. 12. But after he had dipped himself seven times in Jordan, according to the saying of the man of God, and his flesh had come again like unto the flesh of a little child, and he was clean, must it not have seemed to him the fairest and most sacred of rivers? This place has a deeper interest, as being the scene of our Lord's Baptism, where he fulfilled all righteousness, and had the golden waters poured upon Him by the hands of John.

While the western banks are flat and low, the eastern banks are steep, and from them rise the rugged and precipitous mountains of Moab. Numerous ravines intersect this mountain chain, and lofty peaks rise here and there. From one of those summits, "the top of Peor," Balaam, the Seer of Mesopotamia, brought from Pethor, by Balak, to curse Israel, built his altars, offered his sacrifices, tried his enchantments in vain, and then in the rapture of inspired song, exclaimed, "How goodly are thy tents, O Jacob, and thy tabernacles, O Israel! Surely there is no enchantment against Jacob, neither is there any divination against Israel." Num. xxiv. 5; xxiii. 23.

Yonder, too, in the same lofty range, is Pisgah; and from the peak, dedicated to Nebo, the aged prophet, with eye undimned, surveyed the Land of Promise; the Lord miraculously aiding his vision he lifted up his eyes westward, and northward, and southward, and eastward. Northward he saw all the land of Gilead unto Dan; westward he saw the distant hills of Nephtali, and nearer the land of Ephraim and Manasseh. Before him were Judah and Benjamin, Bethlehem, on its rocky ridge, and the venerable fortress of Jebus, while at his feet lay the rich plain of Jericho, the city of Palm Trees. How the goodly land smiled in its beauty and swelled in its grandeur! "Beautiful for situation was Mount Zion." There was the "excellency of Carmel," and the "glory of Lebanon." There were the fair hills of Judea and the soft plains and banks of Jordan, purple in the light, as with the blood of Redemption. How the vision refreshed his soul, and lying down upon the utmost rocks, with angels waiting near, his spirit threw off the vestments of the flesh, and put on the robe of immortal light. So Moses, the servant of the Lord, died there in the Land of Moab, according to the word of the Lord, and He buried him in a valley in the Land of Moab, over against Beth-peor; but no man knoweth of his sepulchre unto this day."—Deut. xxxiv. 5-6.

We were anxious to bathe in the Jordan, but it was deep and swift, and its banks precipitous, and we did not care about being drowned in even so sacred a river. The main channel is not more than twelve or fifteen feet deep, but the river falls nearly a thousand feet in its sinuous course of two hundred miles, and this gives it a very rapid flow, hence the name *Jarad*, to descend rapidly. Only one of our party, a Mr. Johnston, from Scotland, stripped and took the seven-fold bath. Poor fellow. He was the life of our company, full of spirits and vigor, an earnest, devoted Christian, enjoying beyond measure the sacred sites and scenes of Palestine; but crossing the mountains of Lebanon he took a severe cold, which developed into Syrian fever, and he died in Beirût. I did not like to miss the opportunity of getting at least ankle-deep into the sacred Jordan, so with boots off, I made for a point that ran out into the thirty-yard wide stream, getting up to my knees in mud in the effort. I laved my feet in the soft, pleasant waters, but how to get back to solid ground with clean feet was the difficulty. I called an Arab to test every spot around, and at length he found a place where the sand carried him. I followed, putting my feet in his tracks—but alas? down I went into the yellow mud again, and I could only get clean by another wash. For some distance I wandered along the shore, which was so thickly studded with oleanders, feathery tamarisks, willows, and reeds that I could not get through the tangled thicket of trees to the water. I was reminded forcibly of the incident of the borrowed axe falling into the river when the sons of the prophets went down to the Jordan to cut timber which then, as now, grew upon the banks and overhung the rushing waters. At length I found some logs that had been thrown out to recover the body of a Prussian explorer who had perished in the attempt to cross the yellow flood, and then again I washed my feet, bathed my head and face, and drank the sweet, though muddy water.

From the Ford we rode to the irregular clay hills which form the highest bank of the renowned river, and then galloped over the open plain to Er-Riha, a most miserable and filthy village of fifty or sixty huts, situated about six miles from the Jordan, and occupying the site of the ancient Gilgal, the "place of freedom" for the ancient Israelites, where they cast off the slough of their wandering life, and the rite of circumcision was performed. Here the twelve stones taken from the bed of the Jordan were planted as a memorial of the Jordan Passage, and here the tabernacle remained until it was fixed at Shiloh. On we passed, through a forest of thorn trees, to the ruined heaps of ancient Jericho, the city whose walls fell before the trumpet blasts of Joshua's army. We forded the Kelt, the brook Cherith, of which Elijah drank when hiding from the wicked and idolatrous Ahab, here a rushing stream, and camped by the Fountain of Elisha, under the shadow of Quarantania, the traditional scene of our Lord's temptation in the wilderness.

After the day's ride, my first enjoyment was a bath in the clear, fresh fountain, whose waters were healed by the prophet whose name it bears. " And the men of the city said unto Elisha, behold, I pray thee, the situation of this city is pleasant, as my lord seeth: but the water is naught, and the ground barren. And he said, bring me a new cruse, and put salt therein. And they brought it to him. And he went forth unto the spring of the waters, and cast the salt in there, and said, thus saith the Lord, I have healed these waters; there shall not be from thence any more dearth or barren land. So the waters were healed unto this day, according to the saying of Elisha which he spake."—2 Kings ii. 19-22. The waters were so soft and delicious that I can testify to the permanency of the healing, and the abundant growth of the thorny kneekub, of bushes, flowers, and of grain wherever cultivated, show to this day that the land is not barren. In the calm of evening and the quiet radiance of the setting sun, I ascended an elevated mound to obtain a view—one of the most beautiful and impressive in all Palestine. Behind us the lofty and rugged wall of the Judean Mountains. Mount Quarantania, rising up savage and desolate, fit spot for the " forty days' " fast, and fierce assaults of the Evil One ; its almost perpendicular east face, honey-combed with caves, the cells of the hermits of the middle ages, and its summit crowned with a Greek Chapel that marks the spot of the Redeemer's triumph over the Prince of Darkness. Before us, and on either side, as far as the eye can reach, is the Plain of the Jordan, its soil of inexhaustible fertility, but uncultivated and given over to rank weeds, and thorns, and willows, lovely even in utter neglect. The tortuous windings of the Jordan are plainly visible from the flashing waters of the Dead Sea, far up towards Galilee, and away eastward ; rising thousands of feet above the valley, the long range of the Mountains of Moab and Ammon, furrowed with deep ravines, and clad in deep rich purple shade, and glowing with tints of magical beauty; around us heaps of *débris*, entombed dwellings, and palaces of the mighty Canaanitish city, the key of Western Palestine, "Jericho, the city of palms, high and fenced up to heaven," with its walls and gates, its rich temple filled with gold, silver, iron, and brass. Around the very spot where we stood the Israelite host took their seven-days' march when raising the terrible war-cry. The city fell with earthquake shock to rise no more, for over the doomed city the malediction still lingers, "Cursed be the man before the Lord that riseth up and buildeth this city Jericho; he shall lay the foundation thereof in his firstborn and in his youngest son shall he set up the gates of it."— Josh. vi. 26. A curse fulfilled in the days of Ahab upon Hiel, the Bethelite, who attempted to rebuild the city, and "laid the foundation thereof in Abiram his firstborn, and set up the gates thereof in his youngest son Segub."—1 Kings xvi. 34.

About two miles to the south, is that filthiest of filthy towns, Er-Riha, the site of the ancient Gilgal, where the Israelites first pitched their tents, within the Promised Land; where the "manna ceased," and the people "did eat of the old corn of the land;" where the Captain of the Lord's host, "standing over against him with his sword drawn in his hand," appeared to Joshua, to encourage him in the conquest of the land; where the reproach of Egypt was rolled away, and there was no longer among them the uncircumcised; where Samuel held court, and the people assembled to offer sacrifices, long after the Tabernacle had been removed; where Saul was made King of Israel, and the men of Judah, after the death of Absalom, assembled to hail the return of David, and re-instated him upon the throne; where Elijah and Elisha resided, and a school of the prophets flourished; and where—as if the very cradle and birth-place of national life could not be exempted—the tendency to idolatry and apostasy was so manifest as to call forth special denunciation and reproof, from Hosea and

Amos. "All their wickedness is in Gilgal, for there I hated them."—Hos. ix. 15; "at Gilgal multiply transgression."—Amos iv. 4. Near Riha stands an old Tower, on the banks of the Cherith, the site of the Jericho of the New Testament. It was one of the royal cities of Herod, adorned with a sumptuous palace, and other splendid buildings; founded in the midst of a valley of surpassing beauty and fertility, and surrounded by groves of palm and balsam trees, and wide-spreading sycamore trees, that lined the avenues to the city. By the side of one of these roads, blind Bartimeus sat, when Jesus, the Divine Healer, coming from Moab, passed through Jericho, on His way to Jerusalem. Here dwelt the rich publican, Zaccheus, with whom He went to lodge, bringing salvation to his house; and, from a spot recalling most tender, and thrilling, and momentous scenes, "He went before, ascending up to Jerusalem."—Luke xix. 28.

Early next morning we were in the saddle, and riding over the mounds and mouldering ruins of old Jericho, and through a forest of picturesque thorn, which occupies the ground of that vast grove of majestic palms, which once stretched eight miles long, and nearly three miles broad, we climbed up to Jerusalem, over the very road which our Saviour took in his last journey to the city. The road lay along that sublime gorge, the Wady Kelt, through which the Brook Cherith flows, and where Elijah was fed by the ravens, and known in still earlier times as the Valley of Achor, in which
U

Achan was stoned to death for his sin. The ascent is continuous and steep, being no less than three thousand feet in fifteen miles. Hence the Scripture phrases: "going *up* to Jerusalem," "going *down* to Jericho." Skirting the very verge of the Wady, we look into a profound chasm, with massive walls, rising five hundred feet on either side, and we think of the promise, "I will give the Valley of Achor for a door of hope." There is that narrow valley, with its dark overhanging cliffs; the path, rough, winding, and steep, often barred by some huge rock. Yet, however gloomy and long, barren and trackless, God's messenger, Hope, is there, and the gloomy gorge through which we journey—our Valley of Achor in the pathway of life—will be a door of hope.

About midway on our journey, we pass the old ruined Khan, where, according to tradition, the good Samaritan entertained the poor fellow who had fallen among thieves. The falling among thieves is yet common, for it is still a place of robbers. These mountains and narrow rocky defiles are the haunts of plundering Bedouins, and only a little while before, a traveller had been robbed, and stripped of everything except his hat. A strong, vigilant escort is needed. We were guarded by the Sheik, or Robber Chief of the Jordan. These scamps will rob you if you do not employ and pay them to protect you.

We lunched at the "Waters of Enshemesh," one of the boundary marks between Judah and Benjamin, and drank from the cool, sweet water that flows into a stone trough, beneath a Saracenic arch. Here quite a romantic incident occurred between the Sheik and one of the ladies of our party. The hour of parting with our escort was at hand, and, embracing the favorable opportunity, our Robber Chief squatted down by the side of this bright woman. They entered into conversation : he complimented her on her beauty, and she was struck with his noble appearance, and just as she was anticipating an exchange of sentiment, the vision was rudely shattered by his stooping over and whispering, "BACKSHEESH!"

In a little while we reached Bethany, a sweet, retired spot, beautifully situated on the southern slopes of Olivet. No doubt about the hallowed spot; but now it is a ruinous, miserable Arab village, of twenty or thirty stone houses, and its only attractions are its precious associations. They show you the tomb of Lazarus,—an excavation in the rock,—and with lighted candle we crept down a steep winding stairway, of twenty-five or thirty steps, and then reached a square cavity which led down several steps further into a small cave, the traditional tomb. We did not take much stock in Lazarus' tomb, or the house of Simon the Leper, or the "House of Mary and Martha;" but our hearts were filled with the memories of Jesus, and this home in Bethany. Across the cool, quiet Mount of Olives He had often come, weary and worn, and had turned aside to rest Him in that home. And

how gladly they welcomed him! How gladly they
opened the door to Him and gave him the cup of cold
water. Their evening meal was sweeter, when Jesus
was with them, and at nightfall how they loved to sit
at His feet, and hang upon his words! How He loved
that household! When He was about to depart from

MOUNT OF OLIVES.

earth, He led his Disciples out "as far as Bethany," so
that the last spot upon which His eyes rested as He
ascended to his enthronement was the home in which
He had been a loved and honored guest. We climbed
the south-eastern spur of the Mount of Olives, green
with verdure, and bright with flowers, and stood with
reverent awe upon that elevation, from which the
Lord of glory "ascended up into heaven." We rode

along the summit through a wretched Arab village, to what is called the Church of the Ascension—a small octagonal-shaped building, possessing no other interest apart from its name, except, perhaps, a stone, bearing the impress of a foot, which, according to superstition, is the last spot on which the foot of the Incarnate Saviour rested. I cannot regard this as the precise spot of the Ascension, as it is over against Jerusalem. Close at hand is the Church of Pater Noster, standing on the traditional site where the Master taught His Disciples the Lord's Prayer. The Church and Convent have been restored by Aurelia of Bossi, Princess of Tours; and on the walls of a colonnade, surrounding the inner court, the Lord's Prayer has been painted in thirty-two different languages. The view from the summit of the Mount of Olives I have already attempted to describe, but what words can express the emotions awakened by a view which embraces more interesting objects than any other in the world. Bethlehem, Gethsemane, the Valley of Jehoshaphat, the City of Jerusalem, with Mount Zion, Mount Moriah, and Calvary, the Plains of Jericho, the Mountains of Moab, with Nebo and Pisgah, the Valley of the Jordan, and the Dead Sea. Slowly we descended from the summit by a path, no doubt, often trodden by our Lord, passed the Garden of Agony, and crossing the Kedron, we climbed up Zion's Hill, and entered the Holy City.

CHAPTER XII.

ROUND ABOUT JERUSALEM.

An Excellent Guide—Upper Pool of Gihon—Lower Pool—Valley of Hinnom—Field of Blood—The Horrid King—En-Rogel—Pool of Siloam—Fountain of the Virgin—Mount of Offence—Village of Silwan—The King's Dale—Valley of Jehoshaphat—Mohammedan and Jewish Tombs—Tomb of St. James—Tomb of Zechariah—Absalom's Pillar—Three Roads Over the Mount of Olives—The Redeemer's Weeping Over the City—Mount Scopus—The Quarries—Grotto of Jeremiah—Tombs of the Kings—Russian Possessions.

JERUSALEM, as a city, is "compact together," and there is no difficulty in finding one's way from place to place. We were favored with one of the most excellent dragomen, Mr. Bernard Heilpern, in the employ of Cook & Son. He is a Prussian, and came to Jerusalem many years ago as a religious enthusiast, expecting the speedy appearance of Christ to make Jerusalem the metropolis of His kingdom on earth. He has, consequently, studied with great care every foot of the sacred city. It was exceedingly interesting when visiting the Mosque of Omar, to have him point out the location of the twelve gates of the Temple, the site of the Royal Porch, and the Court of the Gentiles; and within this mosque, which he believes was built as a Christian Church by Constantine, it was of intense

ANCIENT STONE COFFIN, JERUSALEM.

interest to have him point out the work of the various parts of this matchless edifice. "Those pillars are from the first Temple; no doubt about it. It is the marble of David." "This is Byzantine work." "That shield is of Persian work. Look at the face of it!" "This is some of the fine work of Herod." "See that face! It is the face of the Roman eagle, and the Muslims have defaced and broken it, for they do not allow images in their mosques." "These tombs the

Mohammedans call the tombs of Aaron's sons. We know very well that the sons of Aaron were not buried in the first Temple. They are, no doubt, the tombs of two Crusaders." "This hole in the rock, which the Mohammedans say was made by the prophet when he went up to heaven, is, I believe, the place through which the blood of the sacrifices descended; and this place which I tread upon, and which you perceive is hollow, and called the Well of the Spirits by the Moslems, is, I believe, where the blood of the sacrifices was received." In the tombs of the Kings, to the north of Jerusalem, with their marble facade ornamented with bunches of grapes and foliage, and great square excavations in the solid rock, with inner and small chambers for tombs all around them, our guide was particularly at home; but when he came to the quarries, the subterranean vaults, then his enthusiasm was unbounded. Underground Jerusalem was more interesting to him—indeed, to many of us, than a good portion of the present city. He led us on and on, through cavern after cavern, to the old city wall, in the south-east corner. There were the marks of chisellings in the rock, just as they were left when the workmen dropped tools thousands of years ago. There were the niches for the lamps and the smoke of their burning upon the rock. We turned aside to get the dimensions of one huge block, partially cut down, but left unfinished. What a history in those dark caverns We were most likely in the place where the stones were made ready by the kingly builder for the goodly temple, that was to glitter on Moriah ; " for the house,

ANCIENT UNDERGROUND PASSAGES, JERUSALEM.

when it was building, was built of stone made ready before it was brought thither, so that there was neither hammer nor axe, nor any tool of iron heard in the house while it was building." Another spot where his soul kindled was amid the ruins of the palace and hospital of the once pure and self-denying order of the Knights of St. John. His ardent spirit stirred within us the memory of the brave deeds of the Crusaders, for here over against the Holy Sepulchre was the centre of their power. The excavations of the *Muristan* have brought to light the ground plan of the spacious palace and hospital, with chapels, galleries, cloisters, courts, arches, pavements, columns, and immense piers of stone, traced down sixty feet below the foundations of the present city to their rock foundations in the Tyropœan Valley, which has been almost entirely filled up with *debris*.

Having thoroughly visited the places of interest in the city, let us make an excursion around the environs of Jerusalem. Starting from the Jaffa Gate we ride down into the Valley of the Gihon, which is here about five hundred feet wide and forty or fifty deep; and ascend to its head or entrance, a little more than the third of a mile above, where we find the Upper Pool of Gihon, a tank about three hundred feet long by two hundred wide, and twenty deep. The reservoir is now dry, but it is supposed that it had some connection with the Fountain of Gihon, whose waters Hezekiah sealed. There is this geographical peculiarity about Jerusalem that almost alone among the great cities and centres of the world, it was founded upon no broad river. Upon the deep and swift flowing Euphrates Babylon sat as queen; Thebes and Memphis owed their splendor to the sacred Nile. The Yellow Tiber founded Rome. The chief city of the world to-day is reflected from the waters of the Thames—the river of ten thousand masts. Jerusalem never had any such river. The prophet pictures an encircling stream when he says: "The glorious Lord will be unto us a place of broad rivers and streams, wherein shall go no galley with oars;" but it is Jerusalem enclosed for defence in the flashing links of a moated river. There was simply this fountain which formed "Siloam's shady rill," that flowed along, a tiny thread of living water. We are standing on the spot where Isaiah met Ahaz, according to the word of the Lord—" Go forth now to meet Ahaz, thou and Shear-jashub thy son, at the end of the conduit of the upper pool in the highway of the fuller's field."—Isa. vii. 3.

The King had heard with terror that Rezin, King of Syria, and Pekah, King of Israel, were approaching his capital, and the prophet's message was: "Take heed, and be quiet, fear not, neither be faint-hearted for the two tails of these smoking firebrands, for the fierce anger of Rezin with Syria, and of the son of Remaliah. Because Syria, Ephraim, and the son of Remaliah, have taken evil counsel against thee, saying, Let us go up against Judah, and vex it, and let us make a breach therein for us, and set a king in the midst of it, even the son of Tabeal: Thus saith the Lord God, it shall not stand, neither shall it come to pass. For the head of Syria is Damascus, and the head of Damascus is Rezin; and within three score and five years shall Ephraim be broken, that it be not

PHŒNICIAN MARKS ON STONES OF UNDERGROUND PASSAGE.

a people. And the head of Ephraim is Samaria, and the head of Samaria is Remaliah's son. If ye will not believe, surely ye shall not be established."—Isa. vii.

4-10. Here also was delivered to the messengers of Hezekiah the haughty message of Sennacherib: "And the king of Assyria sent Rabshakeh from Lachish to Jerusalem unto King Hezekiah with a great army. And he stood by the conduit of the upper pool in the highway of the fuller's field."—Isa. xxxvi. 2.

Descending the valley to where it widens, below Mount Zion, directly opposite the Tomb of David, we come to an immense reservoir, covering a space of three and a half acres, and known as the Lower Pool of Gihon. Here the youthful Solomon was anointed king, as the successor of David. "So Zadok the priest, and Nathan the prophet, and Benaiah the son of Jehoiada, and the Cherethites, and the Pelethites, went down, and caused Solomon to ride upon king David's mule, and brought him to Gihon And Zadok the priest took an horn of oil out of the tabernacle, and anointed Solomon. And they blew the trumpet; and all the people said, God save king Solomon. And all the people came up after him, and the people piped with pipes, and rejoiced with great joy, so that the earth rent with the sound of them."—1 King i. 38-40.

Now we enter the lower section of the valley, a deep and narrow gorge, verdureless and desolate, the "Valley of Hinnom," and fit emblem of perdition. On the right rises the sombre and craggy Hill of Evil Counsel its sides perforated with tombs; midway up the "Potter's Field," the "price of thirty pieces of silver," while on the summit is the traditional site of the country house of Annas, and the legendary tree on which Judas hanged himself. A tradition existed that the soil from the Field of Blood possessed the property of reducing dead bodies to dust within twenty-four hours, and so shiploads of this soil were transported to Italy, and deposited in the Campo Santo, near the Vatican, and also in the Campo Santo at Pisa. Down in the dark and gloomy depths of the ravine, once stood the image of Moloch, that "Horrid King," with the body of a man, and the head of an ox, and whose red-hot arms received the children that were burnt in sacrifice. The Scripture name of the place is Tophet, which means "tabret-drum," from the custom of beating drums to drown the cries of the victims. Who is not familiar with the vivid picture which Milton gives?

> " Moloch, horrid king, besmeared with blood
> Of human sacrifice and parents' tears,
> Though for the noise of drums and timbrels loud,
> Their children's cries unheard, that passed through fire
> To his grim idol—in the pleasant vale of Hinnom,
> Tophet thence,
> And black Gehenna called, the type of Hell."

The Prophet Jeremiah denouncing these idolatrous enormities, says: "And they have built the high places of Tophet, which is in the valley of the son of Hinnom, to burn their sons and their daughters in the fire; which I commanded them not, neither came it into my heart. Therefore, behold, the days come, saith the Lord, that it shall no more be called Tophet, nor the valley of the son of Hinnom, but the valley of slaughter: for they shall bury in Tophet, till there be no place."—Jer. vii. 31-32.

Fourteen years after, this prophecy was verified by King Josiah, who defiled Tophet, filling it with dead men's bones, so that no Jew could enter a valley so ceremonially unclean. Seven hundred years after there was a still more bitter fulfilment, when it was called the "Valley of Slaughter," as the last battle scene between the Jews and the Romans, when six hundred thousand dead bodies were thrown out of the gates, and the doomed receptacle was filled with carcases, "till there was no place." Lower down the valley intersects that of the Kedron, where are pleasant gardens and olive yards. The place is called in Scripture, En-rogel, or the "Fuller's Well." The well is very deep, and is called "the Well of Nehemiah," because, according to the Apocryphal Book of the Maccabees, he received from this well, after his return from Babylon, the sacred fire which had been hidden there by the priests at the captivity. It is also called "Joab's Well," from the circumstance that here the celebrated captain conspired against the King, and by this act forfeited his life. There Jonathan and Ahimaaz lay secreted during the rebellion of Absalom in order to get news for David concerning the counsel of Ahithophel; and afterwards Adonijah, here conspired against Solomon, who was proclaimed King. "And slew sheep and oxen and fat cattle by the stone of

Zoheleth, which is by En-rogel."—1 Kings i. 9. From this conjunction the Kedron Valley runs between the

PERFORATED SLAB IN UNDERGROUND PASSAGE.

Hill of Evil Counsel on the west, and the Mount of Offence on the east, down through the wilderness of Judea to Mar-Sâba, and so on to the Dead Sea

Turning up the Valley of Kedron, which runs along the eastern end of the city, we diverge a little to the left to visit the Pool of Siloam, passing an old gnarled mulberry-tree, the traditional spot where the Evangelical Prophet Isaiah was sawn asunder by order of the wicked Manasseh. The Pool is a walled reservoir, fifty feet long by eighteen wide, and twenty deep. The marble masonry is ancient, and is most likely the spot where, at Christ's bidding, the blind man came to wash his clay-anointed eyes, and having washed received his sight. Above is the little, rippling stream and these are "the waters of Siloah, that go softly," as Isaiah has it, or in the words of Milton:—

"Siloam's brook that flowed
Fast by the oracle of God."

Farther up, under the Hill Ophel, is the Virgin's Fountain. The Turks call it the "Fountain of the Dragon." It is a remitting fountain, and their notion is that a dragon lives within, who stops the waters when he is awake, but during his sleep they flow on. A superstition as foolish as the monkish legend which gives it the name of the Fountain of the Virgin, because here the mother of Jesus was accustomed to come to wash her linen.

The clear cold water is reached by descending twenty-nine steps, cut in the rock. The fountain-head of this water supply is not known, but its overflow runs by a subterranean passage, about seventeen

V

hundred feet in length, to the lower Pool. Dr. Robinson thinks that this "Fountain of the Virgin" is the real Pool of Bethesda, and that its intermittent character is the explanation of the "moving of the waters by an angel." Both Dr. Robinson and Captain Warren crept on their hands and knees along this subterranean channel, making explorations. At both these pools dirty-looking men and women were washing themselves, and bright-eyed Arab women were continually coming and going, with their earthen water-jars on their heads, or their goat-skin bags on their backs. On the opposite side of the Kedron, clinging to the rocky sides of the Mount of Offence, is the ancient and wretched Silwan. It is a collection of filthy huts and caves, once used as sepulchres, but now occupied by a thievish, quarrelsome, and dangerous peasantry. This bleak and sterile hill takes its name from the circumstance recorded in 1 Kings xi. 4-8:—"For it came to pass, when Solomon was old, that his wives turned away his heart after other gods; and his heart was not perfect with the Lord his God, as was the heart of David his father. For Solomon went after Ashtoreth, the goddess of the Zidonians, and after Milcom, the abomination of the Ammonites. And Solomon did evil in the sight of the Lord, and went not fully after the Lord, as did David his father. Then did Solomon build an high place for Chemosh, the abomination of Moab, in the hill that is before Jerusalem, and for

Molech, the abomination of the children of Ammon. And likewise did he for all his strange wives, which burnt incense and sacrificed unto their gods." Between the mountain slopes is the King's Dale—the gardens referred to in Nehemiah, first planted by Solomon, and afterwards known as the "King's Garden."

We continue our journey along the banks of the Brook Kedron. It is dry at all times except in the rainy season, when it runs brimfull. Here the valley which cuts the city off from the Mount of Olives, and the Hill of Offence, is known as the Valley of Jehoshaphat. The Hebrew word Jehoshaphat means Judgment of Jehovah; and because of the numerous conflicts of which the valley has been the battlefield, the Prophet Joel sees in it a symbol of God's judgments, and with graphic force delineates the assembling of the heathen nations in the Valley of the Judgment of the Lord: "Assemble yourselves, and come, all ye heathen, and gather yourselves together round about: thither cause thy mighty ones to come down, O Lord. Let the heathen be wakened, and come up to the valley of Jehoshaphat: for there will I sit to judge all the heathen round about. Put ye in the sickle, for the harvest is ripe; come, get you down, for the press is full, the fats overflow; for their wickedness is great. Multitudes, multitudes in the valley of decision: for the day of the Lord is near in the valley of decision. The sun and the moon shall be darkened, and the stars shall withdraw their shining."—Joel iii.

11-15. This ideal scene is regarded by both Jews and Mohammedans as the spot of the last great Judgment, and so the whole valley is one vast cemetery, and the soil is literally paved with tombstones. On the eastern slope of Moriah is the Mohammedan cemetery, and on the Mount of Olives side is the Jews' cemetery. What a mass of graves! There slumber the dead of many generations. The Moslem tradition is that when Mohammed comes to judge the world, he will sit on a projecting stone of the Haram wall, and stretch his sword across to the Mount of Olives, and all who walk this sword will reach Paradise. The Moslem thinks that the nearer his bones are laid to the sacred Haram wall, the better it will be for him on that great day. The Jews, too, are anxious to be buried on this consecrated spot, and the "whited sepulchres" abound. Among the elaborate burial structures are the Tombs of St. James and Zechariah, and Absalom's Pillar. The tomb of James the Just is a cavern, cut out of the hill-side, with four rock-hewn Doric columns in front.

The tomb of Zacharias is a monument to the memory of the martyr, "who was slain between the temple and the altar;" a four-sided pyramid, with columns and pilasters, each crowned with a plain Ionic capital, while above is an entablature of acanthus leaves. Absalom's Pillar consists of a square platform, a square and circular attic, surmounted with a funnel-shaped dome. Around it are heaps of stones, thrown there by Jews and Moslems, in token of their condemnation of a son's rebellion against his father, and we, too, flung our stone into the heap in detestation of that handsome young profligate's memory. Tradition asserts this to be the pillar which the royal scoundrel himself reared, according to 2 Sam xviii. 18 :—"Now Absalom in his lifetime had taken and reared up for himself a pillar, which is in the king's dale: for he said, I have no son to keep my name in remembrance: and he called the pillar after his own name; and it is called unto this day, Absalom's place." About a thousand feet above this pillar is the firmly-built stone bridge which spans the Kedron, and has stood, most likely, for centuries before the Christian era. Not many rods from this is a walled enclosure, and above the wall we see the tops of cypresses, and venerable olive trees. That hallowed ground is Gethsemane, the scene of the bitter agony and bloody sweat of the "Man of Sorrows."

Three roads branch off from this spot, one running between Olivet and Scopus, another leading directly to the summit of the Mount, and a third running along the lowest terrace, and around the southern end of the Mount. That pathway up the Mount the Saviour often trod, for it was the shortest road to Bethany, and over it David went weeping in his flight from Jerusalem. "And David went up by the ascent of Mount Olivet, and wept as he went up, and had his head covered, and he went barefoot; and all the people that was with him covered every man his head,

310   *Toward the Sunrise; or,*

and they went up, weeping as they went up."—2 Sam. xv. 30.

INVERTED COLUMN FOUND IN UNDERGROUND PASSAGE.

Let us take the road around the southern shoulder. Over this road the Redeemer often passed. Over it on His last journey, He was brought in triumph amid

the waving of palm branches, and the shouts of
"Hosanna in the highest."

Here we have the satisfaction of seeing *one* sacred
place, undesecrated by mosque or church. It is the
spot where the tears rushed forth from the Saviour's
eyes when He beheld Jerusalem. The large building
on the summit is evidently *not* the place. It is
certainly at the rise and turn of the main road, over
the southern shoulder of the Mount. The procession
had started from Bethany, and it is approaching the
City of David. Midway an elevation is reached,
where a portion of the city is seen; then there is a
slight declivity, and the ancient road sweeps by a deep
ravine, and after a winding ascent the shoulder of the
mount is gained, and the whole city breaks in an
instant into view. And what a magnificent vision!
The view is most impressive now, with Jerusalem in
its misery and degradation. The whole landscape
round covered with the tents of the pilgrims; the
valleys and hillsides clothed with the rich verdure of
gardens; the mountain city itself, with its famous
and sacred hills. Mount Zion, the City of David, with
its shops of the goldsmiths, and houses of the priests,
its three famous fortresses, Hippicus, Phasælus, and
Mariamne, towering aloft grandly; the new palace of
Herod, with its gold and silver and precious, stones
shining on every side; its groves and gardens, intermingled with artificial ponds and rivers, and adorned
with countless statues; the Tyropœan, at least sixty feet

deeper than it is at present, its streets running in terraces up the steep sides of the hill; the lower town crowded with narrow lanes. Akra, full of the bustle of restless city life; and on Mount Moriah not only the great fortress, Antonia, with its baths and fountains, and galleries and piazzas, but the magnificent temple, its costly marbles, overlaid with gold, and adorned with flashing jewels; the terraced structure lifted high and shining like the sun in his splendor. Upon all this Jesus looked, and while the grandeur of the prospect thrilled the hearts of the multitude, He "beheld the city and wept over it." He thinks of its wickedness, of tender offers rejected, and mercies insulted. He sees the heavy judgments gathering, and ready to burst like a thunder-cloud upon that doomed capital: the Roman Eagle ready to sweep down upon the city, and Roman armies ready to lay waste its grandeur. He pities—His heart swells with grief; His "eyes with tears o'erflow," and He breaks out, saying, "If thou hadst known, even thou, at least in this thy day, the things which belong unto thy peace! but now they are hid from thine eyes. For the days shall come upon thee, that thine enemies shall cast a trench about thee, and compass thee round, and keep thee in on every side. And shall lay thee even with the ground, and thy children within thee; and they shall not leave in thee one stone upon another; because thou knewest not the time of thy visitation."
—Luke xix. 42-44.

Riding northward along the foot of Olivet, we come to the hill Scopus, on the north-east of the city—the hill from which the legions of Titus obtained their first view of the city, on which they were soon to inflict so terrible a vengeance. The Brook Kedron runs eastward along the foot of this hill, and then, sweeping around Moriah, runs southward to En-Rogel. It takes its rise a mile or so away, to the north-west of the city, and without following it any farther, we climb the hill to the Damascus Gate, a little east of which is the entrance to the Quarries, with their long, deep galleries, and enormous vaults, extending under one side of Jerusalem from Bezetha to Mount Moriah. The natural rock in this labyrinth of excavations has evidently been removed for building purposes, perhaps by Solomon, for the building of the House of the Lord, or by Herod, for the enlargement of the second Temple. We are now on the north of the city, and nearly opposite Herod's Gate is a cavern called the Grotto of Jeremiah, but there is no evidence to connect it in any way with the weeping prophet. About half a mile to the north, and just to the right of the Nablous road, are the "Tombs of the Kings." A court is sunk in the solid rock, and on the side of the court, facing the east, is a porch, over which are ranges of sculptured work, the clusters of grapes and wreaths of flowers being exquisitely executed. Creeping into the sepulchral chambers, we enter a large room, having three doorways on the three different sides leading to other chambers. In these recesses are rows of smaller niches, like the Columbaria of the Romans. These rooms were originally closed with stone doors, wrought with panels highly polished, and hung on stone hinges. These tombs, so elaborate in workmanship, and so highly ornamented, are supposed by some to be the sepulchres of the Asmonean kings, while others ascribe them to Helena, Queen of Adiabene, and her children, who, having espoused the Jewish faith, settled in Jerusalem, during the reign of Claudius Cæsar, and dying in the Holy City, was here buried. Returning toward the city wall, we pass a great "Ash-Heap," which our guide told us might be the ashes carried away from the altar of burnt sacrifices in the Temple. To the north-west of the city are the "Russian possessions," consisting of a superb church, convent, and hospice. There is nothing of special interest here, and we make our way to the Jaffa Gate, having completed the circuit of the city.

CHAPTER XIII.

JERUSALEM TO CAIRO.

A Sabbath in the Holy City—School for Jewish Boys—Union Service in the Mediterranean Hotel—Ramble over the Mount of Olives—View of the City—Gallop to Jaffa—Port Said—Suez Canal—Ismailia—Baggage Seized—Egyptian Scenes—Goshen—Approaching the Capital — Cairo—A Donkey Ride — The Citadel—Mosques—Tombs of the Caliphs—Bazaars—Museum of Boulak—Palace of Shoobra—Excursion to the Pyramids—The Nile—Ascent of the Great Pyramid—View from the Summit—Interior King's Chamber and Queens'—Theories of Prof. Smyth and Others—Second and Third Pyramids—The Sphinx—Return to the City.

A Sabbath spent in Jerusalem is a memorable day. I "was in the spirit on the Lord's day" and felt a strong desire to visit the traditional spot where the Lord was crucified, and where He rose in triumph from his rock-hewn sepulchre, of which supreme event every Sunday is the anniversary.

Accompanied by a Christian friend, we went early to the Church of the Holy Sepulchre. Climbing the hill called Calvary, we found ourselves quite alone, and stood close by the rent in the rock and the hole through the marble slab over the spot where the cross was fixed. I forgot the surrounding ornaments and trappings; the Virgin's face, set in diamonds, and other shows, that burlesque a scene so solemn, and held on that sacred spot for a long season unbroken communion with Him, "who loved me and gave Himself for me," and is now "alive forevermore."

Then we descended to His vacant Tomb. A service was going on at the Latin Chapel near by, and the magnificent music rolled solemnly and gloriously through the aisles, and arches, and chapels of the wonderful building; and, as I saw the passionate devotion of the worshippers, and the costly decorations, I was ready to allow their religious ceremonies, and to admit that even their worship, so full of superstition, might be acceptable to God; especially when my companion, as we were leaving, looking around upon the richly-adorned church, observed, "My! my! These people must have thought a deal of the Saviour, when they built such a structure as this over the spot where He was ignominiously put to death."

In due time we made our way to the Protestant Church, a handsome building, standing in a good position on Mount Zion. The rector gave a capital sermon from the 48th Psalm, second verse. "Beautiful for situation, the joy of the whole earth, is Mount Zion, on the sides of the north, the city of the great King." It was particularly addressed to visitors who were present in considerable numbers and an impressiveness was given to the entire service from the associations of the place. He dwelt upon the things that make our hearts turn to Jerusalem, even in her degradation. It was the source of all civilized law. It was the centre of all true religion. From this place the word of God sounded forth into all the world. Here prophets taught; here Christ lived and did His work; and the awful scenes of His closing life were enacted here. This spot was the crowning point of man's wickedness; and it has been marked from that day in being trodden under foot; and Zion, once full of bursting joy is now in the dust. He spoke of Jerusalem as a type of the Christian Church and of the Heavenly City, the New Jerusalem to come down from God out of heaven. He urged us to pray for the peace of Jerusalem, to remember out-cast Israel, that this ancient people may be brought to a knowledge of the truth, and so Jerusalem become the city that men call the perfection of beauty, and the joy of the whole earth. We were invited to the Communion; and, a rare privilege it was to partake of the Lord's Supper in the city in which it was instituted, and close to the very spot where the little company of sorrow-stricken disciples partook of the feast with Jesus.

In the afternoon I had the privilege of addressing the boys in the school supported by the Society for Promoting Christianity among the Jews. This Jewish day-school is under the supervision of Mr. Else, formerly of Liverpool. He does thorough work, and the school is one of the most effective of the Society's instruments. The "boys" are all sons of Jews, and I was surprised with their accurate knowledge of Old and New Testament Scripture. The school is working its way in the midst of a perfect storm of opposition from Jewish rabbis all over the world, who have said to the pauper Jews at Jerusalem, "No more contributions unless these schools are closed." But the schools live on, and are doing their work.

I enquired of Mr. Else, who is thoroughly up in all Jewish matters, if it were true that the Jews were returning in great numbers to Jerusalem. He replied, "Not at all. Four years ago, during the conscription in Russia, many came; but after the war they went away again." The majority of the Jews in Jerusalem, are the poorest of the poor, and are supported entirely by the voluntary contributions of their brethren throughout the world. These descendants of the patriarchs and prophets, the grandest aristocracy of earth come up to their once proud city for two objects; to study the Scriptures and the Talmud, and then to die and have their bones laid with their forefathers in the Valley of Jehoshaphat. Such is their natural love of country and attachment to the very soil of the Holy Land, that it is still taught that he is most blessed who even after his death shall reach the land of their fathers, be buried there or even have a handful of the soil of Palestine sprinkled over his ashes. There is a tradition among them, that if they die out of Jerusalem, their bodies will have to roll under ground at the resurrection, until they come to the Valley of Jehoshaphat; and, not caring for so long a roll, the old and pauper Jews prefer to come and die in the city of their fathers.

We held a union service at four o'clock in the Mediterranean Hotel. We had arranged for an open air meeting on the Mount of Olives, but the weather was unfavorable, and so the parlor of the hotel was chosen. Three Presbyterian, two Episcopalian, and one Methodist minister took part in the service. Rev. J. J. Lucas, of Futtehgarh, India, gave a most interesting account of the triumphs of the Redeemer's cause among the Hindoos and bore testimony to the high Christian character of the native workers and converts.

Our last afternoon in Jerusalem we spent in wandering over the Mount of Olives. It was so precious to meditate on the love of the Incarnate God, to walk where He walked, sit where He sat, and listen afresh to the heavenly wisdom which He spake on the mountain side. Here He was wont to pray, and here He oft-times resorted with His disciples. On the slopes of this mountain, with the city full in view, He predicted the destruction of the Temple and the overthrow of Jerusalem. Here He delivered the parables of the

Ten Virgins, the Talents, and His description of the Last Judgment. As we sat under the shadow of an olive tree we saw a large flock of sheep, preceded by the shepherd, and how vividly came to mind the words "I am the good Shepherd: the good Shepherd giveth his life for the sheep. But he that is an hireling, and not the Shepherd, whose own the sheep are not, seeth the wolf coming, and leaveth the sheep, and fleeth; and the wolf catcheth them, and scattereth the sheep. The hireling fleeth because he is an hireling, and careth not for the sheep. I am the good Shepherd, and know my sheep, and am known of mine. As the Father knoweth me, even so know I the Father; and I lay down my life for the sheep. And other sheep I have, which are not of this fold: them also I must bring, and they shall hear my voice: and there shall be one fold, and one Shepherd." John x. 11-16. On this mountain, at whose base lay Bethany on one side and Gethsemane on the other, He blessed the Apostle band; sent His message of mercy to all mankind, "Go ye into all the world and preach the Gospel to every creature,' and from it He ascends to glory. He spreads His scarred hands over them in benediction, and while speaking, the glories gather around Him, His form rises, it moves upward thronged by an escort of ministering spirits, until it seems to melt into a glory-cloud that floats high above the heads of His lingering followers, as they stand and gaze upon its fleecy folds, with wonder-stricken faces until the last attendant of the angel train tells them "This same Jesus who is taken up from you into heaven shall so come in like manner as ye have seen Him go into heaven." Acts i. 11.

OLIVE TREE—GATHERING FRUIT.

Sabbatic, pensive, prophetic, and expectant Mount! He is to stand again where His feet last stood on earth! In the evening we had a social gathering in the Mission House, and, before leaving, our kind host took us to

W

the flat-roofed top, and from that commanding elevation in the soft moonlight, which, in the land of the Orient, turns night into day, we gazed for the last time upon the holy city, its streets, and mosques, and minarets, and towers—its hills, and valleys and sacred pools. Farewell! Jerusalem, thy glories have been levelled to the dust; but thou art dear and sacred still. Farewell, Kedron! and "Siloam's brook!" Farewell, Gethsemane and Calvary, and sacred stones on which the Saviour gazed! Farewell, Jerusalem! No more shall these eyes gaze upon thy walls and battlements, but enshrined in my heart of hearts, my thoughts shall be of thee, until I shall behold that city which John saw, not with ill-paved and dirty streets, not with unfinished walls and imperfect masonry, but perfect and entire, descending out of heaven from God! "If I forget thee, O Jerusalem, let my right hand forget her cunning. If I do not remember thee, let my tongue cleave to the roof of my mouth ; if I prefer not Jerusalem above my chief joy." Ps. cxxxvii. 5-6. "Ye that make mention of the Lord, keep not silence. And give him no rest, till He establish, and till He make Jerusalem a praise in the earth." Isa. lxii. 6-7.

Early next morning we were galloping away down the hills and through the ravines toward Jaffa. The nag that had fallen to me was an ill-conditioned beast. Canter he would not, but when forced would go at a rushing gallop. His walk was at a snail's pace, and his trot was so rough as to batter one to pieces. Besides, he must at some time or other, have come into conflict with a camel and fared roughly at his hands, for we could not meet a caravan without his making an effort to rush down a precipice, or over a hill, to get out of the way. Our dragoman kindly proposed to make an exchange and administer a little discipline to this ignoble Arab steed. The pony I thus got was a beauty; would canter up hill and down without losing breath, and the saddle was as easy as a cradle. I took it upon me to lead the party, and the horseback ride of nearly forty miles was accomplished in little over seven hours; while I suffered less than I did the first day's ride of three hours (ten miles from Jaffa to Ramleh). The Austrian steamer was ready to receive us; and, over a sea like glass, we sailed to Port Said. I looked up the Missionary, Mr. Whytock; and, as the little port steamer for Ismailia did not start till midnight, we arranged for a service on the steamship *Adara*. The cabin was filled with captains, officers, and men from the English vessels in port; and we had a profitable waiting before the Lord, being greatly helped in urging those seamen to accept Christ at once as the Captain of their salvation.

The sail up that marvellous achievement of the century, that water-way between the Mediterranean Sea and the Indian Ocean,—the Suez Canal—to Ismailia, occupied from midnight till eight o'clock next morning. There is no scenery. You pass along a straight waterway between monotonous hills of sand, with no vegetation except a narrow fringe of trees on the edge of the canal; a mud hovel now and then on either bank, and here and there a lonely desert grave. The canal is about one hundred miles long, running due north and south, and cost £16,000,000. It cannot yet be considered a financial success, although the increase in the number and tonnage of vessels which pass along it gives hope to the shareholders of ultimate remuneration. The total traffic last year amounted to over 2,000 ships, of four and a half million tons, producing a revenue of $8,000,000. Many high authorities are of opinion that if M. Lesseps had constructed a fresh water canal by tapping the Nile it would have been made at much less cost, and would have reclaimed an extent of land which would have more than repaid the entire cost of construction. All that these desert wastes need is water to make them "rejoice and blossom as the rose." Sea water will not serve the purpose, but the sweet Nile water would have reclaimed and fertilized the arid expanse and added a new province to Egypt. Such a canal once existed, excavated perhaps by the labor of the Hebrew serfs who built Raamses and Pithom for Pharaoh. It was not, however, constructed for the purposes of commerce, but as a protection against invasion, one of the "brooks of defence" referred to in Scripture. The canal begun before the Exodus was intended by Pharaoh Necho for maritime purposes, until he was warned by the oracle to desist. In the time of Ptolemy Philadelphus, this waterway had been so widened and deepened that vessels of war could enter the Nile from the Mediterranean and sail into the Gulf of Suez. This great work, then, is not a new project. The canal runs through four considerable lakes, Menzaleh, Ballah, Tismah, and the Bitter Lakes, which altogether extend about sixty miles. Between Lake Menzaleh and Lake Ballah, at Kanlarah, the waterway crosses the great caravan route between Egypt and Palestine. What feet have trodden those sands! Warriors, conquerors, patriarchs, merchants; Assyrian, Scythian, and Persian armies laden with the spoils of victory; caravans bearing corn, provisions, and spices. Over this oft-trodden track passed the "Midianite merchantmen," their camels bearing "spicery, balm, and myrrh," and with them, Joseph, a slave, to be sold in Egypt; and along this dreary waste fled Joseph, the young Child, and His mother, when warned of God, they departed into Egypt to escape the wrathful Herod who sought the life of this infant King of the Jews. At Ismailia the canal widens out into Lake Tismah, a sheet of water ten miles in circumference; and there you find a fleet of ships in mid-desert—a midland harbor—with a sea of thirsty, scorching, dreary sand all around. Ismailia is a strange mixture of French and Arab life. Charming residences, broad boulevards, beautiful gardens, squares, and promenades on one side; on the other mud huts filled with half-dressed savages.

Coming off the boat I gave my valise into the hands of a good-sized lad to carry to the railway station. But here as anywhere else there are fifty natives to one traveller, each intent on getting your custom. So my baggage was seized by another, and another, and another, until the whole troop swarmed down upon the poor hand-bag. In vain I tried to interfere. Such roaring and tugging, and pulling! I expected to see the leather go into ribbons. But at length an official came to the rescue, and with a large stick he walloped them, striking right and left, until the bones cracked. When he had beaten them all off he put the baggage on the back of one of them and sent him away. The others followed good-naturedly, each asking *backsheesh* for the interest they had taken in the affair. From Ismailia to Cairo you are brought thoroughly into contact with Egyptian scenes and life. At first an arid desert of sand flows around you. Then you pass little villages that are nothing but mud heaps, with swarms of naked children rolling about in the dirt, and old men and women in rags and filth, squatting on the ground. Now the vegetation deepens and the landscape is made picturesque by the graceful palm throwing out its tufts of green, and by white minarets, glistening here and there in the sunlight. We have entered the territory fertilized by the silver streams from the Nile, and everywhere the people are irrigating the fields. Every sort of appliance is used. There is the shadoof, which is simply the old arrangement which used to hang over our wells before pumps came into vogue, a long pole on a pivot post, with a

SHADOOF.

weight at one end and a bucket attached to the other Here the bucket is a basket and the water is lifted out of the canal and emptied into a gutter and so carried over the fields. There is the sakieh, a great cogged wheel with buckets hanging to it. The wheel is turned by a camel,* or cow, or buffalo, with eyes bandaged to prevent the animal seeing that it is walking in a circle, else it would become dizzy and fall. At each revolution of the wheel the buckets are emptied into a trough. A more primitive method is for two men to stand, almost naked, with a basket between them and lift the waters to the higher level where others stand ready to divert it as they wish, closing up one little channel or opening up another with their feet. This was the very method the Israelites used when they dwelt in Goshen and the promise was made concerning Canaan. "It is not as the land of Egypt where thou sowest thy seed and waterest it with thy foot; but a land of hills and valleys, and drinketh water of the rain of heaven." Deut. xi. 11.

We are in the very land of Goshen, where the sons of Jacob pastured their flocks and herds; a district still marvellous in its fertility and perfectly adapted to a pastoral people. But on every side you are struck with the miserable condition of the natives, the toiling and degraded fellaheen. Under their wretched Government, the oppressed masses have nothing but a bare subsistence. The foreign residents are treated with every consideration, but the subjects of the Khedive are nothing more than serfs—patient and

* See page 253.

uncomplaining it is true, but looking cowed and dejected.

On we go from station to station, until Zagazig is reached, a flourishing commercial town, situated on the fresh water canal, and in the midst of a country well watered and well cultivated. The entire valley here is one vast cotton field. On we go toward Cairo.

On one side are the Mokattam hills, and on the other side the Libyan desert stretches away and away. Yonder are three grand triangular forms, which once seen cannot be mistaken, and can never be forgotten. They are the Pyramids! Here are the domes and minarets of the Capital; the train comes to a halt, and the city of the Caliphs stands waiting to welcome us. I have to confess to an ambition. It was the darling wish of my heart to get astride a donkey. I am not a success on horseback. But the donkey, the meek-looking, good-natured little beast, surely one could display fine riding powers on him. Accordingly, as soon as I had secured my room in the Grand New Hotel, charmingly situated opposite the Ebekeeyah, a magnificent garden, the Champs Elysées of the Capital, I was ready to ride to the Citadel to see the sunset. The donkey owners and boys were ready. "Donkey, sir?" "Me good donkey." "Me donkey, George Washington." "Me donkey, Gladstone." And I am hustled, and shoved, and pulled and carried, until I find myself astride one of a size, that if I fall I will not have far to go, and that if I get tired riding, by stretching out my legs, I can do a little walking at the same time. We started for the Citadel, the donkey, myself, and the boy. Away went the donkey at full gallop, the boy behind using his prod, whacking the animal, and vociferating " A-h !" " A-h !" Now, in the old streets there are no sidewalks, and so people, camels, donkeys, carts, and carriages go drifting along in *pele mele* confusion. Imagine the comical spectacle, the donkey at full gallop, wincing and twisting under every stroke of the boy, myself flopping first on one side then on the other, and holding on for dear life; the noise around increasing, " O—A," take care: " Ye Meenak," to the right, " She-nia-lak," to the left; running down goats, dogs, veiled women, and naked children, cracking against the wares of pedlars and the loads of camels, grazing carriages and carts, and having at every moment a hairbreadth escape. It was getting too exhilarating. " Hold on," I shouted to the puffing young Arab; but the more I shouted the faster the boy ran, and the harder he punched. At length we reached the foot of the steep ascent, when the lad came up to my side, dripping with perspiration, and said, " See dat, fast donkey. Me want you to say good boy, good donkey, and so give good backsheesh." He did not know how the perspiration was rolling down my back, and how much I would have given him to have slackened up. But I had got there in safety; to this day I cannot tell how, and can testify, " Uneasy sits the man who rides an ass." We toiled up the ascent, and through the splendid gates of Saracenic architecture, to the highest part of the Citadel. The view from this point is far-famed. Spread out below you is the City of Romance; its countless domes and minarets lifted high in the air and glittering in the rays of the setting sun; to the north-west is Boulak, the fort of Cairo; to the south-west, the old city, with its narrow tortuous streets and lofty houses, the ancient Babloun, or Babylon of the Apostles; and beyond are rich and fertile fields, the gift of the Nile, covered with corn and waving palm trees. The Citadel is one extreme of the Nile valley, the pyramids of Ghizeh on the other, and the breadth of Egypt lies between, with the famous river, a sparkling mirror set in emerald greenness, stretching up and down far as the eye can reach, while beyond stretches the vast desert of Lybia.

While at the Citadel, a visit must be made to the Mosque of Mahomed Ali, a costly structure, with its vast cupola and spacious court and many lamps, set in emeralds and suspended by golden chains, its many-colored marbles, and the whole interior lined with Oriental alabaster. The guide pointed out, with great reverence, the tomb of Mahomed Ali, with the lamps burning continually, night and day. Then I visited the Mosque Tooloon, the oldest in Cairo, and a copy of the Kaaba at Mecca. Cairo being one of the chief cities of the Moslem world, inferior only to Constantinople, it is a city of mosques, there being no less

Cairo from the Ancient Citadel.

than four or five hundred of these sacred structures. But aside from the Mosque of Sultan Hassan, the finest in the city, with its graceful architecture and splendid ornamentation, and the El Azhar, the chief Oriental University, and those already mentioned, there are no attractions to repay the time and cost of a visit. Forbidden by the Koran to imitate animal life, the Moorish artists have devoted all their energies to geometric ornamentation, inscriptions and arabesques, and know how to produce charming color-effects from variegated marble pavements, doors of ivory and amber, and vaulted ceilings of cedar wood.

The tombs of the Caliphs lie outside the city, but they are well worth seeing. They are fine examples of Saracenic Mausoleums. I entered and inspected those of Sultan Barkuk, Kait Bey, and other defunct dignitaries, whose names I have forgotten.

The drive to these Arabian tombs should always be through the Mooskee Street, with its bazaars. What a view one gets of Oriental life! and, in the strange medley one realizes that Cairo is, indeed, the city of the "Arabian Nights." The bazaars are truly wonderful. Among them the Turkish, the Arab, the Egyptian, the Tunis. Some of them are ablaze with jewellery, diamonds, and costly stones. Others have embroidered leather, very beautiful and expensive, and elegant work of every kind. Instead of having everything in a jumble, there are bazaars for specialties. One for cloth, another for shoes and slippers sewed with seed pearls, another for porcelain and glass work, another for tobacco and coffee, another for arms, old

Oriental Street.

and new inlaid with jewels and with gold. There are also shawl merchants, sellers of Persian carpets and of silks.

The museum of Boulak is the great treasure house of Egyptian antiquities. Through the unwearied efforts of the late Mariette Bey it is crowded with relics, specimens of Egytian art, culture, and life, and is without doubt the most valuable Egyptian museum in the world. There are statues life-sized, the very embodiment of life and character as the Nile personified; and busts, among them that of Tirhakah, King of Ethiopia, mentioned in 2 Kings xix. 9.

There are coffins of mummies, the mummies in all states of preservation; the sarcophagi some of wood, some of stone, with linen bands for enveloping the bodies and amulets for decorating them, and funeral objects of every kind. The entire rabble of the Egyptian Pantheon is seen, Osiris, principal deity with his sisters Isis and Nephthys, the Bull-god Apis, the Jackal-headed Anubis, the tutelary of sepulchres and according to Plutarch "the watch of the gods as the dog is the watch of men;" Hathor, the goddess of the pure light of heaven and bearing the sun-disk between horns on a cow's head; Ibis-headed Toth, the god of the learned and of physicians; Besa, a deformed pygmy, god of the toilet, who led the women to conquest in love and the men in war; the Red god Seth, the Typhon of the Greeks, enemy of Osiris of truth, goodness, and purity, the devil of the system, with other gods and goddesses without number. There are the jewels of ancient queens, bracelets, anklets, ear and finger rings, necklaces and clasps, with numerous articles of furniture, utensils, vases, vestments, arms, and weapons. There are stelae, and inscriptions, and papyri that have been steamed, and unrolled and read. How one has unfolded, in these statues and divinities, these relics monuments, and papyri the entire story of art, culture, religion, the life and history of that most intellectual and active people of antiquity, long centuries before the days of Moses! I took special delight in the museum, as I had not been able to ascend the Nile and visit the Temples of Rameses and Denderah and Luxor, nor see the ruins of Thebes, Memphis, Karnak, and Assouan. The museum contains the finest monuments from these places; just as to-day the best specimens of Egyptian sculpture are found not in Egypt, but in the British Museum. New objects are continually being added to the museum. A young acquaintance of mine, through the kindness of some students of Egyptology, had the privilege of gazing on the features and shaking hands with the mummy Pepi, of the sixth dynasty, just discovered at Sakkarah, and yet not made accessible to the public. And still more recently have been discovered in a pit at Deir-el-Bahari, about four miles from the Nile to the east of Thebes, the mummies of the kings and queens of the 17th, 18th, 19th, 20th, and 21st dynasties who reigned in Egypt about fifteen centuries before Christ. The cartouches upon the cases and the funeral inscriptions upon the shrouds in which the remains are wrapped prove conclusively that these kings were

among the most powerful that that ever reigned in
Egypt, for one of them is Thotmes III., the greatest of
the Pharaohs whose conquest extended from Nubia to
the Black Sea, and from Euphrates to Southern Italy,
and another is Rameses II., the fabled Sesostris of the
Greeks, the Pharaoh "who knew not Joseph." Only
think of it, the corpse of that Egyptian tyrant and
oppressor of the Hebrews, brought to light after an
entombment of three thousand three hundred years!

Cairo has some very fine streets. A favorite street
for promenading, as well as driving, is the broad and
beautifully shaded avenue to the palace and gardens
of Shoobra. I had got quite enough of Oriental
palaces, and so did not see the interior of this
palace, which, I believe, blends with good effect the
Turkish and European styles. But I enjoyed the street
life about it. After all, the best place to study Egyptian
life in all its phases, from high-bred ladies with
lustrous flashing eyes, and dainty feet, to the water-
carrier girls, and from the wealthiest inhabitant to
the poorest fellah, is on the street, or before a cafe
or fountain.

But the memorable excursion is to the world-
renowned Pyramids of Ghizeh. We cross the Nile by
a magnificent bridge, and for some distance the road,
shaded by acacias and tall palms, lies along the banks
of that all-fertilizing river. And what a stream it
is! Egypt owes its existence and fertility to this
wonderful river, which flows for over 1.300 miles

x

without a single affluent, to the sea. It is renowned in ancient story. Along its reedy banks, rocked by the zephyrs, was the ark of bulrushes, in which Moses was cradled. Its waters so tranquil and swee

ORIENTAL FOUNTAIN.

were turned into blood when the hard-hearted Pharaoh refused to let God's captive people go free. By its banks the infant Jesus may have dwelt. It is the subject of Divine prediction. Ezekiel calls Pharaoh "the great dragon that lieth in the midst of the rivers." Amos speaks of the "flood of Egypt," and, no doubt, refers to the annual inundation, which, commencing about the end of June, reaches its greatest height in September, diffusing life and joy everywhere. Isaiah prophesied, "The Lord shall utterly destroy the tongue of the Egyptian sea, and with His mighty wind shall He shake His hand over the river, and shall smite it in the seven streams, and make men go over dry shod." How literally has this been fulfilled, for of the seven mouths, five are completely dried up, and the only outlet to the sea is by the artificially-constructed channels, the Damietta and Rosetta. These names can be easily remembered, for our dimity cloth is from Damietta; and at Rosetta was found the famous Rosetta stone, with an inscription in three languages, which has furnished the key to the interpretation of Egyptian hieroglyphics.

Along the old Nile stream we journey until we reach the mud village of Ghizeh, where the road runs straight from the river to the colossal Pyramids. There upon a rocky plateau, on the margin of the great ocean of desert sand, stand these venerable monuments of antiquity. There they stand, with the solitude and silence of the desert brooding over them, their vastness and grandeur incomprehensible, their very immensity seeming to overwhelm us. And now for the ascent. I had an idea that the Pyramids were great mountains of smooth, polished stones, and that by some artificial stairs we reached the summit. But the outer polished stones have been taken away to furnish materials for the edifices of a later epoch; and so the great

corrugated sides run up for seven hundred and fifty
feet and up this formidable staircase of huge blocks
of masonry, each block rising to your breast, you
must mount.

The Sheik of the Pyaramids must be paid a dollar
for the privilege of ascending to the top and of
entering the subterranean chambers. Then you are
furnished with an Arab on each side to pull, one
behind to push, and a water carrier. The toilsome
work begins, and the merry good-humored scoundrels
drag up upward with a will. As you rise, the view
becomes more and more grand. At every pause to
rest, the Arabs squat at your feet, and begin their
everlasting clatter for backsheesh. But I *bought*
their silence. I said, "I don't want you to talk; I
don't want to be disturbed. If you will take me
up carefully, and not say 'backsheesh' to me anywhere nor allow any others to speak to me till
we get down I will pay you well; if not I'll
not pay you a cent." "All right!" they said; and
they kept their pledge. For, if there was the slightest
allusion, I reminded them of the promise and of my
vow. At length we reached the summit, and then
how unrivalled the panorama which unrolled itself.
The day was glorious, and I drank in to the full the
amazing prospect. On one side was the great desert
—wild, weird, solitary, a vast domain of desolation
and death stretching away and away; eastward the
Nile valley, green as an emerald, a rich Oriental land-

scape reaching far over to the Mokattam Mountains; in the distance Cairo, its minarets rising into the air like the ten thousand turrets of some immense Gothic edifice, crowned with the towers and white battlements of the Citadel. Yonder sweeps the broad and glittering river, at once the parent and the cradle of millions of beings. In the far distance, behind old Cairo, is the site of Heliopolis, "City of the Sun"—called *On* in Genesis, and Beth-Shemesh in Jeremiah—the Oxford of old Egypt where Plato and Herodotus studied philosophy and history; where Joseph married the beautiful Asenath, daughter of the Priest of the Temple of the Sun—its celebrated obelisk, old when Abraham came down with Sarai into Egypt—seen, no doubt, by Isaac and Joseph and the weary bondmen as they lifted their eyes from their grinding toil—the scarred veteran—still telling its story of fifty centuries ago. Farther up the river are the Pyramids of Sakkarah, the Necropolis of Memphis—all that remains of the once proud capital of Lower Egypt, for literally fulfilled is the prediction—"Noph shall be waste and desolate, without an inhabitant." "Memphis shall become a desert; she shall be forsaken, and become uninhabitable."

What prodigies these pyramids are! The race who reared them were assuredly a building people. These ancient Egyptians had not the refinement and delicacy of the Greeks, or the constructive art of the Goths, but in massive grandeur they were unsurpassed. The base line of the Great Pyramid is, at present, after the waste and wear and vandalism of four thousand years, seven hundred and thirty-two feet; the perpendicular height is about four hundred and eighty feet. The gigantic structure consists of two hundred and six layers of vast blocks of stone, rising above each other in the form of steps, and Herodotus tells us that after ten years had been spent in quarrying the stones and getting them to the place, it took one hundred thousand men twenty years to construct it. Its base covers over thirteen square acres, and the four sides face exactly the four cardinal points of the heavens. The cubic contents of this huge fabric are more than eighty millions of cubic feet, and the estimated weight six millions of tons. An old Coptic tradition declares, that to annihilate the Great Pyramid would more than consume all the wealth of Egypt.

Here it has stood in its stately grandeur while the great empires of the world have risen, and flourished, and fallen. It stood when Abram and Lot came "to sojourn in the land;" it saw the young Joseph brought a slave into Egypt. It saw the down-trodden Israelites rise up to go out of the land, and heard the rattle of the war chariots of Pharaoh in pursuit. It beheld the invading armies of Shishak and Pharaoh-Necho marching into the land of Israel. It saw the fugitives, Jeroboam and Urijah, seeking refuge in Egypt, and the infant Saviour escaping from the wrath of "Herod the King." It heard the tramp of the conquering hosts of Cambyses, Alexander, Cæsar, Amron, and Omar, and the roar of the cannon of Napoleon. As long as the earth endures it will be the wonder of the world; and long generations coming after us will gaze upon it as the most marvellous work of man. I was roused from my reverie by an old Arab proposing to descend, and climb the adjacent pyramid, which is smooth and polished to the apex, and return in ten minutes for two shillings. I said I did not want him to go. But, said he, "That is my business." I said, "It is a very dangerous business. I could not do it myself." He laughed, and proposed to go. "No," said I; "I am afraid you will fall and break your neck, and then I will be to blame for your death." "Ah," he replied, with ready wit, "you are afraid to break your two shillings." After remaining for some time on the summit, a level platform of fifteen or sixteen feet square, loth to quit the spot, and drinking in for the last time the sublime view, it became necessary to descend. As I approached the edge of the platform and looked down the steep rugged side of the pyramid, it was indeed dizzy and fearful, and the Arabs below seemed like dwarfs. But the guides had the agility of the chamois, the stories at the top were comparatively easy to begin the descent, for while the lower layers are nearly five feet in thickness, the upper ones are only about a foot and a half; so that while it is hard upon the muscles to get down as it is to get up, we reached the bottom in perfect safety, and in less than one tenth of the time it had taken to ascend.

Now we prepare to enter the interior. How the pantaloons have to suffer, and how the lungs labor to inhale pent-up air, and darkness since the days of Pharaoh. The entrance is in the northern face, about fifty feet above the base, and about twenty-five feet east of the centre of the pyramid. The passage dips at an angle of twenty-six degrees, and is cased with finely polished slabs of oriental porphyry, but the guides with lighted tapers creep down the slippery passage like cats, and you are safe in their hands. This passage continues downward from its intersection with the ascending passage, some two hundred feet to a subterranean chamber, about ninety feet below the base of the pyramid. This chamber is the largest in the pyramid and measures forty-six feet long, by twenty-seven wide, and eleven in height. The ascending passage rises at an angle of twenty-six degrees, and has notches in the floor to assist in climbing, and after following it for one hundred and twenty-five feet we reach what is called the Grand Gallery. In this front is the opening to what is called the Well, nearly two hundred feet deep, which was in all probability an outlet for the masons after they had barred the sloping ascent with granite on the inside. Here also commences the horizontal floor of the passage leading to the Queen's Chamber. This apartment is about eighteen feet square, by twenty high. Groping along the narrow, smooth, ascending corridor, we at length reach the chief chamber of the pyramid—the King's Chamber. This royal room is magnificently finished, the granite polish being equal to that of fine jewelry, and measures thirty-four feet by seventeen, and nineteen in height. In the centre, with its head turned to the north stands the mysterious sarcophagus, lidless, and of red granite. Was this empty coffin ever occupied? If this pyramid was built simply to guard the mummy body of King Cheops, it has proved a magnificent failure, for the body is not there. Prof. Piazzi Smith and others maintain that the so-called sarcophagus is really a coffer of exactly similar cubical capacity with the Ark of the Covenant; that it is designed to perpetuate a standard measure of capacity and has been placed in the heart of the pyramid and built in so as never to be removed. The heat of the interior is very great, the beaded drops of perspiration rolled from our faces and we were glad to emerge again into the open air. What endless speculations concerning this remarkable structure! Those long, dark, sloping passages, have been most accurately measured, and every wall and line and over-lapping has been made to symbolize some important event. According to the theories of recent students of this ancient and memorial structure, the veil of mystery has been lifted and the innermost secrets of this grand pillar explored. These philological and hieroglyphic scholars maintain that the venerable structure tells its own date of birth and foundation:—It was erected under the eye of Melchizedek, according to a design furnished by Divine inspiration. It teaches the nature of the orbit of the earth around the sun; the exact proportion of the period of that revolution to the rotation of the earth on its axis; it is a standard of weights and measures on which is founded not only the sacred Hebrew, but the hereditary weights and measures of modern European nations of Saxon and Gothic origin; it is a linear standard, a time standard; it links together science and revelation, and, being a Hebrew-devised structure, it is of Messianic character. The measured height of the Grand Gallery over the other passages representing the Christian dispensation; the pyramid inches symbolize the thirty-three years of the Saviour's earthly life; bringing us right over against the mouth of the well, type of his death and descent into Hades; while the long lofty gallery shows the sway of His blessed religion over the world; the mounting of the steps indicates the manifold conquests of the powers of nature, and the termination of the Grand Gallery at the 1881-2, southern end represents the close of the Gospel age, and the coming of Christ for his saints. These and other vagaries are attached to what sober-thinking people simply regard as only the burying-place of mighty kings.

The Second Pyramid stands a few hundred feet south-west of the first. It is smaller and of inferior workmanship, but the ancient polished casing still exists towards the top so that it is difficult of ascent. It is assigned by Herodotus to Chephren, the brother

ANCIENT EGYPTIAN STATUES.

of Cheops, and called "Shafra, the Great of the Pyramid."

The Third, or Red Pyramid, is very beautiful and

regular of construction, but it is only a little over two hundred feet in height, and is of no special interest. Near by is the Temple of the Sphinx with subterranean galleries of polished marble, and other deep tombs partially choked with sand. Down one of these an Arab descended at least sixty feet, and after brushing away the sand, out came a massive Egyptian face carved in the solid rock. The face was directed upward. I shall never forget the impression as I looked down upon it. Sun, moon and stars may shine upon it, storms beat upon it, but those eyes are directed upward as if gazing ever upon the unseen and eternal. Emblem of what our faith should be, and of that constant "looking unto Jesus," which shall bear us bravely onward through every changing scene.

The last object I gazed upon was that colossal mystery, the Sphinx :—

"Staring right on with calm, eternal eyes."

The mighty head is fifteen feet across and thirty feet from brow to chin. The kingly crown is taken off, the features time-worn and mutilated, the lips thick and heavy, but there it is; emblem of intelligence combined with sovereign power. The fabulous monster remains unchanged in the midst of change. Its stony eyes have looked upon ancient dynasties; upon Persian, Macedonian, Roman, Ottoman conquerors; upon the oldest Egyptian race; upon the sons of Jacob, who pastured their flocks in Goshen;

upon the present toiling and down-trodden fellaheen—
and we and all that now dwell upon the earth shall pass
away, while it shall still look out with sad and stony
eyes upon the incoming floods of humanity. I returned
weary enough to the New Hotel; and every muscle of
my legs and arms was so sore with the tugging,
pulling, and straining, that for three or four days I
could scarcely lift hand or foot without pain.

CHAPTER XIV.

CAIRO TO NAPLES AND ROME.

Population of Cairo—Coptic Christians—Missions—Railway ride to Alexandria—An Oriental Sunset—On the Mediterranean—Sicily—Mount Etna—Stromboli—Bay of Naples—The "Beautiful City"—San Martino—The Museum—Churches—Virgil's Tomb—Sorrento Pozzuoli—Baja—Capri—Pompeii—The Forum and Temples—Streets and Houses—Villa of Diomedes—Objects in the Museum—Ascent of Versuvius—A Magnificent Panorama—The Crater—A Weird Memory—Caserta—Casenum—Roma.

CAIRO is situated on the east bank of the Nile, about twelve miles above the apex of its Delta, and there is an endless charm about its walls and towers, its gardens and squares, its palaces and mosques, with their delicately carved minarets and domes, its broad avenues and narrow unpaved streets. Its population is nearly half a million, composed of Turks, Arabs, Armenians, Copts, Syrians, Africans, Greeks, French, English, Germans, and Americans. As far as the walls are concerned, Cairo is about seven miles in circumference, and it is walled off into quarters, deriving their names from the character or condition of their occupants, as the Mohammedan quarter, the Jews' quarter, etc. There are about 60,000 Copts in Cairo They are the chief employees in the government offices, and are merchants, goldsmiths, jewellers, builders, and tradesmen. They are generally considered more skilful than the Moslems. The Coptic Church in Egypt is in a sad condition, and the clergy are poor and ignorant. The Church Missionary Society of England established some years ago a theological seminary for the training of priests, and made efforts to circulate the Bible among these Monophysite Christians. The Mission was subsequently transferred to the care of the Presbyterian Church of the United States, and the work greatly prospered until the Coptic patriarch, who resides in Cairo, instituted a fierce persecution against all the Copts associating with the Missionaries, causing their children to be beaten and withdrawn from the schools and burning all the Bibles and religious books that he could find. The good work, however, still goes on, and I had the privilege one Sabbath morning of hearing a sermon by a native minister preached to a large congregation of native Christians. There are now quite a number of Christian Churches and Missionary stations in the city.

Our steamer, of the Messageries line, was delayed by an accident at Port Said, and this gave us the time in Egypt which we had lost in coming. But along with the delay came rumors of quarantine in Italy, on account of the plague in the East, and before us rose visions of confinement in some desolate place, dreadful fumigations and all the horrors of inhibition. Telegrams were flying rapidly, and our fears were calmed. The hour when the *Labourdonnais* should leave Alexandria was fixed, and soon we were rattling rapidly, for an Egyptian railway, over the 130 miles between the capital and the great commercial city of Egypt. In the East they do as the pickpockets—"take things easy," and an Egyptian railway is no exception. When once the train stops at a station it requires an endless amount of horn-tooting, and bell-ringing and shouting to get started again. As we journeyed along I witnessed a sunset scene, that was beautiful beyond description. There was the sun, large, full-orbed, hanging like a great globe of gold on the horizon, over the desert, filling the firmament with the most gorgeous hues of purple, pink, and orange, flinging its radiance over the Nile valley, flooding with glory the waving palm trees, and converting the peaks and pinnacles of the eastern hills into towers and structures of lapis lazuli, turquoise, and amethyst. As the golden orb of day sank down behind the ocean of sand, a lovely purple flush diffused its brilliance over the whole circle of the hemisphere. No twilight followed; at once the darkness came and the stars shone out.

Early next morning we were on board the steamer, and at nine our vessel had turned her prow for Naples. The first day was pleasant enough but soon a dreadful storm arose. I seem a regular Jonah, always bringing a storm with me; and this time the equinoctial gales came at least a week in advance, and we were terribly battered by wind and wave. I no longer cherish the impression that the Mediterranean is a comparatively quiet sea. Its waters are classical, and it is a *moving* sea, for one thing seems to bring up another. After three long days and nights the wind abated, and the sea grew calm. Another day and the beautiful coast of Sicily is in sight. Mount Etna lifts up its head. We enter the Straits of Messina, and pass between the famous rocks. On one side the rock of Scylla, a spur of the rugged mountains of Calabria projects into the sea; on the other side the hills of Sicily, and near the famous whirlpool of Charybdis. What says the Latin poet? "*Incidit in Scyllam qui vult vitare Charybdim.*" As we ran the gauntlet of that once terrible sea we began to think that it was not considered so dreadful by ancient sailors as it was by ancient poets. I was up with the first gray light of dawn; and the incomparable scenery well repaid the loss of sleep. On one side Mount Etna, sending up its incense to the skies. Farther on Stromboli, "a lone volcanic isle" lifts its head in isolated grandeur out of the sea, the curling smoke rising from the lofty cone, and mingling with the clouds. Around, the beautiful Lipari Islands are set like gems in the blue sea. More and more the inexhaustible beauties of Southern Italy appear. Islands, bays, and singularly beautiful indentations of the coast; the sea itself a vast mosaic of many colors. At length the Bay of Naples, in all its beauty, bursts upon the view, and the city, beautiful for situation, rises from the incomparable azure of the sea in amphitheatre-like form. The vessel comes to anchor, and we once more set foot upon the soil of Italia.

Naples is most charmingly situated. We entered the magnificent Bay in the evening, with Capri, Ischia, and their sister islands rising like palaces out of the sea, or like sentinels guarding the entrance to the Bay; on either side, the girdling mountains, dotted with towns and villages, the gleaming lights of the city sweeping in a glorious circle around the indented coast, and rising terrace above terrace, and balcony after balcony, to the heights of St. Elmo. I thought it the most exquisite blending of the sublime and beautiful that I had ever beheld. The Italians have given characteristic names to their chief cities. Rome is the Eternal City; Genoa, the Superb; Turin, the Proud; Milan, the Grand; Lucca, the Industrious; Padua, the Learned; Bologna, the Fat; Florence, the Fair; and Naples, "la bella," the Beautiful.

Built at the foot and on the sloping sides of gentle hills, guarded by mountains, surrounded with charming valleys and suburban villas, with a bay whose matchless glories have been sung ever since the days of Virgil and Cicero; with a sea of the deepest blue and hills of the most glorious purple; with the heavens above, the brightest, the zephyrs the softest, and everything that nature can lavish of indescribable and unearthly beauty:

> "An ampler ether—a diviner air,
> And fields invested with purpureal gleams."

Naples is, for situation, pre-eminently the "Beautiful City."

But, on nearer approach, you find a strong blending of magnificence and misery, beauty and ugliness, finery and fashion, with dirt, vermin and deviltry; parks of shrubbery and flowers, charming promenades and lovely avenues, with rank on rank of balconies, and open windows crowded with handsome and gaily-dressed ladies; homes illumined with smiles, and light, and splendor and song; with the narrowest of narrow streets, where the tall, toppling tenements seem to meet overhead, crowded with the dirtiest, worst-smelling, most offensively acting people you ever met. The place is alive with people. Such masses, such throngs, such crowds as walk, ride, struggle, and bustle through the narrow cracks of streets, topped with dwellings five, six, seven, eight, and nine stories high. And, as the streets are alive with people, so the people are alive—at least, one would judge so, by the hunting that is pursued on the streets and door-steps, and every open place. Verily, it is a place of vermin!

First let us take a drive through this crowded city of half a million.

With life the streets o'erflow, exuberant
   As is their soil. There ranged the gaudy stalls
Well piled with fruit and glittering traffic plant
   Their motley ensigns—Pulcinello calls
His faithful votaries—Cappucini chant
   Their Lady's hymn—Calabria's bagpipe squalls—
Monks rant—empirics bawl—in pilgrim weeds
   The bandit tells his plunder with his beads!"

In a high-pitched gig we climb to the highest point of the city. San Martino, formerly a monastery city. The Convent is a rare old place. Its Museum is filled with beautiful works of every description. The church is one mass of marble, the costliest and most beautiful; altar, pavement, statues, all are superb. The view is very fine. From the balcony you look down upon the city, with its flat roofs, its churches, and towers, and palaces. What impressed me was the sounds that came up from the city. All around was quiet, but up from the busy city came the roar of traffic, the rattling of carriages, the hum of voices—some screaming, some singing—the shouting of pedlars, coachmen, and muleteers—an incessant din, a perfect Babel of tongues, a confused babble of innumerable voices. There towers Vesuvius, with its crest of smoke, "a pillar of cloud by day and of fire by night;" at its feet are fertile fields and gleaming villages. Yonder is Castellamare, Sorrento, and other towns memorable in history or famous for beauty; the islands of the Bay; and beyond, far as the eye can see, the glorious Mediterranean.

One of my earliest visits was to the National Museum, with its treasures of Greek and Roman art, and relics of antiquity. The Sculpture Gallery is a perfect world of marble sculptures, renowned masterpieces like the Farnese Bull and Hercules, and copies from world-famous marble forms. I cannot even mention the art-forms that I have noted in my diary as full of grace and beauty. Southern Italy was once the seat of Greek culture, and, in these sculptured bodies of gods and men, and the delicate, fair forms of women, you get a glimpse of the displays of wealth, refinement, and sensuous beauty in the far-off times before the Christian era. The Bronze Room is the finest in the world. The Etruscan Collection of vases, the coin collection, and the Egyptian antiquities are all interesting. The picture galleries contain about a thousand pictures, but none of any particular merit.

The one feature of unfailing interest, aside from statues, busts, household gods, mosaics, and relievos, is the collection from the buried cities of Herculaneum and Pompeii. In the relics, pearls, ornaments, household utensils, brushes, lamps, candelabra, articles of food, rice, beans, eggs, olives, figs, fruits, we have a complete picture of the ancient life, manners, and customs of these long-buried cities.

You see the very loaves of bread, just as they were taken from the oven, the lockets upon the bosom, the bracelets and rings upon the arms and fingers of the fair women that were overtaken by the storm of death. The charred masses of papyri have been unrolled and deciphered, and there they hang, to be read by the learned. A rare and wonderful place is this Museum, its collection is unique and unsurpassed!

The churches of Naples possess no architectural beauty or interest. I visited the Cathedral, celebrated for its silver altars, and the shrine of St. Januarius, the patron saint of Naples, whose blood, kept in a silver vessel, used to liquify once a year, and be carried through the city in solemn and gorgeous procession. The Jesuit Church is sumptuous; and another, whose name I have forgotten, contains the tombs of former kings, and that of the wife of Ferdinand II., who is now undergoing the process of being made a saint.

One greatly enjoys the Chiaja—the *Villa Reale*—a lovely and fashionable promenade—and the Victor Emmanuel Boulevard, a long and charming avenue, which has been rescued from the Bay and turned into a delightful resort, with its long avenues of trees, arbors, groves, fountains, and statues. It is the favorite lounging-place for Naples—city of amusement, luxury, and idleness—where the "sweet donothing" feeling exists in perfection.

The Grotto di Posilipo is a tunnel nearly 3,000 feet in length, cut through the rock; and on the top of this, in a neglected spot, is the reputed tomb of Virgil, the great poet of Latium.

Naples, or Neapolis, "the new city," a name given to it nearly three thousand years ago to distinguish it from Palæopolis, "the old city," was the favorite residence of Virgil, for his words are, "In Mantua born, but in Calabria bred, 'tis Naples owns me now, whose pastoral charms and rural toils and arms I sing."

There are many charming excursions about Naples. One is to Sorrento, the Syren's Town of the Greeks, the Surrentum of the Romans—the birthplace of Tasso embowered amid orange groves, gardens, and vineyards; another is to Amalfi, the scene of such stirring events in the middle ages; another to Pozzuoli, the Puteoli of Paul, where the apostle "tarried seven days" on his way to Rome, once crowded with the patricians of Rome, and filled with memories of such names as Scipio, Marius, Scylla, Pompey, Cæsar, Brutus, Augustus, and Tiberius; another to Baiæ, a city buried beneath the waves, of whose beauty Horace sings; and Cumæ, the home of the Cumæan sybil, from which place came the mysterious Sibylline books, supposed to contain the fate of the Roman Empire.

Capri is a romantic and lovely island gemmed with grottoes, the White Grotto where the waves resemble curdled milk, the Green Grotto, the Stalactite Grotto, and the celebrated Blue Grotto, where every tint is the brightest, most lustrous, most ravishing blue that can be imagined. On the summit of one of the craggy peaks are the ruins of the Villa di Tiberio, where that infamous old Emperor retired to revel in lust and profligacy and cruelty; and the cliff is still pointed out down which he used to hurl his victims a thousand feet over the blood-bespattered rocks into the seething sea.

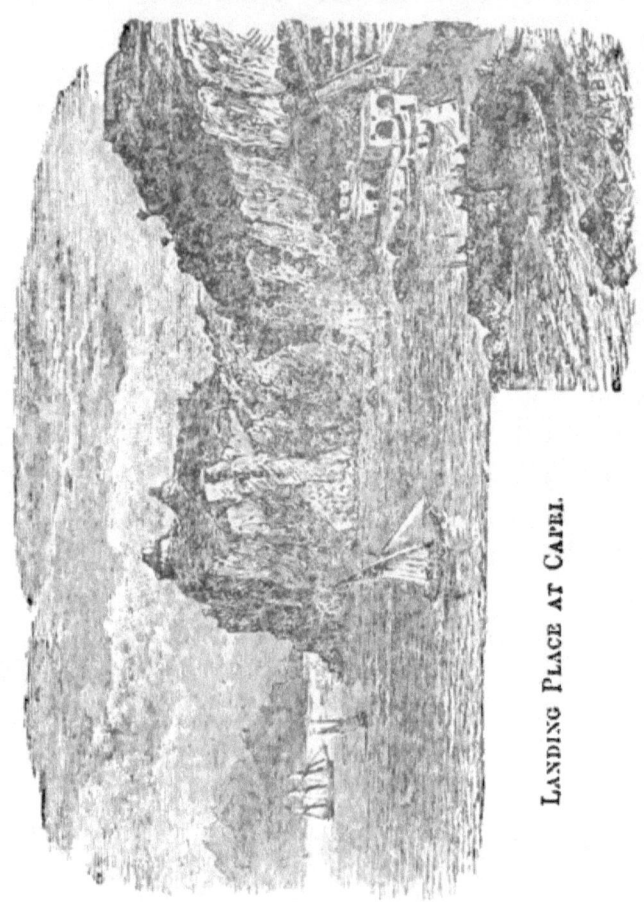

LANDING PLACE AT CAPRI.

But none of these has the interest of a visit to Pompeii, the city of the dead. The excursion is by train. You pay an admission fee of two francs, and are furnished with a guide, who conducts you over the city. What a strange feeling comes over you on entering the streets of a city which was in the full tide of its pride and glory when the blessed Saviour was on the earth, which passed out of existence when the beloved disciple, John, was still living in Ephesus, and which, after eighteen centuries, has been disentombed. We entered by the sea-gate, for Pompeii was built upon the shore of the sea, which has now retired to a

STEPS AT CAPRI.

distance of at least two miles. How impressive to wander up and down through temples, baths, theatres, to tread its narrow, roughly-paved roads, on which we see the very ruts worn by the wheels of wagons that rolled along 1,800 years before ; to feel the corpse-like stillness of the empty homes ; to see the floors inlaid with beautiful mosaics and read the warning *Cave Canem* or the welcome *Salve!*; the walls adorned with frescoes of exquisite beauty, but showing the fearful corruption of morals ; to intrude into the ladies' apartments and see the ornaments of dress, rings, pins, paints, all just as they were laid down twenty centuries ago ! The houses are small, and most of them stand just as they were, but roofless and doorless. Public baths, triumphal arches, and fountains abound. Temples, too, are numerous ; to Mercury, Venus, Jupiter, Hercules, and other gods. The Theatre is in perfect condition, with stage, corridors, and rows of marble seats capable of accommodating many thousand spectators, and close by the Military Barracks, where a large number of skeletons of soldiers were found, who had been faithful unto death. Near the Temple of Isis we heard the murmur of running water, and saw the stream which led to the indentification of Pompeii. A laborer in the middle of the last century found in ploughing a statue of brass, and afterward some workmen employed in the construction of a subterraneous aqueduct, came upon the Sarnus, and found an inscription, which established the fact that the once famous city of Pompeii, where Hercules is said to have celebrated his victories, had been discovered.

In the heart of the city is the Forum, the great lounging-place of the inhabitants, an extensive open area surrounded by shady porticoes; and opening upon it are the principal temples and the tribunal of justice. What impresses the visitor is the small scale of everything at Pompeii. The streets are extremely narrow, but they have a high-raised foot pavement. At the crossings are two or three large stepping-stones. The shops and dwellings are of the most minute dimensions, and the bedrooms are such little nooks, that one wonders how the inhabitants could have stowed themselves away. Even the dwellings of the wealthier inhabitants, as the house of Pansa, the house of Sallust, the house of Glaucus, are on a very limited plan; but how highly ornamented they were! " The smallest apartments were lined with stucco, painted in a most brilliant and endless variety of colors. In compartments simply tinted with a light ground, sometimes embellished with a single figure, or subject, in the centre, or at equal distances, and everywhere exhibiting that taste each individual of Pompeii seems to have been anxious to display. These paintings were very frequently of history, but embrace every variety of subject, some of the most exquisite beauty. Greek artists seem to have been employed; indeed native painters were few, while the former everywhere abounded."

The smallest houses seem to have been laid out with

elegant taste, and supplied with every appliance for luxurious enjoyment; the floors inlaid with mosaics at once cool and ornamental, the walls adorned with frescoes, in the atrium a fountain, and in the rear a garden. In the street-fountains you perceive that the marble is worn smooth where the hand rested, and where the faces pressed against the mouth of the statue.

On the way to the Villa of Diomedes is passed the cemetery, where sepulchral monuments and structures still remain in their splendor. The Romans had a passion for monumental exposure, and were very desirous to have their tombs placed in conspicuous and public situations, especially by the side of the great roads in the vicinity of towns. These sepulchres are as clearly marked on the east side of Pompeii as they are along the Appian Way. We threaded the subterranean chamber of the house of Diomedes, where the bodies of eighteen of the household were found. Hither they had betaken themselves for shelter and refuge, and no doubt died from suffocation. Various ornaments were found with their skeletons, and finger bones still adhered to trifling articles they had wished to preserve. The streets show trade-signs, and unfold the whole picture of the life of the city 1,800 years ago, when suddenly it was shrouded from human sight. The very mementos of sin are perpetuated; whole streets, that were given over to licentiousness, and walls with inscriptions and paintings that are nameless in indecency. Thus men and women are swept away as with the besom of destruction, while the story of their uncleanness and corruption is read through all the centuries. The ancient inhabitants are gone, but we can still actually step into their shops, enter their most private apartments, see their occupations, pleasures, sins, for the story of their life remains with the awful warning, "Be sure your sin will find you out."

The Museum contains, besides marbles, bronzes, implements of silver, brass, and stone, earthenware vases, and almost every article of household furniture or convenience; a complete toilet with combs, thimbles, paints, rings, almonds, dates, nuts, eggs, raisins, figs, and bread well baked, in fact old enough to be somewhat stale, and other objects of interest, many skeletons of the thousands who perished in the overthrow. There is the Roman sentinel who grasped his sword, and stood sternly at his post amid the sulphurous rain and dreadful thunders of that day. There is the skeleton of a woman who had fallen in the street, her right hand clutching a bag of money. A mother and daughter are seen, and the form of a beautiful woman with rings on her fingers, and the very tissue of her garments distinguishable. These bodies are not repulsive to look upon; they are rather the perfect cast and model of the form, than the body itself. The overthrow was not effected by a flood of burning lava, else marbles, bronzes, frescoes, everything would have been completely destroyed; but rather, by showers of ashes and scoriæ, and torrents of liquid mud, which encased all objects as in a mould. When the excavators came upon the bodies, of which about six hundred have already been found, where the mould was perfect, and the cavity, made by the flesh and bones crumbling away, remained intact it was filled up by pouring in liquid plaster of Paris. When this hardened and the ashes were removed there was the perfectly-moulded form, the exact counterpart of the human victim in the attitude and dress of the last supreme moment. Oh! what a day was that when the black smoke burst from the mountain, and, hiding the sun, overshadowed the whole land! Amid the Egyptian blackness came blue and sulphurous flashes of flame, followed by the terrible rain of ashes, and hot stones, and streaming torrents of black liquid mud, that rolled in rivers down the mountain sides, filled the streets, overwhelmed the deserted houses, and overtook the fleeing, panic-stricken inhabitants with a catastrophe like that which swept away the guilty Cities of the Plain. There is the old enemy looming up black and threatening, and how vividly comes home to our imagination the terrible drama, the mountain belching forth its smoke and torrents of lava, the falling of ashes like a funeral pall, the horror and consternation of the inhabitants overwhelmed with the terrors of earthquake and volcano.

I took a carriage to Annunziata, and the road lay

amid garden groves of orange and fertile vineyards. The rich, volcanic soil is covered everywhere with verdure and beauty. And yet there is the overhanging mountain, the old enemy ready to repeat its work of desolation. The railway which hurried us back to the city runs through deep cuttings in the old lava beds, between the mountain and the shore; stratum after stratum of mixed hue in which blue predominates. The entire district is volcanic, but everywhere is fertility and a teeming population. I should not like to dwell in such a place. Yet the people live carelessly on in their doomed dwellings, heedless of the danger, and fortified, perhaps, as I was during my brief stay, with the idea that things will last out their day in the place. Another grand excursion yet remained —the ascent of Vesuvius. This I had reserved for my last day in Naples. But, to my regret, I found that the railway was not sending a day excursion up the cone. The volcano of late had been unusually active. The disastrous earthquake on Ischia may have had something to do with the increased activity. At any rate the forge of Vulcan was in full blast. On our approaching Naples from the sea, long before the mountain was in sight, we saw the vast column of smoke rising and spreading for many and many a league. In the evening as the sun went down and the darkness gathered we saw the great red mouth of the crater, and the glowing lava gathered, and slipped, and glided like fiery serpents down the mountain side.

For these and other reasons there happened to be not a sufficient number to form an excursion by the Railway Company, so I made up my mind that I would try the old way of ascent—to go by train to Resina, hire a guide and horses to ride to the foot of the cone, and then clamber on foot as far as my strength would allow, through the slag and loose ashes, toward the crater. But I happened to go into a shop, and as I was looking at some pictures to my surprise there entered

CRATER OF MOUNT VESUVIUS.

some friends of Boston, among them Dr. and Mrs. Cullis. They also desired to make the ascent, and we were not long in making up the party. We deposited our twenty-five francs, and were soon in a large carriage rattling over the rough pavement through the noisest, dirtiest, and most crowded quarter of the city towards the mountain which, beautiful as it is at a distance, began to assume, on nearer approach, a dreary rugged appearance. Then came the long stretch of three and a half hours up the mountain side. As we toiled upwards in long zig-zags, what a magnificent panorama spread itself out before us. At our feet the great city itself, softened by distance, with its gardens and palaces, and over it the frowning and precipitous rock on which St. Elmo stands; the long sickle-like sweep of the shore, gay with suburbs, bright with towns and villas; the graceful curve of the unrivalled Bay, a sheet of soft but intense blue, dotted with white sails and islands set like emerald gems, while shimmering down upon all was the lustrous light of an Italian sky. A mist was sweeping up the slopes of the mountain, but the landscape below was bathed in a flood of mellow, unsullied, transparent light. Far as the eye could reach gleamed the brilliant Mediterranean, its waters like a perfect kaleidoscope, now a bright green, now a dark green, now a blue like the sky, now darker and deeper, and now all these colors combined, "a sea of glass mingled with fire!" We ascend the blackened sides to the observatory in the midst of a perfect wilderness of lava—fields, hills, valleys, deep ravines, all lava, twisted and fluted into all and every shape. Interspersed with barrenness and death are luxuriant verdure and smiling gardens. At length we reach the foot of the cone, and commit ourselves to the tender mercies of a railway that runs up, not quite perpendicularly, into the clouds.

The railway ascent to the top of the cone having

been made, we take to our feet, and scramble knee-deep in the ashes for twenty minutes or so when we come to the hard crust, around the crater's mouth. The " old inveterate smoker " was unusually active and his eye burned and glared like the eye of Cyclops. Sulphurous vapors rise and strong mephitic fumes threaten to suffocate us. We see the fires beneath. The guides attach a piece of paper to the ends of their walking-sticks, and at once it bursts into flame. We give them pennies and small coins, and they make impressions of them on the hot lava, which we bear away as souvenirs. The soles of our boots grow hot, the red-hot lava is beneath us, and only a thin crust separates us from the mass of fire. One of our party had a strong purpose to look into the very orifice of the volcano; but when he saw the vapors rising all around him, the numerous cracks and crevices, yellow and red-stained, and felt the hot breath of the fiery furnace, his ardor cooled. He thought he had gone far enough, he felt that he was at the very entrance of the infernal regions, and was glad to retrace his steps. The view of the crater is a wild, strange awful sight and has left a weird memory not unlike that of the famous Geysers of California, a desolate, dark, Plutonian region which seems to have been dedicated to Satan from the names given to the springs—" The Witch's Caldron," a horrible mouth of unknown depth; " The Devil's Punch Bowl," a large basin seven feet in diameter; " The Devil's Den," dark as Erebus; " The

Devil's Kitchen," where the black water bubbles and seethes, hisses and roars. Almost anywhere in the wild gorge, if you run your staff into the burnt soil steam will issue forth. Earthquakes are frequent, angry underground rumblings are heard; noise and fumes fill the air, boiling, frying, fizzing, simmering, steaming, sputtering, hissing. The Mountain of Fire has its hundred orifices, and the Steamboat Geyser sounds like a high-pressure boiler blowing off steam which rises a dense volume into the air. We leave the explanation of this California wonder with the philosophers and scientists; but Vesuvius had to me the strange fascination of the Geyser Canyon. The return to the car was much more easy than the ascent; laughing, and almost breathless, we made tremendous strides through the deep loose volcanic dust, the momentum carrying us on with increasing speed, our bodies every moment in danger of a headlong career. The railway descent appeared more dangerous than the ascent. It was like going down the side of a house a mile high. But we put away fear, and sang "Crown him Lord of all," "Hold the fort," "I need thee every hour," "Jesus, lover of my soul," and other sacred airs, to the great delight of our Italian companions and guides. Yes, every spot of earth belongs to Christ, and on the very summit of Vesuvius Jesus is Lord of all. We rolled quickly down the mountain side, and, weary enough reached our hotel about nine in the evening. Early next morning I was on the way to

Rome. Vesuvius was sending out its clouds of smoke which rolled down the mountain side till they reached a lower stratum of air, and then spread out over all the plain. The landscape looked more charming than ever as I felt that I was looking upon city and vineyards, mountain and shore, perhaps for the last time; and I tried to photograph upon my memory the surpassingly beautiful panorama. On we came to Caserta, the Versailles of Naples, with its royal palace and famous fountain; then to Capua, with its ramparts and churches, the old town which Hannibal conquered, then the second city in Italy, now dwindled to a miserable village; then to the ancient Casenum, with its colossal amphiteatre and its monastery, magnificently situated on a lofty mountain in the rear of the town, the site of an ancient temple of Apollo. The road leads along the slopes of the Apennines, and presently we are in the midst of walls, gateways, remnants of temples, triumphal arches, and other relics of antiquity. Yonder is a mighty aqueduct whose sweeping arches extend for miles and miles along the plain; all around are columns and masses of ruins. There is no mistaking these monuments. We are in the Campagna around the Eternal City. We dash past walls, and grass-grown mounds, and mouldering ruins until the train comes to a halt before a large station, and the guards call out "Rome!"

CHAPTER XV.

THE ETERNAL CITY.

Old Rome—The Forum—Mamertine Prison—*Via Sacra*—Arch of Titus—Coliseum—Arch of Constantine—Baths of Caracalla—Ruins of Cæsar's Palaces—Forum of Trajan—The Corso—Panorama of the City from the Pincian—St. Peter's—A Climb into the Ball—Interior of the Cathedral—The Vatican—Picture Gallery—Sistine Chapel—Vatican Museum—Library—Famous Statues—Theatre of Marcellus—Protestant Cemetery—St. Paul's—Church of Il Gesu—Santa Maria Sopra Minerva—Pantheon—Other Churches—Scala Santa—Museum of the Capitol—Palace of the Conservatori—Guido's Aurora—Barberini Palace—Doria—Corsini Borghese—Ghetto—Appian Way—*Domine Quo Vadis*—Catecombs—Tomb of Cecilia Metella—A Sabbath in Rome—Protestantism in Italy.

No city in Europe is so interesting and exciting to visit as Rome, the ancient centre of Western civilization, the City of the Republic and of the Empire, the proud City of the Cæsars. Next to Juerusalem, it stirs the profoundest feelings of the soul. In its monuments and remains of ancient grandeur are recorded the history of twenty-five centuries—nearly half of the entire duration since the days of Adam in Eden. The objects of interest are so endless and various that it is bewildering to attempt a description of those seven hills on which are stamped the impress of nearly thirty centuries. Rome Consular, Rome Imperial, Rome Pagan, Rome Christian, Rome Papal. Where shall we begin? Not with St. Peter's. Although Rome is the seat of the vastest ecclesiastical jurisdiction on the face of the earth, its wealth and power culminating in the most splendid edifices and columns, celebrating dogmas from the Immaculate Conception to the Infallibility of the Pope, nevertheless one is more interested in ancient than in modern and Papal Rome. Suppose we place ourselves in the very heart of old Rome, where the Senate had its assemblies, where the rostra were placed and the destinies of the world were discussed—the Forum Romanum. Standing in the excavated space let us glance around. We are at the foot of the Capitoline Hill, on which stood the Capitol and the famous temple, "the everlasting gates of Capitolian Jove." That old wall is a part of the Tabularium, built B.C. 78, for the reception of the Archives of the State.

We are amidst the remains of illustrious temples. Those ten pillars are the Basilica Julia, built by Cæsar, A.D. 40; and the three fluted columns the Temple of Saturn. Those eight formed part of the Temple of Vespasian. Near by is the Temple of Concord. One wonders that temples so famous in history should be so crowded together, and that each should occupy so small a space. Rising in the centre is a solitary pillar, the column of Phocas, of which Byron sings, "The nameless column, with a buried base." But it is no longer nameless or buried. Recent excacavations have brought its base to light, and resting on the ancient pavement of the Forum, it shows that this former centre of Roman life was in the seventh century still free from ruins. Here, "at the base of Pompey's statue," occurred the tragedy of Julius Cæsar, and here Mark Antony pronounced his oration. Close at hand is the Temple of Jupiter Tonans, and near by the Rostrum, where orators addressed the populace—

"Where the unworded accents flow,
And still the eloquent air breathes—burns with *Cicero*."

There stood the Golden Milestone, in which was marked the distances to all the chief cities of the world, and from which rayed out paved roads to every part of the empire. In the midst was the arch of Septimus Severus, a sumptuous marble structure erected in honor of that emperor and his two sons, Caracalla and Geta, who had achieved victories in the East over the Parthians and Persians. It was in front of this arch that the statue of Marcus Aurelius stood which now adorns the square of the Capitoline Museum. Behind this elaborately ornamented structure is the

Mamertine Prison. This is the fatal spot where, as the triumphal procession began to ascend the slopes of the Capitol, the most illustrious of the captives were led aside, and in that horrible dungeon, black and tomb-like, doomed to die.

> "Well might the great, the mighty of the world,
> They who were wont to fare deliciously
> And war but for a kingdom more or less,
> Shrink back, nor from their thrones endure to look,
> To think that way ! Well might they in their pomp
> Humble themselves, and kneel and supplicate
> To be delivered from a dream like this !"

It was excavated by Ancus Martius from the solid rock under the Capitol. It is a cold, dark cell, enclosed within walls of enormous tufa blocks. In the floor is a small opening, down which we descend into an inner and more horrible dungeon, the lower prison, called *Robur*. Let Sallust describe it: "A place about ten feet deep, surrounded by walls, with a vaulted roof of stone above it. The filth and darkness and stench make it indeed terrible." Here Jugurtha, King of Mauritania, was starved to death by Marius, and here the accomplices of Cataline were strangled, when Cicero came forth and said to the people in the Forum: " *Vixerunt* "— " They have ceased to live." Here, also, Appius, Claudius and Oppius, the decemvirs, committed suicide. Here Vercingetorix, the gallant enemy of Julius Cæsar, suffered, and also Simon Bar Gidras, the last defender of Jerusalem. The Papal legends have it St. Peter was imprisoned here too, and a spring of water is pointed out as having burst miraculously from the rock to furnish water for the baptism of one of the guards converted through his instrumentality. An indentation in the wall is also shown as the place against which the hard-hearted jailor jammed the head of the apostle—thick-skulled, hard-headed Peter!

Here tradition has it that St. Paul, the aged, was imprisoned before his execution. If so, no wonder the damp, chill air of that subterranean vault made the veteran hero ask for the cloak which he had left at Troas. From this place it is believed he addressed his immortal farewell to the Christian world: "For I am now ready to be offered, and the time of my departure is at hand. I have fought a good fight, I have finished my course, I have kept the faith. Henceforth there is laid up for me a crown of righteousness, which the Lord, the righteous judge, shall give me at that day; and not to me only, but unto all them also that love his appearing." 2 Tim. iv. 6-8.

Now we ascend the Capitoline, which towers above the temples in the Forum, and take a look at the Tarpeian Rock, from which traitors had to leap to their execution. We stand in the very centre of all the glories of old Rome, and overlook the ground on which so many illustrious actions were performed. We trace the windings of the Sacred Way. How many triumphant legions have trodden that pavement! How many captive and humbled kings!

What throngs of cars and glittering chariots! On this spot Rome enthroned her heroes. Right around us are the famous hills from which Rome took the name of the seven-hilled city. We stand on the Capitoline. Yonder is the Palatine; beyond, the Aventine; beyond that, the Coelian. To our right is the Quirinal; beyond that is the Esquiline; and between them the Viminal. These are the hills enclosed within the walls of Servius Tullius. Of course, we must see the Wolf, nourished and kept sleek and fat, in commemoration of its illustrious ancestress, that sustained the half-mythical founder of the city.

Descending again to the Forum, let us traverse the *Via Sacra*, the street which led from the southern gate of Rome to the Capitol, and over which the victorious generals and conquerors of nations passed in their stately processions to the crowning sacrifice in the Temple of Jupiter. The very dust we tread stirs as with life, for these huge blocks of lava, that form the ancient pavement, have been trodden by the feet of all the illustrious men of Consular and Imperial Rome. Here, crowded together, are the remains of basilicas, temples, arches, rostra statues, and monuments of splendor. On one side is the Esquiline, where were the residences of Mæcenas, Horace, and Virgil; on the other side the Palatine, the very cradle of Rome—the original city of Romulus, now a labyrinth of ruins, the ruins of Cæsar's Palaces and the Golden House of Nero. To the left we see the Basilica of Constantine, whose three colossal arches are said to have suggested to Michael Angelo the plan of St. Peter's. This site was previously occupied by the *Temple of Peace*, which was the great museum of Rome under the Empire, and contained the treasures brought from Jerusalem, and the works of art that had been collected in the palace of Nero. This temple was burned down in the time of Commodus.

"*In Summa Via Sacra*," on the highest spot of the Sacred Way, is the Arch of Titus, of Grecian marble and exquisite proportions, erected by the Senate, A.D. 70, to commemorate the fall of Jerusalem. The sculptures on this imposing and famous monument are nearly perfect. You see the captive Jews, the Ark of the Covenant, the golden candlesticks, the silver trumpets, and other sacred utensils; and, as you stand under the arch, you think of all Rome making holiday, as the proud Conqueror and his train passed over these very flagstones on which we stand, bearing all the holy things from the Temple of Jerusalem as spoils to the Capitol.

On the frieze is the sacred river Jordan, borne on a bier as an aged man. The bas-relief of the seven branched candlestick is so perfect that in mediæval times this beautiful monument was called the Arch of the Seven Candlesticks. In the centre of the arch, Titus is borne to heaven by an eagle. To this day no Jew will pass under this arch, but turns aside with downcast eyes and averted countenance, and spits violently in detestation as he passes by. To the left is the Temple of *Venus and Roma*, the last Pagan temple which remained in use in Rome. It was closed by Theodosius in A.D. 391, and all that now remains of it is the cella, facing the Coliseum, and a mass of Corinthian cornice; but the ground around is strewed with fragments of columns which once joined the Grand Portico.

Now we have reached the world-famous Coliseum, "a noble wreck, in ruinous perfection," alive and teeming with historical recollections. Begun by Vespasian, who built as far as the third row of arches, it was completed by Titus after his return from the conquest of Jerusalem, and he is said to have employed twelve thousand captive Jews in its erection. What a structure it is! So vast, that one can hardly picture it in the imagination, or take in its height and sweep. Its circumference is more than sixteen hundred feet. It is an oval, 620 feet long, 573 in breadth, and 157 feet high. What splendid masonry! Now a mouldering ruin, scarce one-third of it remaining, stripped of its marble, and colored walls, and iron clamps; yet, what remains has been computed to be worth over half a million pounds sterling. As I climbed to the highest tiers, and looked over the empty space, the *podium*, containing the places of honor for the Emperor and his family, the senators, and the vestal virgins, once covered with costly marble, the arches glittering with gold and gems, I thought of the dedication festival, when 5,000 wild animals fought with gladiators, and the arena was red with the butchery, the galleries crowded with excited spectators, the Emperor, the senators, the vestal virgins, the knights, and common people ; I thought of the after scenes, in the days of persecution, when 100,000 voices roared, " The Christians to the lions. The Christians to the lions!" and brave men and timid women surrendered themselves to the devouring wild beasts.

EXTERIOR OF THE COLOSSEUM.

Magnificent abode of pleasure and of wickedness! There it stands, a monument of the cruelty of old Rome, and of the faith of the early martyrs. There it stands, built as if not for time but eternity, in its solitude, its awful beauty, its majesty, the most impressive sight conceivable. Not a day was I in Rome in which I did not visit the Coliseum, and to see it by moonlight is a vision which can never be forgotten.

> " Arches on arches ! as it were that Rome,
> Collecting the chief trophies of her line,
> Would build up all her triumphs in one dome,
> Her Coliseum stands ; the moonbeams shine
> As 'twere its natural torches, for Divine
> Should be the light which streams here to illume
> The long-explored, but still exhaustless mine
> Of contemplation ; and the azure gloom
> Of an Italian night, where the deep skies assume
> Hues which have words, and speak to ye of heaven,
> Floats o'er this vast and wondrous monument,
> And shadows forth its glory. There is given
> Under the things of earth, which Time hath bent,
> A spirit's feeling, and where he hath leant
> His hand, but broke his scythe, there is a power
> And magic in the ruined battlement,
> For which the palace of the present hour
> Must yield its pomp, and wait till ages are its dower."
>
> —CHILDE HAROLD.

In front of this great sweep of walls are the remains of the basin and the fountain called *Meta Sudans*, where the gladiators, after tearing and being torn, used to wash ; and here the Via Triumphalis leads to the Via Appia, passing under the triple arch of Constantine, one of the most strikingly beautiful of Roman arches, of fine proportions, but its delicately cut bas-reliefs and decorations were plundered from an arch originally erected in honor of Trajan. Upon its pilasters stand, with folded hands, the stately captive kings and warriors of Dacia, whom Trajan brought to Rome. Not far away are the Baths of Caracalla, a very city of tumbling walls and arches, whose ruins, a mile in circumference, are an imperishable monument of the unparalleled splendor and luxury of Rome when she was supreme mistress of the world. What rooms of splendor! The floors and ceilings of the immense establishment of mosaics, the walls faced with costly marbles, or decorated with frescoes and innumerable statues, that peopled the arcades and colonnades with beauty. There are the walls of the Calidarium, or hot bath, the Frigidarium, or cold bath, the Tepidarium, or warm bath. The mighty structure could accommodate 16,000 bathers at one time; and in these halls of pomp and luxury the Roman youth frittered away their hours, and spent the night in the indulgence of gross and revolting sensuality. The views from the summit of these walls are enchanting; hill, vale and city in ever-varying combinations, the lovely Alban and Sabine mountains, the melancholy stretches of the Campagna, the Eternal City with its palaces and domes, and over all the bright blue sky of Italy. It was from the summit of these mountain walls and dizzy arches that Shelley gave to the world his great drama, " Prometheus Unbound."

Now we return to the Via Sacra, and close to the Arch of Titus ascend a flight of steps to the lordly Palatine, the original site and centre of the metropolis of the world. Back to the period before Romulus, in the earliest age of that country, that which preceded the birth of Rome, can be traced the history of the Palatine. Tradition connects this hill with the fabled colony of the Trojans, who settled in Italy under the pious Æneas. Here the shepherd-king Evander is represented by Virgil as welcoming Æneas. Here dwelt the half mythical founder of Rome. Augustus was born here, and to this ancient seat of the Kings he transferred his residence. Here was the golden house of Nero. Here rose palace after palace of imperial splendor. The quarries of the world were ransacked for costly marbles, pure and white, or veined with purple and gold, until Palatium, the name of the hill, became synonymous with palaces. Now we see but the silent memorials of past grandeur. Everywhere are ruins and desolations, roofless columns, shattered walls, fragments of mosaics; but the classical memories and associations of the spot charm the imagination, and the heart is impressed with the surrounding witnesses of departed empire.

"Behold the Imperial Mount! 'Tis thus the mighty falls."

We strolled about among arches, towers, chambers, halls, in the very centre and home of kingly pomp, and examined objects in ivory, bronze, and terra cotta; figure heads, vases, broken columns, architectural carvings, and sculptures, that once adorned these palaces of empire, and arches of triumphal power. What a spot in which to muse upon the transitoriness of earthly grandeur! Rome, fountain of all mighty memories, once queen of the earth, how hast thou fallen! And yet her ancient mantle of renown still cloaks her ruins, and we forget her present misery, weakness, and sins, in the memorials of her vanished splendors.

The Palace of Vespasian was built on the top of that of Augustus, and we descend into rooms underneath, excavated from that palace, begun shortly after the battle of Actium. In the palace of the Cæsars is the Basilica, or Ancient Law Court, and this ruin was the actual place in which St. Paul was brought in fetters before the adulterous and blood-thirsty Nero. Beyond the Basilica is the Tablinum, or great hall of the palace; then the Peristyle, an open court surrounded with arcades, ornamented with statues. Now we reach the *Triclinium*, or dining-room, off which is the *Nymphæum*, its pavement of oriental alabaster with a beautiful fountain, surrounded by little niches once filled with bronzes and statues, and just beyond is the *Vomitarium* with its basin, to which the royal feasters retired with feather to tickle their throats, and then return with renewed appetite to the banquet board. Verily these old Romans were sumptuous fellows! There are also the ruins of the *Palace of Tiberius*, and the vast ruins of the *Palace of Caligula;* ruins of small temples, the famous temple of Cybele, "Mother of the gods," *Temple of Apollo*, Temple of *Juno Sospita*, of *Minerva*, a temple of moonlight and a shrine of Vesta—ruins, nothing but ruins.

> "Cypress and ivy, weed and wall-flower grown
> Matted and massed together, hillocks heap'd

B l

> On what were chambers, arch crushed, columns strewn
> In fragments, choked-up vaults, and frescoes steeped
> In subterranean damps, where the owl peep'd,
> Deeming it midnight."   —CHILDE HAROLD.

We gathered some wild flowers, and descended weary enough with our day's stroll over the Palatine.

Another monument of old Rome is the *Forum of Trajan*, the marble fragments of which tell of former magnificence. The four rows of pillars are the columns of the Basilica Ulpia. Towering over the Forum is the beautiful Column of Trajan, a wonder of art, on whose spiral bands of bas-reliefs are carved not less than two thousand five hundred human figures, besides numberless other objects. The sculpturing is by Apollodorus, and the forms, illustrative of the Dacian wars, increase in size toward the top, so as to preserve the same proportion throughout when seen from below. It is nearly 150 feet high; and where once stood the statue of the Emperor holding a gilt globe, is now the bronze figure of St. Peter. Very similar to this is the column of Marcus Aurelius, its relievos representing the wars of that Emperor. The column is now surmounted with a statue of St. Paul!

For a view of the city, let us drive through the principal street—the Corso—and past some of the charming fountains, with which Rome abounds, adorned with rock-work and statuary. The Trevi is magnificent, the central figure of which is "Neptune," careering with his watery steeds, and Tritons blowing their horns about him. The water of this fountain is in great regard far and wide, and the traveller who takes a parting draught is sure to return again to Rome. We like the winding road up the terraces of the Pincian, or hill of gardens. This is the fashionable drive and promenade—the Hyde Park of Rome—and a little before sunset it presents a gay and brilliant scene. From this place of gardens, and fountains, and statues, where Lucullus once luxuriated, and the infamous Messalina, the fifth wife of Claudius, revelled, what a panorama of the city is obtained— its domes and palaces gleaming in the golden light of the setting sun like a New Jerusalem! What is that structure rising in matchless beauty, and standing out in noble grandeur against the sky—the sweet blue sky of this lovely land? It is the dome of St. Peter's, the most famous church of Christendom, the world's cathedral, the greatest structure ever built by man. To the right is the Vatican, in front is the Castle of St. Angelo, to the left is the steep crest of Janiculum, where stood the temple of the war-god Janus, its gates closed only in time of peace. That vast circular dome, the most magnificent in the world, is the Pantheon, a temple built by Marcus Agrippa, B.C. 27, and dedicated "to all the gods." Through all the mass of buildings we trace the windings of the yellow Tiber, until it is lost in the wide Campagna, while the silver line beyond marks the sea melting into the horizon beyond Ostra. A turn or two through the grounds, embellished with statues, columns, pines, and cypresses, and sparkling with fountains, and a view of the charming gardens of the Villa Borghese, and the sun has set so that we must hasten to our hotel.

Among all the churches of Rome the most notable is St. Peter's. We cross the Tiber by the Ponte St. Angelo, built by Hadrian, A.D. 130. This bridge has on it ten figures of angels, each bearing some symbol of the Passion—the nail, the spear, the crown of thorns, etc. These angels have been called the "Breezy maniacs" of Bernini. Facing the bridge is the famous Castle of St. Angelo, originally Hadrian's tomb, transformed into a fortress in the sixth century. It takes its name from the massive figure of the archangel Michael sheathing his sword, as that high personage was seen by Pope Gregory while he was praying for the cessation of the Great Plague, standing on the summit of the Mausoleum, sheathing a bloody sword while a choir of angels were chanting with celestial voices. A little further on we enter the Piazza Rusticucci, and there bursts upon us the sweeping colonnades, having in the centre the granite obelisk, brought from Heliopolis by Caligula. Who has not heard the story of "Wet the ropes?" It had its origin in what occurred when this huge monument of 500 tons weight was being erected by Pope Sixtus on its present site. On the pavement round this obelisk the points of the compass are marked off, and the signs of the Zodiac. On each side a great fountain sends up its sun-lit spray, which falls with ceaseless splashing into marble basins, and farther to the left and right are the imposing colonnades, which form a covered way. The two hundred and eighty-four Doric columns are in four series—a perfect forest of columns—and on the roof of these covered passages are one hundred and twenty-six colossal statues of saints. All this is the work of Bernini.

Now we ascend the magnificent flight of steps and pass through the central entrance, over which is the Loggia, where the Sovereign Pontiff is crowned, and from which he used to give his Easter benediction. What a glorious temple! We are awed by the immensity and magnificence, the proportions and grandeur of the marvellous structure, and dazzled by its gorgeous beauty and splendor. The guide-books give the measurements, and they are truly amazing; but such is the wonderful symmetry and harmony of the structure, that you do not realize its colossal proportions. Its size grows on you, especially as you note on the pavement the length of other great churches like St. Paul's, Milan, Florence Cathedrals, and St. Sophia's, at Constantinople. Measure those little cherubs' fingers, they are good-sized arms; and look at the bronze figure of Peter, which seems from the door two or three feet high, but is nearly double life size. The central nave is surpassingly grand, and is flanked by marble arcades, and aisles, and transepts, enriched with variegated marbles and mosaic copies of famous pictures. We cannot attempt to describe the Bronze Canopy, and High Altar, and Tribune, and Sacristy, and Choir Chapel, with its music like the morning stars singing together, when the great organ and choir roll out their swelling billows of harmony. Let us hasten to ascend the Dome, which is 630 feet in circumference, and rises over 300 feet above the high roof, which, with its smaller domes and structures, appears a village in itself.

As you ascend, you find that you are in illustrious company, for on the walls are the tablet inscriptions of many royal personages who have climbed up into the ball: the Prince of Wales, the sons of the Emperor of Russia, Queen Isabella of Spain, Empress of Mexico, and many others. Note also the monumental inscriptions over tombs, and sarcophagi—among them one to the "Great and Clement Mary, Queen of Britain."

From the galleries within the dome you get a striking view of the interior, and look down upon men and women, who appear like little dwarfs walking about. On and up we climb to the Lantern, then up a narrow staircase right into the Ball of St. Peter's. The view from this point is not very striking as it is confined to the eight or ten persons huddled in with you; but the outlook from the Lantern, on such a day as that with which we were favored, is enrapturing. Below is the seven-hilled city; in the distance, the deep blue shadows of the Alban and the Sabine Mountains; beyond, far as the eye can reach, the shining expanse of the Mediterranean; and all around, like a sea, the vast sweep of the Roman Campagna, once a garden of fertility and beauty, but now become, after a thousand years of papal misgovernment, a pestilential marsh and howling wilderness.

Now we descend, and again traverse the interior of the structure, which surpasses all description, and seems more like a great work of nature than the achievement of man. No wonder that three centuries were required to bring the edifice to its present form, that its erection cost over sixty millions of dollars, exhausting the treasures of forty-three Popes, and requiring the sale of indulgences, against which Luther thundered, to bring in the vast sums needed. It is a matchless show-room. I visited it several times. On the last day a mass was being celebrated for the soul of the Pope's brother, when the music was surpassingly fine, and the pageantry throughout very imposing.

From St. Peter's we enter the Vatican, ascending to the Picture Galleries by the grandest staircase in the world, the *Scala Regia*, decorated with frescoes illustrating the history of the Popes and guarded by Swiss soldiers in their picturesque costume. I was disappointed in the extent of the collection in the Gallery of Pictures; but each picture is a delight and full of effective expression. I cannot dwell on the immortal creations of Raphael, his "Faith, Hope, and Charity," "The Madonna di Foligno," the angel in the foreground being one of the most marvellous figures ever created by art; "The Coronation of the Virgin," and "The Transfiguration," the last picture that came from the painter's hand, and the grandest in the world. Titian's "Madonna and Saints," Guido Reni's "Martyrdom of St. Peter," Paul Veronese's "Dream of St. Helena." "The Last Communion of St. Jerome," that master-piece of *Domenichino*, one of the most celebrated pictures in the world, second only to the Transfiguration; "The Resurrection," by Perugino; and the works of Guercino, Murillo, and such masters. The Loggie of Raphael is called Raphael's Bible, the frescoes being all scenes from the Bible, forty-eight being taken from the Old Testament and four from the New. It is a master-piece of decorative art. The "Camera" of Raphael are four rooms of frescoes executed by that master. Here are the famous "Battles of Constantine," "Triumph of the Church," and "The School of Athens," a picture in which the great characters of antiquity, the kings of thought, are embodied and stand out clear and unmistakable. In the centre on the steps of a portico are seen Plato and Aristotle, on the left is Socrates with his pupils, on the right is Archimedes drawing a problem upon the floor, in front is Diogenes, and behind are Zoroaster and Ptolemy. Now let us proceed to the Sistine

Chapel, the ceiling of which was painted by Michael Angelo. It is his crowning work. He was two years in accomplishing the task and his eyes became so set in his head that he could not read a letter until he placed it above his forehead. The ceiling is in nine sections, which embody the great events from the Creation to the Deluge. The architect as well as the painter is shown in the columns, pillars, and cornices of the majestic structures by which these scenes are connected. The lower portion of the ceiling is divided into triangles occupied by the Prophets and Sibyls in alternation. What majestic figures are Isaiah and Ezekiel and Daniel! Once seen they can never be forgotten. Zachariah is an aged man, Jeremiah is bowed down in grief, while the Sibyls are full of power. The "Last Judgment" occupies the entire altar wall. It occupied the artist seven years, and a marvellous but truly terrible picture it is. In the upper half we see Christ the Judge surrounded by Apostles, Patriarchs, Saints, and Martyrs; in the lower half are naked beings given up to despair and anguish, and to their hellish tormenters. Among the rising dead in hell is the face of Biagio da Cesena. He was master of the ceremonies of Pope Paul IV., and had complained to the Pope of the picture on account of the indelicacy of the naked figures. In revenge the artist painted his face as Midas, with ass's ears, and when, in real distress, he came to Paul IV., the Pope asked, "And where has he put you?" "In hell," was the answer.

"Ah!" said the Pope, "then I can do nothing for you. If it had been in purgatory I might have got you out, but over hell I have no power." And there he is to this day. We cannot explore the mysteries of the eleven thousand chambers of the Vatican, or go through that portion inhabited by the Pontiff who keeps himself a prisoner in that palace home. The Vatican museum is a collection of antiquities and statues, one of the finest in the world. The entrance is through a narrow corridor more than two thousand feet in length, the sides of which are covered on the right with Pagan, on the left with early Christian inscriptions. Along the gallery of inscription are Sarcophagi, vases, torsos, cornices, bas-reliefs, and specimens of everything dug up under and about Rome. Ten rooms are fitted with Egyptian antiquities, and twelve with Etruscan terra-cottas, cinerary urns, vases, jewels, and ornaments. But who can describe the gems of sculpture, the marvels of art that adorn the vestibules and cabinets! There is the *Minerva Medica*, which alone is worth a pilgrimage around the earth to see; the Torso Belvidere found in the baths of Caracalla, before which Michael Angelo, old and blind, used to stand and pass his fingers over the mutilated lines, and enjoy through touch the grandeur of this breathing stone; the Antinous, considered by many artists the most beautiful statue in the world; the Laocoon, that wonderful group, the father, the two sons, and the serpents, with their awful

Sketches of Travel. 395

folds, formed out of a single block; the Apollo Belvedere, brother of Minerva; the immortal thought, the immortal action; the Perseus by Canova the sleeping Ariadne, the Colossal form of Hercules, with busts of emperors, philosophers, and poets, and figures of heroes, gods, and goddesses. The library of the Vatican is an enormous collection, there being no less than twenty-three thousand Greek, Latin, and Oriental MSS., but it is somewhat disappointing to go through it as no books or manuscripts are visible all being enclosed in painted cupboards.

During my stay in the Eternal City I gave the mornings to galleries of art and churches, the afternoons to drives in and about the city.

Let me give you an afternoon's excursion. We drive through the Corso, past the column of the Immaculate Conception, erected by Pius IX, in 1854, in honor of that dogma, and the Propaganda buildings, the great missionary centre of Romanism, erected by Pope Gregory in 1662.

In this college, youths of all nations are educated as Missionaries for any part of the world. We visit the Theatre of Marcellus, a huge edifice, the oldest theatre in the world, built by Augustus, B.C. 20, and said to have accommodated 20,000 spectators; also, the Temple of Vesta, a picturesque round building of Parian marble with twenty Corinthian columns, covered by a slight roof. It consists of one simple apartment, lined with white marble, a pearl of beauty and fair type of a vestal virgin. Near by is the house of Rienzi, "the forum's champion and the people's chief," and next at hand the Ponte Rotto, a re-erection of the Pons Æmelius begun B.C. 142, and standing upon this, we see the ruins of the famous Pons Lublicius, the oldest bridge in Rome, and which the "brave Horatius" kept against the army of Lars Porsenna. A ride of half an hour brings us to the famous St. Paul's without the gate. It is built on the site of a church erected by Constantine to commemorate the martyrdom of St. Paul. It is a most gorgeous and imposing structure. Not an inch, from floor to ceiling, but is covered with marble the most costly and beautiful—columns of oriental alabaster, altars of malachite, splendid mosaics, richly decorated shrines, celebrated sculptures, and marbles from the famed quarries of the world, make up the picture of this splendid show-room, erected at a cost of millions in a suburb deserted, and with scarcely a human habitation near. We returned by the way of the Protestant Cemetery. What pathos in that little spot, shaded by cypress trees, and carpeted with violets. We paid homage to the memory of Gibson, the English sculptor, and Shelley the poet, whose heart is buried here; and poor Keats, on whose tombstone we read the words which he desired to have engraven there, "Here lies one whose name was writ in water." Close to this quiet spot is the Pyramid tomb of Caius Cestius, who, some thirty years before Christ, mimicked the Pharaohs in his form of sepulchre. How suggestive is the thought that near this sepulchural pyramid on which the eye of St. Paul must have rested as he was led to execution, beyond the city walls, on the very spot where rested his dying glance, and near the soil watered by his blood, sleep our dead countrymen who have passed away in a foreign land, and whom Papal Rome suffers there to rest. From the fields in front of the cemetery rises an extraordinary formation, the Monte Testaccio, an isolated mound, 165 feet high, the rubbish-heap of ancient Rome.

One of the most gorgeous of the churches in Rome is the vast church of Il Gesu. It is magnificently adorned with marbles, mosaics, silver altars, columns of lapis lazuli, and precious stones that dazzle the eye and bewilder with their splendor. In this church lie the remains of St. Ignatius Loyola, in an urn of gilt bronze, adorned with precious stones, and above the altar, in the hand of a figure of the Almighty, is a globe of lapis lazuli said to be the largest in existence. Not far away is the Santa Maria Sopra Minerva, a church built upon the ruins of Pompey's temple to Minerva, and remarkable as being the only Gothic Church in Rome. On the left of the high altar is Michael Angelo's "Christ with the Cross," the right foot marred by a bronze shoe, a necessary protection against the kisses of the devout. The statue is one of Angelo's divine and gentle creations. The form is delicately moulded; the face is one of ineffable attraction, and as he stands in gentle majesty, holding a heavy cross, the story is told of Him who bore it and was crucified upon it, "for us men and for our salvation." Here is the tomb of Fra Angelico da Fiesole, the angelic painter, and in the choir are the tombs of two Medici popes. Near this church is the most perfect relic of ancient Rome, the Pantheon. It is a vast circular structure, exquisitely proportioned, and surmounted by the most magnificent dome in the world:—

> "Simple, erect, severe, austere, sublime,
> Shrine of all saints, and temple of all gods."

Twenty-seven years before Christ's birth was this temple built, and it stands almost perfect and intact to-day the "pride of Rome." On this pavement trod the feet of Augustus and Agrippa. From these pagan altars of gold ascended incense to divinities of old that have long since crumbled into oblivion. It is lighted by a circular opening in the dome forty feet in diameter, and the effect is very striking. The dome itself is an exact hemisphere, and a "thing of beauty." The bronze doors, the vast colonnade, and walls twenty feet in thickness give a faint idea of the massiveness of this structure, which has withstood so long the ravages of time, but the decorations of bronze, and marble have been stripped to enrich modern edifices. The Pantheon was consecrated as a Christian church about the year 600, by Pope Boniface IV. It has become the burial place of celebrated artists, and here sleep Raphael, Caracci, Taddeo Zucchero, Baldassare Peruzzi, and others. There is also a sumptuous monument to King Victor Immanuel. I did not visit all the four hundred churches of Rome, eighty of which are dedicated to the Virgin Mary; neither have I space to describe those that I did visit.

The Church of St. John Lateran is, however, too important to pass without brief notice. It is the Metropolitan Church of Rome. Its adjoining palace was the residence of the popes for a thousand years. Five Councils have been held within its walls. Its famous chapels are the Torlonia, richly decorated with marble and gilding, and the Corsini, the marble walls of which blaze with precious stones. Beneath the chapel is a vault, lined with sarcophagi of the Corsini, and its altar is surmounted by a magnificent Pieta, by Bernini. No sacred form in marble impressed me more than this. Surely there never was chiselled such a hand as that of the dead Christ!

San Pietro, in Vincoli, the church which holds the chains of St. Peter, contains the famous statue of Moses, by Michael Angelo. On either side of the figure of the great law-giver and prophet are the statues of Rachel and Leah, emblematic of active and contemplative life: but we carry with us, and shall through life, that form of unapproachable sublimity, with long flowing beard descending to the waist, with deep-sunk eyes, and brow of majesty with its horns of power.

St. Clements consists of an upper church, very old;

a lower church, built in the fourth century, first discovered in 1857; and below that, a heathen temple discovered in 1867. Its layers of stone belong to early Christian, Imperial and Republican Rome. The frescoes in the lower church are very interesting, and represent the dawn of Christian Art, while there are several pillars of the rarest marbles in perfect preservation.

The Santa Maria Maggiore is one of the oldest churches in Christendom, and the most perfect of the Basilicas at Rome. It contains the great relic, the Santa Culla, taken from Bethlehem, and has also preserved, in two little bags, the brains of St. Thomas à Becket. There are five doors leading into the magnificent nave, one of which is the Porta Santa, only opened once in twenty-five years, when the eager worshippers press into the church and to the altar by a way most of them never before trod, and never will again.

The Conventual Church of the Cappuccini has among its pictures the singularly striking one by Guido, of the Archangel Michael trampling upon the Devil—the fiend's face being a portrait of Pope Innocent X., against whom the great painter had a grudge. There is the famous cemetery, consisting of four chambers, filled with sacred earth brought from Jerusalem, ornamented with mummified bodies and bones of six thousand monks, set in mosaics, and architectural devices, altars, bas-reliefs, columns, arches, all of human limbs, and topped with grinning skulls.

The last of the Romish churches that we shall refer to is the *Scala Santa*. I was shown in Jerusalem the place in the Palace of Pilate, from which these marble steps were taken. They were brought to Rome by the Empress Helena, mother of Constantine the Great, and are so sacred, that they may only be ascended on the knees. While I stood before this staircase, I counted between forty and fifty pilgrims toiling up these steps, with tears and prayers at each step, just as Luther did when the light broke in upon his soul, in the words of inspiration that flashed with more than noonday radiance upon him, " The just shall live by faith." Numerous indulgences have been granted by different popes to the penitents who ascend it on bended knee with prayer.

The Rev. J. H. Piggott, Wesleyan Missionary at Rome, to whom I am indebted for many kindnesses, and who accompanied me to the church, read the conditions, printed in Italian, in which this pious act was prescribed as a penance, and the indulgence to be obtained thereby, viz., nine years of indulgence for each one of the twenty-eight steps ascended. Pius VII., in 1817, declared that it might also be applied to souls in purgatory. So then every one who ascends these wood-covered steps on his knees, kissing the marble over the aperture cut in the wood, that mark the drops of the Saviour's blood, can by each such pilgrimage, not only shorten his stay in purgatory by two hundred and fifty-two years, but also perform a like service for some beloved defunct! O Romanism! full of darkness, and ignorance, and superstition!

As we are not yet done with galleries of art, we cannot do better than take you to the Museum of the Capitol. As we ascend the asphalte steps to the platform of such glorious traditions, let us note the two lions of Egyptian porphyry, and take another look at the she-wolf kept there in honor of the legendary foundation of the city. At the head of the staircase are the colossal statues of the twin brothers, Castor and Pollux, and in the centre of the court-yard stands the splendid bronze equestrian statue of Marcus Aurelius. On the left side of the Capitoline Piazza is the Gallery of Sculpture.

On the ground-floor are several rooms devoted to ancient inscriptions and sarcophagi, with high reliefs; and the walls of the staircase are lined with broken pieces of the Pianta Capitolina, bits of marble, covered with the ground plan of Rome in imperial times, and throwing light upon the site and relations of forums, temples, and porticoes.

We enter at once the Hall of the Dying Gladiator. In this room are the Antenous, the Amazon, the Lycian Apollo, and the Juno. They are all marbles of marvellous beauty, but the Dying Gladiator is one of he greatest of all sculptures, and as you gaze upon this noble form of the wounded Gaul, how a sense of its irresistible power steals over you! The Hall of the Faun derives its name from the wonderful Faun of Praxiteles, in rosso antico, found in Hadrian's Villa. It is the image of a young man in an attitude of grace and easy rest, his garment, a lion's skin, thrown over his shoulders. An enchanting master-piece in which "the marble flows like a wave." There are also Satyrs, and Centaurs, with symmetry of feature. In the Hall of the Emperors are nearly a hundred busts of Emperors, Empresses, and other royal personages; and in the Hall of Illustrious Men, are about as many more busts of Philosophers, Statesmen, and Warriors.

In the centre of the former hall is the celebrated sitting statue of Agrippina, grand-daughter of Agustus, the beautiful wife of Germanicus, the mother of the infamous Caligula. How interesting to look at the heads of these rulers of the world—the curly-headed Marcus Aurelius, the uncomely head of Julius Cæsar, the midge-like head of Augustus, the bull-head of Caracella, and the dull head of Hadrian! That wonderful Mosaic, Pliny's Doves, is here, and that statue of unrivalled excellence (the work of a Greek chisel)—the famous Venus of the Capitol. The Palace of the Conservatori is on the other side of the Piazza. The court at the entrance is full of relics. Among other things, the enormous feet and hands of a statue to Apollo, forty-five feet high; and the colossal statues of Julius Cæsar and Augustus. There is also the figure of a horse attacked by a lion, and several granite columns.

marble, and porphyry. The Protomocteca contains a collection of busts of eminent matrons.

We cannot dwell upon the bronzes and terra-cottas, the vases and cones. The third room contains the famous bronze "Wolf of the Capitol." A feeling of awe creeps over one as he carefully observes the rent in the right hind-leg, and remembers that Cicero describes this figure, and tells us that the injury inflicted was caused by a stroke of lightning in the time of the great Orator. The Picture Gallery has a beautiful St. Sebastian, by Guido, and some fine works of Guercino, as the Persian Sibyl, a sad impressive face. Augustus and Cleopatra; he is of fine expression, and she of gorgeous form and dress. St. Petronella is an immense picture. Paul Veronese has the Virgin and Angels, and the Rape of Europa, the White Bull, with a garland of flowers across its brow, while the queenly woman sits upon his back in sensuous loveliness, arrayed in silks, and gold, and precious stones.

The Palazzo Rospigliosi, holds as its art treasure Guido Reni's world-renowned ceiling painting, Aurora. What a painting! There is Apollo, god of the sun, his body flushed with living hues, and blazing in a sea of golden light. Before his chariot is the Queen of the Morning, strewing flowers and attended by her train of dancing Houri, heaven-robed, and fair as the morning! A mirror in the room is so arranged that you can sit down and look into it and drink in this radiant creation without breaking your neck in looking up. In this gallery are Domenichino's Triumph of David, and a Garden of Eden after the Fall; also a great picture of the Death of Samson, by Ludovico Caracci. This palace is built on part of the site of the Baths of Constantine, and in the garden are marble busts and statues of antique workmanship and beautiful bas-reliefs, the spoils from those famous baths. These palaces of the Roman nobility, with their massive walls and barred windows and spacious courts, their frescoed ceilings and floors paved with mosaics, have become the receptacles for the immortal canvas of Italian masters and the imperishable sculpture of the Grecian chisel, and, on certain days, are thrown open to the public.

The Barberini Palace has Albert Durer's *chef-d'œuvre*, Christ disputing with the Doctors; and Guido's Beatrice Cenci, with the perfect face and look of unspeakable grief, one of the greatest works of man. The Doria Gallery contains some grand portraits and magnificent pictures, among them Titian's Three Ages of Man, Raphael's Bartolo and Baldo, and Claude Lorraine's The Mill. The foreground is made up of the most perfect scenery, an "ideal" landscape. In the Corsina Palace you find the usual number of Madonnas and Magdalenes, Crucifixions and Martyrdoms, but there is a Sunset by Both; Vanity, by Carlo Saraceni; a Hare, by Albert Durer; St. Agnes, by Carlo Dolce; An Old Woman, by Rembrandt, that are very highly finished and choice pictures. The

Borghese Gallery is by far the largest and most superb private gallery in Rome. The twelve rooms contain at least eight hundred pictures, and there are several gems of consummate genius. Raphael's Entombment is here, and his portrait of Cæsar Borgia, a face excessively handsome, but cold, cruel, and vindictive; also, her own portrait by herself. Domenichino's masterpiece, the Cumæan Sibyl, is here also, and his other celebrated picture, the Chase of Diana, where the verdant goddess, queenly, graceful, and commanding, is awarding a prize to one of her nymphs. The Four Seasons, by Francisco Albani, are favorite pieces, and Titian's Sacred and Profane Love, has all the great Venetian's matchless warmth of coloring and correctness of design. It represents two figures, one a youthful form of utmost beauty unclothed; the other, dressed in the richest attire, with the sunshine of heaven resting on her pure and serene brow. There is no end to picture galleries and visiting studios in Rome. I drove through the Ghetto, the Jews' quarter, its narrow streets reeking with filth, where amid squalor and degradation is pointed out the old house in which St. Paul lived and taught.

The ride along the Appian Way to the Catacombs, and on to the tomb of Cecilia Metella, is a never-to-be-forgotten one. Passing out of the Gate of St. Sebastian we reach the Arch of Drusus, a monument of Augustan architecture, made of huge masses of stones, with but very little sculpture. All along the way are tombs and Columbaria. A *Columbarium* is a tomb containing a number of cinerary urns, in semi-circular niches, like pigeon-holes, whence the name. We halted at the Church of *Dominie Quo Vadis,* and saw a copy of the mythical footprint which Christ is said to have left here on the marble. This is the

TOMBS ON THE APPIAN WAY.

legend:—As St. Peter, on the persecution which arose from the accusation that the Christians had set fire to Rome, was fleeing for his life, he met the Master, travelling toward the city, and enquired of him, "Lord, where goest thou?" The Saviour replied with a gentle reproach, " I go to Rome, to be crucified a second time." Whereupon St. Peter, ashamed of his cowardly weakness, and filled with trembling and joy, returned and boldly met the martyr's death. Not far from this church are the Catacombs of St. Calixtus. The entrance to the Catacombs is from an open field, in which the work of excavation is still going on. Anywhere over this invisible city, a few yards under the soil, you come upon ruins, or openings down into this great city of the dead.

We light our candles, and following the guide descend into the labyrinths below. The passages, hewn in the soft rock, are like the alleys and streets of a city. Both sides of the galleries are perforated with tombs, or oblong niches carved out—three to six in number, one above another. Each of these hollow

ENTRANCE TO A CATACOMB.

shelves held a corpse. We tread on hallowed ground. Here the martyred dead were laid to rest. Here the saints of God sought refuge—" they wandered about in sheepskins, and goatskins, being destitute, afflicted,

GALLERY WITH TOMBS.

tormented (of whom the world was not worthy); they wandered in deserts, and in mountains, and in dens and caves, there they died in triumph and were laid to rest in these rock-hewn sepulchres of the earth." It is estimated that here are at least four millions of graves, and these mazes of narrow passages would stretch, in one continuous line, 900 miles.

It would be a serious matter to lose your guide or your light here. As I threaded the passages, or

SUBTERRANEAN ORATORY, CATACOMB OF CALLIXTUS.

entered the small chapels and family tombs, I longed for the companionship of the scholarly author of one of our standard works on the Catacombs, Rev. W. H. Withrow, M.A., who writes with the beauty, and purity, and vigor of Prof. Goldwin Smith, the Addison of our day, and who would have trodden these narrow and winding passages, as familiar to him as the streets of his native town ; who would have revelled in the inscriptions carved on every sarcophagus, found wonderful meaning in the allegorical and biblical representations ; and taken delight in every favorite symbol of these early Christians; the anchor, expressive of hope, the dove, the phœnix, the palm-bird, the fish, the ship, palm-branch, olive-leaf, sun, and vine.

Coming out of the Catacombs, we drive on over this time-worn pavement, past the Circus of Maxentius, and the circular tomb of Cecilia Metella, daughter of Quintus Metellus Creticus, and wife of Crassus. It is built of great blocks of hewn stone and in mediæval times was transformed into a round tower seventy feet in diameter. The inscription in front of the mausoleum is as clear and distinct as if carved only yesterday; yet it was cut nearly three thousand years ago.

A little further on and we enjoy uninterrupted views of that gray, ruin-strewed, fever-stricken, yet marvellously fascinating Latin plain, the Campagna. We did not go as far as the Three Taverns, where the brethren came to meet the great Apostle of the Gentiles, and accompany him into the city of the Cæsars ; but as our carriage rattled over the old blocks of stone, and we looked up to the sweet blue skies and over the broad marshes, with the sweeping arches of the Claudian and Marcian aqueducts extending far along the scene, backed by distant and purple mountains, that threw their darkening shadows over the vanished palaces of Pompey and Domitian, we thought of the victorious generals, the orators and senators, the emperors and kings that had trodden this pavement and looked up to the same sweet sky, and over the same wide landscape. And vividly rose before our mind one greater than all these, who passed this way, not with chariots and horses, but whose feet trod these very identical large flat stones on his way to Rome. What road in all the earth is so rich in memories as this?

I had the privilege, like Paul, of "preaching the Gospel to them that are at Rome." A very good congregation of Italians were assembled in the Wesleyan Chapel, and, as I preached, sentence after sentence was interpreted by the Rev. Mr. Piggott, whose long residence in Rome has made him a thorough master of the liquid and silvery language.

In the evening of the same Sabbath I heard the eloquent Sciarelli. No Church is making greater efforts for the evangelization of Italy than the Methodist. The warm, social character of the services, seem peculiarly adapted to the people of this lovely land, and some of the most gifted, learned, and eloquent of the native preachers are Wesleyans.

Protestantism is growing in Italy, although the spirit of persecution is not yet dead. The scattered evangelical communities often suffer from riotous and violent attacks. When I was in Italy, in Marsala, Sicily, the very town where Garibaldi landed twenty years ago, the little Wesleyan Church was assailed with the avowed intention of killing the missionary. He barely escaped by the roof, and the furious devotees of Rome vented their rage on the seats and furniture, which were carried into the Cathedral square and a bonfire made of them. The rioters then entered the Cathedral and received the solemn blessing of the priests. These facts startled the whole country, and when the member for Marsala put a question on the subject to the Home Minister, he received the reassuring reply that the guilty parties would be punished, and liberty of conscience maintained throughout the land. A daily paper commenting on the outrage, put the question, " Are these the last shots of a retreating army or the first skirmishing of an advancing one ?" Even in Marsala there came a strong reaction in favor of the *evangelici*, and public services have been resumed with even a larger attendance than before. God hasten the regeneration of this sunny land!

CHAPTER XVI.

HOMEWARD.

Rome to Florence—Valley of the Arno—The Duomo—Campanile—Baptistery—Ghiberti's Gates—"Sasso di Dante"—Santa Annunziata—Michael Angelo's Bride—Santa Croce—Illustrious Men—San Marco—Savonarola—San Michele—Mausoleum of the Medici—Uffizi and Pitti Palaces—The Tribune—Art in Florence—Pisa—Its "Leaning Miracle"—Genoa—Its Palaces and Campo Santo—Turin—A Day in Milan—The Cathedral—San Ambrogio, "The Last Supper," by Leonardo da Vinci—London—Death of Dr. Punshon—Home Again.

TAKING the night express from Rome to Florence we reached the city of flowers and the flower of cities just as the sun was lifting himself gorgeously over the summits of the encircling hills and flinging his radiance upon the palaces and temples, monuments and arched bridges of this elegant Italian Athens. What a picture, than which there is nought more beautiful upon the face of the earth! The city, with its towers and domes, standing in the broad Valley of the Arno, bounded on either side by lofty romantic mountains.

The blue peaks of Carrara close a prospect westward; and on the other side the Appennines, rising gradually and softly from the plains tower up thousands of feet in exquisitely graceful and undulating forms, their summits bare, their sides intersected with romantic glens; their lower slopes villa-jewelled and gemmed with white farm-houses amid fertile gardens and groves of cypress, olive, and fig. Yonder is the height of Fiesole, an old city of Etruscan origin, with its lofty campanile, at its feet Florence and the Val d' Arno, the winding stream shining like silver, and over all the purply-gold splendor of a lovely sunrise. It is the very landscape, given to so beloved a fame, that even Milton longed for sight that he might once more gaze on the beautiful Arno, and its enchanting valley; the fair Florence, and its thousand villas, "like a pearl set in emerald."

Entering the city you are struck with the picturesqueness of its narrow sunless streets, and high houses, its many towers and spires, its glorious dome and graceful campanile, its quaint bridges spanning the river, and massive palaces. The Arno itself is disappointing; it is an insignificant muddy stream, but the arches of the bridges, the palace gardens, and statues on either side, and stately open arcades, make up a picture that cannot be forgotten; a very vision of beauty. And as we gaze in trance of rapture—

"On golden Arno, as it shoots away
Through Florence's heart beneath her bridges four."

At once you perceive why the city is called the Athens of Italy. Every piazza is rich in monuments of architecture and sculpture. The Loggia dei Lanzi alone contains, besides the two colossal lions and the six vestals, all Greek sculptures, the bronzes Perseus of Cellini, and such celebrated groups, as the " Rape of the Sabines," "Ajax Dying," and " Hercules and the Centaur."

Three great things of Florence, sacred to the memory of three of her greatest men, Brunelleschi, Giotto, and Ghiberti, stand close together, the Duomo, the Campanile, and the Baptistery. The charm of the Duomo is its majestic simplicity. The exterior is covered with precious marbles, vast mosaics, which have a superbly rich effect; but the inside is quite plain, and all the more impressive because of the absence of that garish splendor, that confused richness of details which usually belong to Italian Churches. The pavement is composed of beautiful marbles in white, red, and blue. The dimness within is a glorious dimness, but with the splendors of painted windows that seem made of sapphires, rubies, emeralds, and gold, and set in a border of adoring saints, angels, and prophets, transfuse and transfigure the daylight streaming through them into prismatic hues, as water turned to wine. The dome covered with frescoes is the largest in the world and it is said that when Michael Angelo set forth to Rome to build St. Peter's he looked back at this and said, "Like it, I will not make it; better I cannot."

The Campanile rises alone, quite distinct from the Cathedral, a grand and beautiful square tower, lifting itself upward three hundred feet, "like an unperplexed fine question heavenward." It is an undreamed of wonder, a lovely and impressive poem in stone. It has stood, the delight of five centuries, a combination of solidity with aerial grace and indefinable delicacy. His frescoes are marvellous, and he it was who when the Pope asked of him a specimen of his skill to be judged of with other efforts by the best painters of the period contented himself with drawing, with a brush of red colors, by one turn of his hand, a circle so round that no compass could have designed it more perfectly. Here he has diffused his artistic soul through the very stones and lines, for the four sides of this splendid ornament are inlaid with marble mosaics, and in the windows are slender twisted columns, cunningly carved in leaf, and fruit, and flower, while all about it are niches for statues and bas-reliefs, set in medallions of carving that symbolize, from base to summit, a history of human culture. Near the base is the story of man's creation, and then his slow growth in civilization and the arts; above the cardinal virtues, and higher still the beatitudes and the sacraments, all of the sacred number seven, a glorious chord of mingled human effort and Divine aid, set forever above the city with its hurrying life, and the bells every hour, with their deep round liquid notes, tell worthily the story in melody as the artist has told it in stone. The Baptistery is a small Pantheon, once lighted by an opening in the dome, but now it is dark and sombre.

This octagonal edifice with its magnificent gates, their designs and ornaments in bronze, is known the world over. It was one of these gates, the one facing the cathedral, that Michael Angelo declared was worthy to be the gate of Paradise. They are the work of Ghiberti, and the designs are Bible scenes. The reproductions of these bronze doors are seen in the South Kensington Museum, but they are not so impressive as these almost miraculous originals.

Such fidelity of finish, such force of expression and grace in the sculptured events of Scripture, as the Fall of Jericho, Miriam with her timbrel and other well designed scenes, such skill of execution displayed in the endless combinations of fruit and flowers, birds and animals, are truly wonderful. No wonder Raphael used to study and copy these figures! Near by in the court of Duomo is the "Sasso di Dante," where he used—

> "To bring his quiet chair out, turned
> To Brunelleschi's Church, and pour, alone,
> The lava of his spirit when it burned,
> While some enamoured passer used to wait
> A moment in the golden day's decline,
> With 'Good-night, dearest Dante.'"

The Santa Annunziata is magnificent, its roof exceedingly rich, its high altar of solid silver and dazzling with precious stones. Its gorgeous chapel contains the picture miraculously painted, as the people believe, by the angels. The Church of Santa Maria Novella is called Michael Angelo's Bride. Santa Croce is the Westminster Abbey of Florence. It is large and stately, and has a marble facade. In this "temple of silence and reconciliation" lie, or are commemorated, many of the famous dead of the Flower City. Michael Angelo's tomb is here, and figures of sculpture, painting, and architecture sit mourning round this sarcophagus. What a mighty genius, "unique in painting, unparalleled in sculpture, a perfect architect, an admirable poet, and a divine lover!" His David was made out of a block of marble which had been marred in the hands of another artist, and such was his skill that he left some of his predecessor's work untouched, so that it became a common saying in Florence that Michael Angelo had raised the dead. He lived to the advanced age of ninety years, and then, to use his own words, "died in the faith of Jesus Christ, and in the firm hope of a better life." Here also is the too late monument to the divine poet, Dante. Further on is Alfieri's monument, cut by Canova, the sacred shrine of another sweet poet. Here also is the tomb of Galileo, "sturdy Protestant of the pre-Protestant ages"; and the monument of Niccolo Machiavelli, "out of whose surname," says Macaulay, "we have coined an epithet for a knave, and out of his Christian name a synonym for the devil." The versatility of the Italian mind has always been considered a marvel, and more than one example of this is found in the great men of Florence. Take for illustration Benvenuto Cellini, whose pictures and sculptures are found in many galleries. He made jewelled chalices for churches, and diamond buttons for the great. He was the designer of that stud of silver donkeys, with panniers belonging to Queen Victoria, which I saw in the silver room of Windsor Castle, and used to this day as salt-cellars at the state banquets in St. George's Hall. Though no real soldier, yet, with insufferable vanity, he figured at fights and sieges, and had his dagger out in every street row. All this time he was by trade only a goldsmith. There is a still more striking exemplification of this quality of versatility in Leonardo da Vinci, who was born in a Florentine village. That illustrious genius, whose fame as a painter and sculptor will endure to the last syllable of recorded time, was not only a carver, a goldsmith, a musician, an inventor of musical instruments, and composer of music; an author, a poet, an athlete, a mathematican, leading the way to the invention of the barometer, the stereoscope and the telescope; but also a projector of cannon, of gunpowder, of catapults, of scaling-ladders and war engines of all kinds; of lock-gates for canals, of wind-mills, of tread-mills, windlasses, of the camera obscura, and last, though not least, of the common wheel-barrow!

Remarkable frescoes of the Giotto school are being discovered and restored in some of the chapels, and on the centre ceiling of the church. The theory is, that to preserve them from Vandal wantonness of outrage they were covered over with whitewash, nearly two inches thick, and with equally Vandal indifference, suffered so to remain for centuries. Now the work of uncovering and restoration is going on, and what splendid frescoes are the half obliterated and pale wrecks of these grand old masters.

San Marco is a specimen of Florentine architecture of the thirteenth century. It is the home of the great painter, Fra Angelico, where his finest pictures are kept. In this church is the pulpit from which Savonarola thundered, and the adjoining convent sheltered that patriot, scholar, apostle, and martyr. Who is not familiar with the story of this almost inspired man. With commanding speech he uttered his fiery denunciations of the corruptions of the Papacy, and his protestations against the unparalleled godlessness of his age and country. Under his influence the reformation of morals in the city was great. He was threatened, but the words of the vigorous reformer were, "Lay me on the altar; let my blood flow; let my body be burned; but let my testimony be remembered among men, that iniquity shall not prosper forever." The perfidious Pope, Alexander VI., having in vain tried to silence the preacher, famed for his eloquence, next sought to bribe him. "Give him a red hat and so make at once a cardinal and a friend." But the monk answered from the pulpit, "I will have no other red hat than that of martyrdom, colored with my own blood." He saw what was before him, but shrank not. When brought out to be burned, he was degraded from being a priest, and when the last vestment was removed the Bishop pronounced the degradation, "I separate thee from the Church militant, and from the Church triumphant." "Nay," said the martyr, "thou canst not separate me from the Church triumphant." He then mounted the pile, uttering the sentence: "Oh! Florence, what hast thou done this day?" A strong wind was blowing, and in his fiery chariot the right hand of the martyr, unconsumed, was seen moving in the midst of the flame, and blessing the city that clamored for his blood. The reaction soon came, and to-day his memory is an inspiration to the Italian people, and his words, "*Italia renovabitur*" are words of prophecy and of life.

San Michele is one of the glories of Florence, and has all around its exterior of white marble, statues of angels, saints, virtues, prophets, that are regarded as the finest works of the ancient Florentine school. But for beauty and richness of *Pietre dure* the Medicean Chapel, belonging to the Church of St. Lorenzo, excels everything. It was originally intended by Ferdinand I. for the reception of the Blessed Sepulchre, which was to have been rescued from the hands of the infidels; but failing in this, it became the burial-place of the great Medici family.

The walls of this mausoleum are covered with the richest mosaic, a pomp of marble, and the shrines of these Grand Dukes are profusely ornamented with precious stones. The tomb is a plain small chapel designed and adorned by Michael Angelo. At the feet of the statue of Giuliano de Medici are the famous symbolic figures Day and Night; but the *chef-d'œuvre* of genius is the figure of Lorenzo, a grand human life portrayed in marble, and at his feet the colossal forms of Morning and Evening.

But thus far we have only had a glimpse of the splendors and artistic treasures of this glorious old Tuscan city. To understand why Florence has been rightly called the Athens of Italy, the cradle and home of civilization and the fine arts, we have only to visit the galleries of the Uffizi and Pitti Palaces. These are by far the richest collections of works of art in the world. Stairs, vestibules, corridors, halls, cabinets, saloons, crowded with the paintings, drawings, and sculptures, of five hundred old masters, as well as the most celebrated artists of the world! And the centre, and crown, and jewel of all, the inner sanctuary, the holy of holies of art, is the Tribune, a little octagonal room, filled with the very masterpieces, the rarest wonders of art! Here is "the statue that enchants the world;" that ancient piece of sculpture, found in Hadrian's Villa, at Tivoli, the Venus de Medici, its form the ideal of loveliness, with ineffable and virgin expression of countenance. The dignity of a goddess is in her carriage, there is a loftiness in her mien, and a maidenly modesty in her bearing, that has an irresistible fascination, and we drank in the indescribable charms of a beauty in which there is nothing unrefined or gross. Here is that delicately chiselled figure of a perfect symmetry and beauty, the Dancing Faun, by Praxiteles, and that other remarkable Greek sculpture, the Wrestlers, and the Slave Whetting his Knife, a powerful, earnest, striking form and face! And the paintings, how wonderful! You look upon them with amazement. They command the eye, and they charm the imagination, they awe the soul, they uplift the being! There are pictures in that room that haunt the memory with their loveliness, the impress of them is indelible. Such as Raphael's Fornarina, a picture with a touch of divine sweetness; and his Madonna, with her serene brow, and sacred face of maternity; Michael Angelo's Holy Family, the Samian Sibyl of Guercino, and Titian's Venus.

Two large rooms are filled with portaits of artists, and here you can study the countenances of all who have ever had a name. In the cabinet of gems are precious stones and jewels, ablaze with splendor. The corridor leading to the Pitti is a long covered gallery over the Ponte Vecchio that spans the Arno, and is lined with fine engravings, of which there are ten thousand; also original drawings, and pen sketches of the old masters, in number thirty-three thousand. The tapestries are brilliant and fresh in their coloring as the paintings, and there are six hundred pieces of Gobelin. Every room contains tables of Florentine mosaic *in pietra dura*, as well as of the most precious marbles. There are also superb cabinets inlaid with flowers, composed of pearls and gems, lilies, passion flowers, roses, mosses, and ferns; birds of turquoise, lapis-lazuli, coralline, agates, jasper, amethysts, crystal, alabaster of exquisite beauty, and every combination of tints. In the Pitti Gallery alone are five hundred paintings, each one a real treasure, besides bronzes, cameos, and engraved stones; medals, gems, blazing in every hue; porphyry tables, with vases and flowers in mosaic; baths in Persian lapis-lazuli, Oriental alabaster, furniture in ebony, and jasper, and malachite, and brocatello di spagna, and lovely statues, among them the celebrated Venus, by Canova. The Boboli Gardens adjoin the Royal Palace, and they are very extensive, including hill and valley, groves and fountains, lakes and islands, bowers, grottoes, and statues. A drive through the streets, and this is all that we can give you of beautiful Firenze. My departure from this lovely city was hastened by a despatch from the Rev. Dr. Punshon, requesting me to come at once to him. At Rome I had received a letter from him, telling me that because of illness he was unable to reach the Eternal City, and suggesting Florence, the city of his love, as our meeting-place. And when the telegram reached me that he was unable to proceed any farther I hastened forward to Genoa. The railway takes one through the finest landscape of Tuscany. Fields covered with emerald verdure, and glittering in the yellow sunlight, winding streams, and sparkling rivers, valleys of vineyards and fig-trees, and silvery olive foliage; dark forests, waving from distant hills, crowned with the ruins of some old Etruscan Castle; the spires, and domes of town and city, mountain and valley, bright soil and sea, all sleeping in the rosiest light of a Tuscan heaven, served to make up a picture unequalled even in this land of beauty.

We pass through Pisa; but have only time to get a glance, at the famous group of buildings. The Leaning Tower, an airy structure rising one hundred and eighty feet in height, and leaning thirteen feet out of the perpendicular; the Cathedral with its Mosque-like dome, and bands of black and white marble; the Baptistery, with its pulpit of marble fret-work and exquisite echo, and the Campo Santo, an oblong cloister, surrounded by spacious arcades, and its earth brought over from the Holy Land. Thence the road lay along the Mediterranean, and the mountains grow dim and distant, except a coast-line of hills, which shone in places in the whiteness of their own Carrara marble. All that afternoon the sea lay glittering before us, now and then snatched from the eye, by hill or tunnel, the sinuosities of the road, or fantastic rocks of a thousand shapes, only to steal upon it again in sudden and bright surprise.

At length the sun went down behind the Western

waves, and the pale and veil-like mists that succeed
the sunset, gathered over the scene. Soon the queenly
moon rose on high, and the wild and romantic coast
slept in her silver light, while below dashed, and
glittered the waters of the great island sea. We
reached Genoa shortly after midnight.

I did not, during our four days' stay in the "Superb
City," owing to the illness of Dr. Punshon, do much
sight-seeing. But I visited a few of the many ducal

BIRD'S-EYE VIEW OF GENOA.

palaces for which Genoa is famed, and strolling through
their stately rows of pillars about a central court of
marble, where a fountain is always making music,
climbing their broad stairs, of the whitest marble, and,
entering their spacious rooms, it was not difficult to
realize their regal splendor in the days of Genoese
greatness, when their princely occupants ransacked
the earth to adorn them with all that art boasted most

precious, or royal luxury held most dear; paintings wrought in gold, antique marbles that spoke of the bright days of Athens, carpets and stuffs of the East, her own silver workmanship, mosaics of Florence, draperies of Venice, Carrara and alabaster vases, fountains wreathed in flowers, and sending up their diamond and fairy spray. In the Municipal Palace we were shown the handwriting of Christopher Columbus (the penmanship of Mark Twain notoriety), his bust, and other mementos of the heroic and venturous seaman, the discoverer of the New World. In the same place is carefully treasured up the violin of Paganini, the famous Genoese fiddler.

I cannot speak in enrapturing terms of the pictures seen in Genoa. The Campo Santo is, however, a place of rare and striking beauty. In that land, where art once ruled supreme, the very cemeteries are galleries of statuary, and here many of the monuments to the dead have angel and human forms with limbs after the mould of the Faun of the Capitol, and the Discobolus.

A fine panorma of the city, with its roofs and spires its narrow streets and lofty houses, and the magnificent harbor, with the far-shimmering gleam of the Mediterranean, is obtained from the summit of the girdling hills; but no more enchanting view can be desired of sea and shore, harbor and square, palace and cathedral, rising terrace above terrace from the lovely Gulf, than that which we enjoyed from the cars, as we were leaving the city, and climbing to the high table-land above.

Turin, our first stopping-place, is a five hours' ride from the sea, through magnificent scenery, and is under the shadow of the glorious Alps.

I had procured tickets from Florence to Venice, the widowed bride of the Adriatic, and had expected to feast my eyes on the "Sea City," afloat on the placid waves, to see the Palace of the Doges, and the Bridge of Sighs—"a palace and a prison on each hand"—the grand square of St. Mark, the patron saint of the ancient and dreaming city; to glide noiselessly over the water-streets in a gondola, and hear the song of the gondolier, each one a gay Othello, and behold a fair Jessica in each maiden, with roguish eyes, and cloud of raven hair; but I had given up all for the sake of my beloved and illustrious friend who was ill. Dr. Punshon, however, insisted that I must not miss the Cathedral of Milan, and, as the city was only three hours' distant, I gave a day to the ancient capital of Sardinia.

Milan, the grand, is situated in the midst of the vast and fertile plains of Lombardy, and her Cathedral, a miracle in stone, known as the eighth wonder of the world, towers above the city, and dominates over every other object.

There it stands, in the great square, so massive, so solemn, so vast, yet so delicate, so graceful, so airy, a wilderness of glittering pinnacles cut against the sky;

a gemmed, and laced, and carved device, crystallized as in mid-air; a forest of spires shimmering in the amber sunlight, a graceful vision in marble, dripping solid splendor on every side! Entering the vast and shadowy interior you find a cruciform, with double aisles, and arch beyond arch, column after column, in vast proportions. The fifty-two pillars of support are each twelve feet in diameter, and their summits have, in the place of capitols, canopied niches, filled with statues. Wherever you look is a marble statue—each statue a study, the work of a Raphael, an Angelo, or a Canova, with attitude full of grace, and face radiant with expression. The floor is in mosaic of many-colored marble. The gorgeous windows are ablaze with colors and pictured scenes.

Now we mount to the marble roof, adorned with a hundred Gothic turrets. All around fretted spires spring high in the air, and marble statues attract your gaze. Higher still you mount to the very summit of the tower, and then look around you. It is a far-famed prospect from this marble "flower garden;" and deep blue shadows, rose-tinted hues, and snow-white peaks of the far-off Alps, lending to it a golden distance, give that solemnity and ethereal charm of mountain vision without which no landscape is perfect. The sun was shining brilliantly in a sky darkly and intensely blue, while dim and delicious hues gathered over the mighty and silent mountains so many miles away; and all between was a green table-land of vines, and gardens, sparkling streams running snake-like, and hamlets white as the sea-shore sand—just such a landscape as a Claude, or a Rosa loved to paint. Below you, the city raised its roofs, palaces, and spires, to the sun, and, at your feet, this poem in marble, with statues, statues, statues! The entire Cathedral, from floor to roof is marble, and interior and exterior have, it is said, niches for seven thousand statues. From base to summit, over doors and windows, in nooks and corners, over arches and transepts, on spires and pinnacles, wherever a niche or pedestal can be found, is a marble statue.

Descending, I examined the sculptured form of St. Bartholomew, flayed alive, and carrying his skin over his shoulder; and paid homage to that noble and pious Bishop of the Church, S. Carlo Borromeo, by visiting his tomb, of Carrara marble, blazing with gold and precious stones; paying five francs more to see, amid the treasures of croziers and crosses of solid silver, and lockets of gold, brilliant with precious gems, the old cruicifix which he carried before him through the city, when he pleaded for the staying of the plague in 1576.

Bidding farewell to the Cathedral, that presence of beauty, majesty, and solemn grandeur, I had time to visit the old Church of San Ambrogio, founded in the fourth century, the church in which the Lombard Kings and German Emperors were crowned with the iron crown; the Church, too, in which Augustine heard from St. Ambrose the words of truth which pierced his heart, so that he became a child of God, and a royal diadem in the hand of the Lord. The old Lombard architecture is quaint and rude, but one gazes long at those ancient bronze doors, said to be the very ones which St. Ambrose shut against the Emperor Theodosius.

In the refectory of the suppressed monastery of Santa Maria Della Grazia is that picture, which has always been worshipped by masters in art, "The Last Supper," by Leonardo da Vinci. It is painted on the end wall, and is thirty feet long, by ten feet high. The picture is crumbling, and is much marred by the hand of time; but the Divine face of the blessed Master is there in all its beauty, grandeur, and majestic sweetness—a face surely as near the face of the God-Man as can be conceived by an immortal thought.

Not far away is the Brera Palace of Science and Art; sixteen rooms of which are given to paintings, some of them of no inferior order. A visit to the Victor Emmanuel Octagon Gallery, a kind of Crystal Palace, with elegant shops on every side, a drive to the Public Gardens, and through some of the principal streets, and we return through valley, and plain, and rice fields, under the shadow of vast, dreamy, bluish, snowclad mountain ranges to Turin.

The long journey from Northern Italy to England, was one of intense anxiety, owing to the extreme illness of the sufferer, whom we were bearing homeward.

We dreaded especially the passage through the Mont Cenis Tunnel. The sensation in going through it is at any time awful and instructive, and one can never forget the rumble of that deep bass note; but our patient bore it well, and the grand mountain scenery seemed to revive his spirits. His was the feeling, kindred with that of Canon Kingsley, when he says: "Beauty is God's handwriting, a wayside sacrament; welcome it on every fair face, every fair sky, every fair flower, and thank for it Him, the fountain of all loveliness, and drink it in simply and earnestly with all your eyes— it is a charming draught, a cup of blessing."

Through sunny France we came, and on to London. A few days were spent with him in his own home, and I was ready to return to Canada, when with bewildering surprise came the shock of death. His departure was like one of those sudden sunsets in the East,—

> "The sun's rim dips, the stars rush out,
> At one stride comes the dark."

When all was over, and all that remained of this "polished shaft" had been laid in the grave, I returned to Liverpool and embarked for Quebec. The homeward voyage was as long and miserable as buffeting winds and storms, perils of fog, and perils of ice could make it; but at length our vessel steamed up the St. Lawrence and brought us in safety to our "desired haven."

The record of my journey is completed, and in closing there is a fitness that my last words should be those of devout gratitude to Him, who in many thousand miles of travel through Europe, Asia, and Africa, has preserved me from accident, and brought me back in fully restored health to the land of my pride, the people of my affection, and the home of my heart.

In Memoriam.

REV. WILLIAM MORLEY PUNSHON, LL.D.

A Special Providence—William Morley Punshon—His Early Life—Opening Ministry—Great Popularity—Excessive Labors—His Work in Canada—True Greatness—Bereavements—A Memorable Conversation—Return to England—Great Responsibilities and Heavy Sorrows—Failing Health—Continental Tour—Severe Illness at Genoa—Homeward Journey—Sudden Death—Universal Sorrow—Funeral—Affection's Tribute.

I CANNOT close this volume without offering my humble tribute of affection to that great name which has so suddenly become a memory. It was my unspeakable privilege to be a companion of that great and noble personality during the closing weeks of his life. I shall ever regard it as a special Providence that I was found in the heart of Europe in mid-winter where I could hasten to the bedside of this God-honored minister, and render to him some comfort and sympathy in the supreme moments of his life. I count it a privilege, too sacred for words, that I was permitted to share the friendship of so great and gifted, so good and honored a man. From the day that Dr. Punshon came to Canada, he took me to his heart, and no one can persuade me that by mere chance there was sent to him, as he lay sick in a foreign land, with the shadows of eternity upon him, one whom he had always cherished with the kindness of a son in the Gospel—who had been with him in the Gethsemanes of his sorrows—who had journeyed with him thousands of miles, knew all his inner experiences, and to whom he could open all his heart.

The Christian world will soon, we are glad to know, be furnished with a fitting memorial of the character, the gifts, and unparalleled career of one who was not only known and loved and honored throughout the Methodist world, but also far beyond the limits of his own denomination. It is for me in these hastily-written pages to furnish some particulars of his last illness and closing hours, and drop my wreath of immortelle over the grave of a dearly-loved friend.

William Morley Punshon was born at Doncaster, England, May 29th, 1824. His parents were earnest Wesleyan Methodists, and he inherited the blessing promised to the seed of the righteous. He early gave indications of extraordinary gifts, exhibiting a remarkable memory and a singular aptitude for acquiring knowledge. Deeply affected from childhood by religious influences, at the age of seventeen he underwent the great moral crisis of his being. His decision for God and conversion were through the instrumentality of the late Rev. Samuel Romilly Hall, and throughout life he cherished the most filial affection for that eminent minister. While yet in his teens, he began to preach, and while residing with his uncle, the late Rev. Benjamin Clough, a devoted Missionary, he began a course of preparation for the ministry of the Gospel. Accepted as a candidate for the Wesleyan ministry, he was sent to the Theological Institution at Richmond; but shortly afterwards, to meet an emergency which had arisen in the Maidstone Circuit, he was sent out into the work with a haste which only his extraordinary gifts, attainments, and graces could justify. At once he took rank as a young man of wonderful promise; and while at Whitehaven, Carlisle, and Newcastle he became the most famous pulpit orator in the North of England. He was a born orator. "His robust build, his powerful and well-mastered voice, his frank address, his native and yet highly cultivated elocution, his animated and appropriate action, his happy, ardent temperament, his keen yet healthy and restrained sensibility, his vivid, versatile imagination, all fitted him to move great gatherings by breathing thoughts and burning words. His rhetoric was naturally brilliant; rich in color and profuse in imagery. To his genius, barrenness would have been a meretricious affectation, as the poetic element formed so large a part of his mental constitution. His images were illustrations. However gorgeous the medium through which he made the light of truth to stream, that medium was always translucent; never dimming, but ever intensifying the heavenly beam. He took unsparing pains in the preparation of his discourses and addresses; but their one aim was usefulness, conviction, edification, 'the furtherance and joy of faith.' And this was their general result. However elaborate the structure of a sermon or a speech, there was no unhelpful ornamentation: the stately shaft and flowering capital invariably *supported* something, sustained some solid truth, and beautified what it upheld."

While in Sheffield and Leeds his popularity was still increasing; and about this time, when only twenty-seven years of age, he burst with meteoric brilliancy on the mighty metropolis, and by his two great lectures in Exeter Hall, established his renown as an orator, not a whit behind the chiefest in the land. His ministrations were eagerly sought for and lavishly bestowed throughout the length and breadth of the kingdom; and in addition to his own circuit work, in his unselfish generosity, he undertook to raise, by lecturing and personal solicitation, the sum of fifty thousand dollars to aid in the erection of Wesleyan chapels in English watering-places. This self-imposed labor of love was accomplished within five years. He also raised in six months, by his lecture on "The Huguenots," five thousand dollars for a heavily burdened chapel in Spitalfields. Bestowing his gigantic powers and generous sympathies upon every religious and philanthropic movement, his health gave way, and three years were passed in sore physical prostration. But, retired to a considerable extent from public life, the warm poetic fire burned within him, and he gave to the world his "Sabbath Chimes," which have been to thousands of suffering children of the household of faith, like the sound of church-bells. This volume of sweet poems shows that he struck with gentle charms the poet's tuneful lyre as well as wielded the orator's spell. In 1867, Mr. Punshon was appointed as the English Representative to the Canadian Conference, over which he was also elected President. He spent five years in Canada, and to his commanding influence, his force of character, intellect, and unsparing energy Canadian Methodism owes much to-day. His zealous ministrations and labors are commemorated in all the great movements of the Church—the endowment of the University of Victoria College, one of his first acts after coming to Canada, being to consecrate to this object his entire official salary for a year and a half; the establishment of two theological schools; the interest infused into Missionary work, and the establishment of a Foreign Mission to Japan; the organic union, consolidation, and unprecedented growth of the Church. The Church building enterprises of the Connexion received a mighty impulse from his labors, and to his indomitable energy is largely due the erection of the Metropolitan Church, Toronto. He elevated the tone and heightened the power of the Canadian pulpit by infusing into the ministry of all the churches the spirit of his own earnestness, his reverent love of truth, and his holy ambition to make the fullest use of all the faculties with which God had blessed him.

His breadth of character and Catholic spirit, his statesmanship and administrative ability, his brilliant imagination and poetic sensibility, his dramatic genius and unrivalled oratory, commanded the admiration of all; but only those who enjoyed the privilege of close intimacy can fully appreciate his loveable personal qualities and the living purity of the man. From the day that he came to Canada he took me to his heart with strong affection, and he was to me more than a friend, a father so true, so ready to counsel, and give me all the benefit of his rich experience, so full of gentle goodness and geniality of heart. The splendor of his oratory charmed and fascinated me, but it was only after I had been a guest for weeks in his own bright and beautiful home that I began to see the regnant greatness of his character, his tenderness and affectionateness, his goodness, his modesty and humility. His real greatness was in his character more than in his transcendent gifts. The qualities of his heart, his simple Christian trust and close clinging to the cross impressed me as even nobler than his genius. I more than loved him—I revered him. I was in Toronto when his double sorrow came upon him. In the first moments of bereavement he sent for me, and I shall never forget the anguish of grief that surged through his great, manly heart. He was overwhelmed. After pouring out his complaint he grew calmer, and asked for reading and prayer. The passage which he requested to be read was the account of the Saviour's agony in the garden of Gethsemane. He had not been driven from the anchor-ground of faith in Christ, and in his Gethsemane he found balm and comfort in the story of His sufferings, " who, being in an agony, sweat great drops of blood." He cultivated an appreciative and sympathetic acquaintance with his brethren, and could call nearly every one of them by name as well as tell where they were appointed. Magnanimous in every instinct he was incapable of detraction, and would never speak in depreciation of the humblest brother. His spirit was most loving, and his love of the brethren was sincere and unaffected. He made his influence felt throughout every department of the work, and not only visited the chief centres of population but gave his assistance to the most remote rural districts.

His journeyings on this continent, in the aggregate, exceeded one hundred thousand miles. It was my good fortune to accompany him in his journey to the Pacific Coast. His great fame had gone before him, and the entire tour was a complete ovation. It was an exciting thing to see the mobile people of the West sit bewildered and carried away with breathing thoughts and burning words such as they had never heard before; and as he mounted from height to height of oratorical grandeur, and reached climax after climax, if from the pulpit, they would be all subdued and melted; if from the platform, they would break out into cheering, and rising to their feet pour forth rapturous plaudits that shook the house. He seemed to lift up as never before "Christ and Him crucified." How he commended to those strangers His Master as a Saviour, and besought sinners to be reconciled to God! The very service which he rendered as a lecturer was in the cause of the pulpit. His subjects were nearly all sacred; and he sought to "please men for their good to edification." He never laid aside the gravity and dignity of the Christian minister, or said anything whereby the ministry might be blamed. He often told me that the pulpit was his throne, that preaching was his supreme work, and that on the platform he never lost sight of his character as a preacher of the Gospel; and I have seen letters from persons who dated their religious awakening to hearing his lecture on "Daniel in Babylon." What always struck me was his great humility and the unaffected modesty with which he bore his unsurpassed renown. In closest intimacy with him from day to day, when his popularity was greatest, I saw no pride in him;

he was simple and guileless as a child. He always thought of himself soberly, and though I have been with him in his unsurpassed efforts, in the very floodtides of his resplendent career, yet such was his innate meekness and unfailing modesty, that I never remember an instance in which he seemed other than unconscious of his marvellous gifts and unparalleled success.

I shall never forget, on our way to the Yosemite Valley, one night we stopped at a place called Chinese Camp, and strayed out together in the fields under the bright Californian sky. He had a poet's temperament, and this was one of his seasons of peculiar sensibility, and he gave me the history of his life, his early struggles and aspirations, his mother's death, his conversion, his spiritual conflicts, his entrance upon the ministry, his discouragements, depressions and success in the work, the sorrows that had come upon him, and the means which his Heavenly Father had taken to keep him very low. There was nothing of self-exultation; he spoke in the "meekness of wisdom," yea, with the very "meekness and gentleness of Christ." It was late when we returned to our hotel, but the impression received while he poured forth the story of his life under that bright, silent, star-lit sky, will abide with me through life. His spiritual sympathies were tender and profound, and he ardently longed for fruit of his labors. When he was a regular pastor, the prayer meetings that followed his Sunday night services were often seasons of great power, and marked by an ingathering of souls. In later years he had always to encounter crowded congregations, and this somewhat diminished the spiritual effect, for only those immediately about him knew the awful fear, the nervous anxiety, and agony almost to fainting, that had to be overcome before he ascended the pulpit. He preached for me one evening in Richmond Street Church, on the understanding that it was not to be known that he was to officiate. It was a sacramental service, and oh! the spiritual sweetness and power! There were the same well-rounded sentences; the tropical wealth of illustration, the blaze of rhetoric, the marvellous oratorical power and force of emphasis, but there was the living earnestness of the man and the love of Christ constraining him. He counted it his crowning joy to lead a soul to the Saviour, and no doubt now, before the throne, he rejoices in many stars in his crown saved through his ministry.

On his return to England he was at once elected to the highest offices of trust, and in 1875 he was appointed one of the Secretaries of the Foreign Missionary Society. He cheerfully girded himself for the arduous duties of this office, and carried the burden of its great anxieties and responsibilities. There was a continual and excessive strain upon his powers and sensibilities. He had been prematurely forced into leadership of the Church. His official obligations were many and great, for, having the perfect confidence and love of the brethren, the weightiest honors and responsib'lities were placed upon him. Then his engagements in every cause, as the most popular platform man of the time, were exacting and enormous. Sorrow and anxiety, too, pressed down his tender and sensitive spirit. His life was saddened by successive griefs and bereavements. When I reached London he had just made another pilgrimage to the grave's mouth.

His physicians then insisted upon his taking rest, and he thought of accompanying me to the East. But he felt that he could not be spared from the Mission House until a month later, when the accounts would be closed, and so we arranged for a continental tour, in which we were to meet at Rome. But going to Walsall to fulfil an engagement to preach, he had a very severe attack of heart-trouble, and was compelled to give up work. He then started on his continental trip, visiting Paris, Lyons, Avignon, and Marseilles. At Cannes he spent two or three days in delightful communion with his life-long friend, Rev. William Arthur. From Nice he, with his wife and son, started to drive by carriage over the beautiful road to Mentone, when the dreaded "mistral" came upon them with great fury, in clouds of dust and blasts of wind, and they were obliged to turn back. That night, at Mentone, he became alarmingly ill. His diary bears the following: "March 23rd.—How little we know what is before us! Retired to bed restless and out of sorts, yet no worse than I had been aforetime; but about half-past two in the morning was seized with a most severe attack of difficulty of breathing, with crepitation, which lasted in its severity for nearly three hours. I do not think I could have lasted much longer, without relief. Got a little relief about six, but suppose I have not for a long time been nearer the eternal world. There was, the doctor said, a good deal of bronchial congestion, and there was some blood coloring the expectoration, accompanied, as was the attack at Walsall, with heart disturbance and intermittent pulse. Alarmed the whole party, my poor wife notably." From this attack he recovered sufficiently, after twenty-four hours, to go on to Genoa. This is his record, the *last* in his well-kept diary: " March 25th.—The doctor saying I might move, we ventured on to Genoa, arriving there shortly after sunset. A poor and rather troubled night." " March 26th.—The party saw sights, but I kept indoors." Here he had another attack of spasmodic breathing and great depression. He had sent me a message that he was sick, and feared that he could not reach Rome, and at Florence I received another despatch, asking me to come to him at once. I found him at Genoa, alarmingly ill. His nights were occasions of great suffering. The physician who had been called in said that he had organic disease—enlargement of the heart—and that the trouble was aggravated by dyspepsia.

As there were no signs of improvement, his London physician was telegraphed for, and, on the arrival of Dr. Hill, he expressed his desire to turn his face homeward. He seemed to have a presentiment that he would never recover, and he had a dread of dying in a foreign land. We endeavored to persuade him that it was merely the peculiarly depressing character of his disease, but his instincts were true. On Friday, the first of April, we started for Turin. He bore the five hours' journey well for one so ill, but on reaching Turin he complained of pain in the back of his lungs. His physician made an examination, and found that there was congestion there. Saturday and Sunday he rested, and was quite cheerful in the midst of his sufferings. On Sunday night he had another terrible paroxysm. Oh! that long, weary, suffering night, when the seconds lengthened into minutes, and the hours seemed like days! In the morning we assisted him to dress; but his whole system was prostrated, and I shall never forget his suffering look as he turned to his beloved wife, and said, "Oh! I am so ill!" Still he could not give up the idea of making another stage homeward. He longed for the comforts of his much-loved Trauby, and for nearness to his dearest friends. We took tickets for Macon. The railway journey over the Alps, amid the magnificent mountain scenery which he loved so much, acted as a tonic, and with every sense alert he would point out to us some valley of rarer beauty, or some snow-mantled summit of more soaring grandeur. As the evening approached it became a question whether he should not ride on through the night to Paris. He could not be more

oppressed and restless in a railway carriage than he
had been in bed, and when his physician who accompanied him found that his heart beat quite strong and
full, it was decided to go on. And so he made that
long twenty-three hours' ride, so tiresome even to one
in full health and vigor; and in the gray morning the
weary suffering one, rode through the streets and
boulevards of the brilliant French Capital to the hotel
to which we had telegraphed for rooms. After a day's
rest he came to London; and I shall never forget the
radiant smile of satisfaction with which he entered his
own home. And there we gave thanks to God who
had given him strength to accomplish the long journey
from the shores of the Mediterranean. His mind at
rest, surrounded by familiar and loved objects, for the
first day or two symptoms of improvement appeared;
but the disease which was manifesting itself all along,
congested pneumonia, now reached its height. Dr.
Radcliffe was called in as consulting physician, and he
was getting what he himself styled "heroic treatment." All this time his mind was in full activity; and
in the intervals of rest from oppressive breathing and
extreme nervous depression, he was bright and cheerful. There was the glow of sympathy, and a quiet
humor sparkled in his eye and illumined his speech.
He manifested the most delicate consideration for the
comfort and feelings of all around. Yet, withal, there
was a deep undercurrent of spiritual feeling that turned
continually heavenward and Christward. I said to

him one evening, "Why do you talk despondingly about the future, you are not afraid to die?" "No," he answered, "but I have a love of life." "But you have had the highest human satisfactions—you have had the deepest sorrows, why should you wish to live?" After a moment's pause, the characteristic reply was, "It is the rapture of living. Besides," said he, "I do not like to feel that my work is ended." Noble man! He had consecrated all the energies of his great mind and heart to the service of the Church, and to the glory of that Lord and Master who had joined together so many gifts in one life, and lent that life to the world.

As I think of him now in the shining Heavens, with his blessed Lord, summering high in bliss with God Himself, and remember our seasons of communion, his pantings after God, his beautiful resignation, cheerful hope, distrust of self, and simple trust in Christ, I feel that the sanctifying Spirit was indeed making him meet for the immortal inheritance. He was so afraid lest he should manifest any impatience. He had been schooled in sorrow and had learned not to murmur. Mrs. Arthur mentions one of the touching incidents of his stay in Cannes. They had visited the potteries at Vallerais, and as they stood round the potter with his wheel, and watched the facility with which he changed the form of the clay in his hand and impressed his mind upon it, she looked up in amazement and met

Dr. Punshon's eyes all suffused with tears, and he said,—

"Mould as Thou wilt my passive clay!"

He was being moulded and fashioned—a vessel to adorn the palace of the King. He disclaimed all goodness in himself, and would say, "I feel utterly unworthy, but my trust is in Christ." He took special delight in prayer and the reading of God's word, and on the last of his earthly Sabbaths he found great comfort in the 22nd Psalm, and commented on the 8th verse, "He trusted on the Lord," literally "he rolled himself on God," and spoke of the security it gave to have the "Almighty God beneath us!"

Special prayer had been offered for him in the Brixton Chapel, where he was wont to worship; and in the Metropolitan Tabernacle, Mr. Spurgeon prayed for him as his beloved brother, pleading "Lord, he whom thou lovest is sick. Make haste to help him." And when I brought him a message of love and sympathy from Mr. Spurgeon, who bade him be of good cheer, telling him that his own seasons of sickness were times of deepest despondency, he seemed to be cheered and strengthened.

On Tuesday night, the 12th of April, he rested quite well, and on Wednesday morning the physician found him so much better that he did not think it necessary to make an afternoon call. But toward evening he became restless, got out of bed and walked unaided, like a man of strength, to the chair in which he died. There was failing heart-power, and the sound of the Bridegroom's approach fell on his quick and watchful ear. As we gathered round him he asked for prayer, and himself joined in supplicating grace and strength according to his need. He seemed to know that he was going, and said: "You have come to see me die." We all sought to cheer him with assurances that he would soon be better. I said, "Never fear, dear doctor; when you go you will have an abundant entrance into the kingdom." His mind reverting to death-bed testimonies, he replied, "*I do not ask that. Let me only have peace. My testimony is my life.*" The physician had been sent for, and when he arrived he sought to arouse the heart's activity. He was suffering from *cardiac dyspnœa*—difficulty of breathing from enfeebled heart action: still no immediate danger was anticipated. Our eyes were holden. But shortly after midnight he had become suddenly worse, and the heart that had always rallied hitherto refused to do its work. He knew the change, and turning to the doctor asked, "Am I going?" His physician, with a sigh, answered that nothing more could be done. Then his heart turned to the human in love and to the Divine in trust. His devoted wife, who had watched over him with unspeakable affection day and night through all his illness, with breaking heart, asked, "Have you a message for me, my darling?" And he said, "I have loved you fondly; love Jesus, and meet me in heaven." One of the two sons, Morley, was with them, but the Benjamin of the household was absent, and she asked, "And Percy?" "Tell him to love Jesus, and meet me in heaven." "And yourself, how do you feel?" "I FEEL THAT JESUS IS A LIVING REALITY—JESUS! JESUS! JESUS!" One heavenly smile, one rapt and upward glance, and the head dropped—there was silence broken only by the sob of a widow, and WILLIAM MORLEY PUNSHON was no more —his spirit had passed upward to the bosom of God.

For him we need shed no tears or rend a garment in token of our grief. He has departed to be "with Christ," which is "far better." Gone in the maturity and plenitude of his powers—gone from his work and from us who loved him so well. In the full tide of his usefulness, when he seemed to be needed most, the Church has been bereft of its chief ornament. His sun has gone down in the splendor of high noon, and no words are more fitting and appropriate to his departure than his own eloquent reference to the death of the sainted Alfred Cookman: "He went home like a plumed warrior, for whom the everlasting doors were lifted as he was stricken into victory in his prime; and he had nothing to do at the last but mount into the chariot of Israel and go 'sweeping through the gates, washed in the blood of the Lamb.'"

The unlooked-for calamity fell like a thunderbolt upon the public mind. Everywhere the tidings were received with astonishment and the profoundest sorrow. The mourning was universal. It was as though "one lay dead in every house."

His death was not only a vast and unlooked-for loss to the Methodist Church, it was a national calamity, and like that of Lord Beaconsfield, which occurred about the same time, seemed to cast a shadow over the whole face of English society.

Expressions of sympathy and reverential grief came pouring down upon the smitten household like the leaves of a forest in autumn; and a great cloud of incense arose before the throne of God and of the Lamb on behalf of the widow, and the fatherless, and the bereaved Church. The most eminent Churchmen and Nonconformists alike paid their tribute of respect to his beloved and honored memory, "for his praise was in all the churches." Canon Fleming wrote, "None of his legion friends can mourn more sincerely than I. He belonged to us all, but now he belongs to Christ forever, and we must wait to follow and renew in unbroken fellowship our Christian friendship on earth." The Rev. Charles H. Spurgeon wrote to the striken widow, "We are all mourners with you. The entire Church laments its grievous bereavement. He who stood foremost as a standard-bearer has fallen! I feel like crying, 'Alas, my brother!' Yet, thank God, he is taken from us without a spot on his escutcheon! He has fought a good fight. Dear sister in Christ, I congratulate you upon having had such a husband. Peace be to you as you think of him in the heavens. Our grief is full of hope, yea, a present triumph chases away the pressing sorrow. We shall go to him though he shall not return to us. Your dear husband's kindness to me makes me feel that I have lost a brother, and it comes closely home to me when I consider that he is taken and I am left, though I should have thought him much the stronger man. It will soon be our turn to go home, and where else should children go?"

His funeral was such a one as mighty London seldom sees. The solemn concourse was immense. Brixton Chapel was densely crowded, and the address of the President of the British Conference, Rev. E. E. Jenkins, was one of exquisite tenderness, extraordinary discrimination, appropriateness, and mental and spiritual power. And when with deep emotion he spoke of the Mission-House, with its vast responsibilities and the critical condition of its resources, and of having to go back there to miss him, a mighty sob seemed to surge through the great congregation. He was attended by thousands to the grave, hundreds of ministers following their fallen comrade to his last resting-place; and there, with aching hearts and silent tears, they laid away all that remained of him who had stood confessedly and pre-eminently the greatest preacher of British Methodism, and one of the chief orators of the world. His remains were laid in Norwood Cemetery,

"Hic cineres ubique nomen"—
"His ashes here, but everywhere his name,"—

a name untarnished as the sun and resplendent with lustre, for he was the Apollos of the modern Church ; and of the modern pulpit, the anointed king.

Dr. Punshon departed this life April 14th, 1881, at the age of fifty-seven years. The day after the funeral, when all was over, Mrs. Punshon, opening his drawer, came upon his private diary, and this is his last entry, made just before leaving home :—

"My health is suffering much from reaction, after my long suspense and recent sorrow. Went last week to Walsall, to fulfil an engagement, and had so sharp an attack that I was unable to preach, and now am enjoined absolute rest for some time. I feel all the symptoms of declining health—am much thinner; my digestive apparatus entirely out of order, and a fearful amount of nervous exhaustion. I am in the Lord's hands, and, in my best moments, can trust Him with myself for life or death. But I am weak and frail. My langor makes me fretful, and my unquiet imagination often disturbs my faith. I feel that I must go softly. I should like, if it be the Lord's will, to serve the Church of my affection yet for ten or twelve years; but He knows what is best, and will bring it about. Oh! for a simpler and more constant trust—a trust which confides my all, present and future, into my Father's care."

Yes, " He knows what is best," and so the Master whom he so much delighted to honor, has taken His servant from the cares, and anxieties, and untiring labors of the Church below, to the higher service of the Church above. He is gone from us. The "polished shaft" is broken, the bright and shining light of the Church is quenched. Palsied is the eloquent tongue; that voice of marvellous modulation and startling emphasis we shall hear no more, no more. "But he being dead, yet speaketh;" his testimony is his life, and that testimony calls us to a higher consecration and a fuller development of all the energies of mind and heart to the service of the Redeemer. How mysterious are the ways of Providence! I little thought when I started on my journey Eastward that it was on a mission of loving service to one whom the whole Church of Christ delighted to honor. His closing hours were linked with holy memories of his joys and sorrows in Canada; and his name is embalmed in many Canadian hearts, in a deep and undying affection.

How I love to recall every word spoken, every pressure of the hand, every token of endearment, every glance from

"The sweetest soul
That ever looked through human eyes."

There are memories too sacred and precious to be placed in a book, but are claimed for the heart, and such are the memories that I shall ever cherish of that great and noble and kingly man whom I have been permitted to call my friend. It has seemed to me that this record of the scenes and incidents of my journeyings toward the sunrise lands would be incomplete without some reference to that overwhelming sorrow which shadowed my homeward way, and the tidings of which fell like a personal bereavement on so many thousand hearts and homes. And though

> "He bears a truer crown
> Than any wreath that we can weave him;"

yet this simple *In Memoriam* is affection's homage to departed worth. His is one of the few "immortal names that were not born to die," and though we shall no more hear his burning and electric words, yet the spiritual sentiments and noble lessons that fell from his pen and from his lips will live forever in our hearts, and be the constant inspiration to a higher and holier life.

> "Offer thy life on the altar;
>   In the high purpose be strong;
> And if the tired spirit should falter,
>   Then sweeten thy labor with song.
> What if the poor heart complaineth,
>   Soon shall its wailing be o'er;
> For there in the rest that remaineth
>   It shall grieve and shall weary no more.
>
> "Then work! brothers, work! let us slumber no longer,
> For God's call to labor grows stronger and stronger;
> The light of this life shall be darkened full soon,
> But the light of the better life resteth at noon."
> —*Punshon's Pilgrim's Song.*

THE END.

www.ingramcontent.com/pod-product-compliance
Lightning Source LLC
Chambersburg PA
CBHW051856300426
44117CB00006B/419